To my traveling

companions at

NBTS

which played a critically

positive role in my

my journey in ministry

+
scholarship

John Huber

Oct 16, 2017

"In this account of the brief missionary career of Pliny Fisk, Hubers has given us an intricate analysis of the ways in which an imagination schooled in the Bible, the Enlightenment, New England Protestantism, and the lives of missionary heroes could impose and maintain an objectifying and estranging distance even from the most hospitable 'other.' This book will be a fascinating case study (and warning) for anyone interested in the possibility of fruitful inter-religious encounter."

—**MARK N. SWANSON**
Lutheran School of Theology at Chicago

"The story of Pliny Fisk (1792–1825), ABCFM's first missionary to the Middle East, is as salutary today as it was tragic then. Shaped by the Orientalism of the times, blinded by the presumptions of Western superiority, and constricted by the doctrinal straitjacket of his Calvinism, Fisk's social isolation was guaranteed, and his failure as an emissary of the Gospel assured. A perpetual outsider, detached and critically aloof from the religious and cultural others among whom he lived out his missionary vocation, he is a pitiful figure. His story and its lessons bear hearing in our time of nationalistic hubris fueled and ignited by ignorance. For those who have ears to hear, eyes to see, and the humility to self-examine, there is much to ponder. Hubers is to be thanked for writing a story that is surprisingly contemporary in its lessons."

—**JONATHAN J. BONK**
Director, *Dictionary of African Christian Biography*; Research Professor of Mission,
Center for Global Christianity & Mission, Boston University School of Theology

# I Am a Pilgrim, a Traveler, a Stranger

# American Society of Missiology Monograph Series

Series Editor, James R. Krabill

The ASM Monograph Series provides a forum for publishing quality dissertations and studies in the field of missiology. Collaborating with Pickwick Publications—a division of Wipf and Stock Publishers of Eugene, Oregon—the American Society of Missiology selects high quality dissertations and other monographic studies that offer research materials in mission studies for scholars, mission and church leaders, and the academic community at large. The ASM seeks scholarly work for publication in the series that throws light on issues confronting Christian world mission in its cultural, social, historical, biblical, and theological dimensions.

Missiology is an academic field that brings together scholars whose professional training ranges from doctoral-level preparation in areas such as Scripture, history and sociology of religions, anthropology, theology, international relations, interreligious interchange, mission history, inculturation, and church law. The American Society of Missiology, which sponsors this series, is an ecumenical body drawing members from Independent and Ecumenical Protestant, Catholic, Orthodox, and other traditions. Members of the ASM are united by their commitment to reflect on and do scholarly work relating to both mission history and the present-day mission of the church. The ASM Monograph Series aims to publish works of exceptional merit on specialized topics, with particular attention given to work by younger scholars, the dissemination and publication of which is difficult under the economic pressures of standard publishing models.

Persons seeking information about the ASM or the guidelines for having their dissertations considered for publication in the ASM Monograph Series should consult the Society's website—www.asmweb.org.

Members of the ASM Monograph Committe who approved this book are:

Paul V. Kollman, University of Notre Dame
Roger Schroeder, Catholic Theological Union
Bonnie Sue Lewis, University of Dubuque Theological Seminary

# I Am a Pilgrim, a Traveler, a Stranger

*Exploring the Life and Mind of the the First American Missionary to the Middle East, the Rev. Pliny Fisk (1792–1825)*

By John Hubers

*Foreword by Peter E. Makari*

American Society of Missiology Monograph
Series vol. 30

PICKWICK *Publications* · Eugene, Oregon

I AM A PILGRIM, A TRAVELER, A STRANGER
Exploring the Life and Mind of the First American Missionary to the Middle East, the Rev. Pliny Fisk (1792–1825)

American Society of Missiology Monograph Series 30

Cover art: Artistic rendering by Adam Hubers. Used with permission. Original image from Alvan Bond, *Memoir of the Rev. Pliny Fisk, A.M. Late Missionary to Palestine* (Boston: Crocker and Brewster, 1828) https://archive.org/details/memoirofrevpliny00bond.

Pickwick Publications
An Imprint of Wipf and Stock Publishers
199 W. 8th Ave., Suite 3
Eugene, OR 97401

www.wipfandstock.com

PAPERBACK ISBN: 978-1-4982-8298-7
HARDBACK ISBN: 978-1-4982-8300-7
EBOOK ISBN: 978-4982-8299-4

*Cataloguing-in-Publication data:*

Names: Hubers, John.

Title: I am a pilgrim, a traveler, a stranger : exploring the life and mind of the first American missionary to the Middle East, the Rev. Pliny Fisk (1792–1825) / by John Hubers.

Description: Eugene, OR : Pickwick Publications, 2016 | American Society of Missiology Monograph Series 30 | Includes bibliographical references

Identifiers: ISBN 978-1-4982-8298-7 (paperback) | ISBN 978-1-4982-8300-7 (hardcover) | ISBN 978-4982-8299-4 (ebook)

Subjects: LCSH: Fisk, Pliny, 1792–1825. | Missionaries—Palestine—Biography. | Missionaries—United States—Biography. | Middle East—Religion.

Classification: LCC BV3202 H85 2016 (print) | LCC BV3202 (ebook)

Manufactured in the U.S.A.                                                09/28/16

# Contents

# Foreword[1]

THE HISTORY OF NORTH American Christian mission in the world is a subject that can be both inspiring and deserving of closer critical examination. It is a history and experience, as John Hubers asserts, that "engenders a reorientation." For some, it is tempting to idealize and romanticize the missionary and their work. For others, it is easy to discount and criticize the missionary enterprise as paternalistic or imperialistic. There is validity in each, and it is only responsible for missionaries, and their sending boards, to engage regularly and attentively in self-reflection and assessment.

In this impressively researched book, Dr. Hubers seeks to discern whether Pliny Fisk, one of the American Board of Commissioners for Foreign Missions (ABCFM)'s first two missionaries sent to Western Asia, personally experienced a transformation in his understanding of mission through encounter with the people he met, similar to the kind of epiphany and transformation that Dr. Hubers himself experienced when he served in mission in the Middle East. The goals that a missionary sets out hoping to accomplish and the ideals s/he bring often change, in some cases radically, when standing in a new place, meeting the people there, and learning about the Christian, faith, and other-identified institutions that already exist—and in some cases are thriving.

1. Dr. Peter E. Makari, PhD, has served as Executive for the Middle East and Europe with Global Ministries of the United Church of Christ and the Christian Church (Disciples of Christ) since July 2000. For two terms, he also served ecumenically as the Co-Chair of the National Council of Churches' Interfaith Relations Commission (2008–2013). He earned an MA in Middle East Studies from the American University in Cairo (1993) and a PhD in Politics and Middle East Studies from New York University (2003). He is the author of *Conflict and Cooperation: Christian-Muslim Relations in Contemporary Egypt* (Syracuse University Press, 2007).

The Board on whose staff I serve is one and the same as the ABCFM, the first North American mission board. Founded in 1810 by Congregational churches in New England, it continues to exist today, incorporated as Wider Church Ministries of the United Church of Christ. Institutionally, not only has the ABCFM undergone a "reorientation" over the course of its institutional life, but as a prominent mission board, our approach to mission has been transformed by our encounter with people, churches, and institutions, to become more "appreciative" and to become more respectful—to strive to engage in a more mutual mission.

Today, we as a board and church are conscious that our 200 years as part of the North American missionary movement is only a part of the history of Christian mission. Of course, the first Christian missionaries were those of the first century CE, the followers of Jesus. We also assert that mission is about the relationships we enjoy with people and institutions around the world—not so that they are changed to see things our way, but in order to contribute together to the establishment of a better manifestation of God's peaceful and just vision for all people and creation.

That sense of mutuality and accompaniment represents a major transformation from our early days of seeking to "convert the heathen." The terms "missionary" and "mission" certainly continue to carry much accumulated baggage, and some of that baggage still applies. The impact of different missionary movements and efforts, over time and across the spectrum of theological understandings of mission, is varied but there are negative consequences, to be sure. These are manifest in several ways, including the occasional difficulty of international ecumenical relations resulting from a sense and history of exclusion or of ignorance about indigenous churches' presence; the perpetuation of misunderstanding, misrepresentation, and active hostility that can arise among people of different faiths, perhaps most visible in the media in Christian-Muslim dynamics; and the association of indigenous and global Christians with the foreign policies of Western (the so-called "Christian") countries, which have been especially disruptive in the Middle East.

Fisk's story is one of encounter. In a time when travel and communications were much more time-consuming and difficult, the missionaries in Western Asia provided new perspectives on the world, and were a source of knowledge and information that was not otherwise available to North Americans. Despite advances in technology and ease of travel, the same is true today. It is through relationships and encounter that we can understand the world differently. Dr. Hubers has helped us to do that with this book, pointing to the combination of characteristics of non-judgmental intellectual curiosity and humility as traits that can lead to active participation in the global community, and ultimately, transformation.

Peter E. Makari

# Acknowledgments

THE FOLLOWING WORK WOULD not have been possible without the patient and loving support of my wife, Lynne, who gave up a "normal" life with a semi-normal husband to allow me to pursue the needed research on trips East as well as inward to that place where the nineteenth century was more home to me than the twenty-first. Gratitude is also offered for the gracious assistance offered by the archival staff at Middlebury College, Vermont, the Congregational Archives in downtown Boston, Andover Newton Theological School in Newton Center, Massachusetts, Dartmouth College in Hanover, New Hampshire, Houghton Library and Archives at Harvard University, and Columbia University's Burke Library at Union Theological Seminary in New York City. Their enthusiasm for my project gave me extra incentive to do the work necessary to bring it to fruition. I must also mention my gracious, encouraging mentor and adviser, Dr. Mark Swanson, whose patient guidance helped me put aside the preacher in me to allow the academician to emerge.

# Abbreviations

ABCFM   American Board of Commissioners for Foreign Missions

ANTS    Andover Newton Theological School, Merrill Department of Rare Books and Special Collections, Franklin Trace Library in Newton Center, MA

ATS     Andover Theological Seminary

BLA     Burke Library Archives (Columbia University Libraries) at Union Theological Seminary in New York City

CLA     Congregational Library and Archives, Boston, MA

DFL     Davis Family Library, Special Collections, Middlebury College, Middlebury, VT

HLH     Houghton Library at Harvard University, Cambridge, MA

# 1

# Introduction

## THE TRANSFORMATIONAL NATURE OF MISSIONARY SERVICE

HISTORICALLY MISSIONARIES HAVE BEEN transformational agents. In some cases this has drawn a critical response as it is believed that the change they bring is destructive of values that give internal coherence to indigenous cultures. In other cases they are praised for changes that operate as incarnational seeds of healing and hope. Missionaries themselves often speak of another kind of transformation. This is a perceptual alteration that occurs as their encounter with other cultures and faiths allows them to see the world through new eyes. Many would identify this as the most profound change, particularly so when it involves a revolution in their assessment of the religious other.

For missionaries whose conceptualizations represent the more conservative side of the theological spectrum this can be a wrenching experience, as it may mean attributing greater value to a religious identity they had previously anathematized. In some cases this may lead to their questioning the validity of their missional purpose. More often, it engenders a reorientation in a more dialogical direction. This was my experience during the twelve years (1976–1978; 1986–1996) my wife and I spent in cross-cultural ministry in the Arabian Gulf states of Bahrain and Oman. Many others who have shared our experience would agree.

## SHIFTING MISSIONARY PERCEPTIONS

The question that has intrigued me for some time about this phenomenon is whether it was also the case for earlier American missionaries. My attempt to discover an answer to that question prompted me to write a paper exploring the ministry of the pioneering Reformed Church in America missionary to the Arabian Gulf, Samuel Zwemer, which appeared in the *International Bulletin of Missionary Research* in July of 2004.[1] What I discovered in doing research for this paper is that Zwemer did undergo a transformation of sorts in his perception of his Muslim neighbors, allowing a polemically defined categorical approach to evolve into something more appreciative of Muslim humanity, diversity and spirituality. It was a movement from "polemic to a hint of dialogue" in anticipation of later developments in Christian-Muslim relations.

Kenneth Cracknell discovered a similar phenomenon in research he did for a book he published in 1995 with the title *Justice, Courtesy and Love: Theologians and Missionaries Encountering World Religions, 1846–1914*. Cracknell's interest was less shifting missionary perceptions of the religious other than the broader issue of the Christian theology of religions. "Within [this book]," he says, "we examine one aspect of missiology: the vital question of the significance of other peoples' religions within the purposes of God."[2] But the approach he took to his research put his discoveries within the framework of my own interests, as his work involved examining the evolving perceptions of a collection of nineteenth and early twentieth-century western missionaries and theologians. It is in his description of the difficulties such a study entails that I take inspiration for my own research.

> On the one hand such an undertaking demands searching analysis of the views and opinions inherited by individual missionaries before they went to their chosen "mission fields;" and on the other, scrupulous attention to the way in which their new environments altered their perceptions and caused major shifts in their own thinking.[3]

This is the primary concern of what follows; to undertake a "searching analysis of the views and opinions" of an early American missionary prior to his departure for his chosen field of service in order to examine

---

1. Hubers, "Samuel Zwemer and the challenge of Islam, 117–18.

2. Cracknell, *Justice, Courtesy and Love*, 1.

3. Ibid.

whether or not a personal encounter with the subjects of his missionary interest "altered [his] perceptions and caused major shifts" in his thinking. The focus in this case will be on how he perceived the religious other in the framework of his missiological task.

## SUBJECT OF INQUIRY: THE REV. PLINY FISK

The subject chosen for this study is one of a pair of missionaries sent to the Ottoman Empire in 1819 by the American Board of Commissioners for Foreign Missions (hereafter ABCFM) with a primary purpose of exploring possibilities for a missionary engagement with the peoples of the Holy Land. His name was Pliny Fisk. His traveling companion was his friend and fellow Andover graduate, Levi Parsons. What makes Fisk a particularly interesting subject for an inquiry of this nature is the fact that he made this trip at a time when only a handful of Protestant missionaries had journeyed to this region, none of them American. His story in this case provides a unique opportunity to examine the transformational nature of a cross-cultural missionary encounter in its pioneering stage.

## AN ORIENTALIST MODEL

The model of analysis I have chosen to determine the nature of Fisk's transformational experience takes its inspiration from Edward Said's observations about orientalism in the western scholarship of the era. What is most pertinent here is the distinction Said draws between what he calls "vision" and "narrative."

> The Orientalist surveys the Orient from above, with the aim of getting hold of the whole sprawling panorama before him— culture, religion, mind, history, society. To do this he must see every detail through the device of a set of reductive categories (the Semites, the Muslim mind, the Orient, and so forth.). Since these categories are primarily schematic and efficient ones, and since it is more or less assumed that no Oriental can know himself the way an Orientalist can, any vision of the Orient ultimately comes to rely for its coherence and force on the person, institution, or discourse whose property it is. . . .
>
> Against this static system of "synchronic essentialism" I have called *vision* because it presumes that the whole Orient can be seen panoptically, there is a constant pressure. The source of the pressure is *narrative,* in that if any Oriental detail can be shown to move, or to develop, diachrony is introduced into the system

> . . . History and the narrative by which history is represented
> argue that vision is insufficient, that "the Orient" as an uncondi-
> tional ontological category does an injustice to the potential of
> reality for change [emphasis added].[4]

According to Said, this 'static system of "synchronic essentialism"'
that he designates "vision," is such a fixation of the orientalist discourse
that it effectively "defeats" the possibility of a less rigid, more humanizing "narrative," even when the discourse in question emerges from an
existential encounter.[5] This is a primary thesis of his work.

John M. Steadman anticipated Said's observations in his book *The
Myth of Asia,*[6] published nine years before *Orientalism*. Steadman noted
how there has been a long history of bias in western scholarship towards
what he calls "ideation" that creates a unitary vision of the Orient that
obfuscates more than it enlightens.

> Many a writer on Asia treats the Orient as though it were a
> single entity (which it is not) and thus postulates a unity that
> has no real existence outside his own imagination.[7]

Neither Said nor Steadman had missionary literature as their primary focus of concern. Said, in fact, attributes the orientalist project to
"secularizing elements in eighteenth-century European culture" (even
while acknowledging that such elements drew their discursive power
from "the old religious patterns of human history and destiny" leading to a "naturalized supernaturalism").[8] But parallels to the vision that
undergirded the early nineteenth-century American Protestant mission
effort are hard to ignore. Here, too, there was a tendency to "see every
detail through the device of a set of reductive categories." Here, too, "ideation" came into play with an inclination to treat the Orient "as though it
were a single entity," or, perhaps more accurately a *collection* of idealized
entities (Muslims, Jews, Oriental Christians). Examples of this kind of
broad-brush categorization of the religious other abound in missionary
literature of the era, including the following excerpt from an essay that

4. Said, *Orientalism*, 240.

5. In Said's words: "The defeat of narrative by vision—which is true even in so pa-
tently story-like a work as *The Seven Pillars* is something we have already encountered
in Lane's *Modern Egyptians*." Ibid.

6. Steadman, *The Myth of Asia*.

7. Ibid., 1.

8. Said., *Orientalism*, 121.

Fisk's biographer, Alvan Bond, wrote on "Mohamedanism" when he and Fisk were fellow students at Andover Seminary:

> [T]his religion prevails among those who are generally of a jealous, arrogant and savage disposition, and infatuated with a blind devotedness to their cause that reason has little or no influence on them.[9]

Parallels to Said's "vision" are readily apparent here. Yet, surprisingly, few scholars of Christian mission history have made use of Said's insights as a hermeneutical tool.

## Said's Absence from Missiological Literature

In an article that appeared in the July 2004 edition of *The International Bulletin of Missionary Research,* Herb Swanson writes that "a survey of issues and concerns debated by missiologists over the past twenty-five years . . . shows Said to be largely absent from the missiological literature."[10] Swanson attributes this reticence to several factors: 1) missiological students who are unaware of the debate swirling around *Orientalism* as it has largely taken place in fields of study that do not normally draw their attention, 2) a reluctance to use an approach that is perceived to be an "unremitting attack" on the West, thus suggesting a polemical approach they wish to avoid, and 3) "writing Said off" as a postmodern critic of passing interest.[11]

Swanson believes this to be an unfortunate development. I would concur. It is unfortunate because Said's insights can open a window on attitudes and practices that have hindered the development of the kind of contextually sensitive relationships we wish to cultivate in inter-faith encounters today. Noting how Said's work "has had a powerful impact on global intellectual thought,"[12] particularly among Asians, Swanson urges a much wider use of Said's paradigm-shifting insights in missiological research.

> Communication of the Gospel, we now understand, always requires sensitive appreciation for context. Said's *Orientalism* has

---

9. Bond, *The Present State of Mohamedanism*, Series 7/Dissertations, Dec 17, 1816, ANTS.

10. Swanson, "Said's *Orientalism* and the Study of Christian Missions," 107.

11. Ibid.

12. Ibid., 111.

become one important source for reflection both on our own histories and contemporary situations and on our relationship as Christian communicators to those with whom we would communicate.[13]

## Orientalism and Missions: Areas of Intersection

Swanson sees four possible areas of intersection between Said's work and missiological studies. The first is Said's emphasis on "the relationship of knowledge and discourse to power."[14] This cuts to the heart of Said's primary purpose, which is to expose the influence of Orientalist discourse on the Western political, cultural and economic domination of Asian peoples. Here, says Swanson, the question is "How has missionary discourse in both words and deeds embodied and used power?"[15]

The second area of intersection is the way reductive orientalist categorizations "function as blinders that restrict the 'orientalists' vision so they tend to see the worst in the East and the best in the West." The third is the way an orientalist "textual attitude" creates an illusionary knowledge that falsely assumes "that the swarming, unpredictable, and problematic mess in which human beings live can be understood on the basis of what books—texts—say." The fourth is an "intimate estrangement"[16] created by the inability of resident orientalists to move beyond their generalizations to engage their subjects in that contingent space that is most definitive of positive social intercourse.[17]

While the first area of intersection is crucial to an examination of the relationship between Western missions and Western imperialism, it will not be a major area of concern in this book. This is due primarily to the fact that it lies outside the interest of this project, which has to do with examining attitudinal transformations in the life of one American missionary. It is also not a major area of concern because the power equation it suggests was reversed. This is what Ussama Makdisi infers in his assessment of what he considers to be the largely inconsequential evangelizing efforts of Fisk and Parsons as well as others sent by the ABCFM to the region in these early years.

13. Ibid.
14. Ibid., 110.
15. Ibid.
16. Ibid.
17. Ibid.

The extraordinary reversal of position permeates the missionary correspondence. The privileged men belonging to established churches preaching in English to broken Indians in North America had been transformed, indeed had voluntarily transformed themselves, into largely isolated individuals speaking in halting Arabic to firmly entrenched Christian communities living in the shadow of the Ottoman Empire.[18]

Although he is much more critical of the imperialistic overtones of the pioneering missionary work of Fisk and Parsons,[19] Samir Khalaf would echo this assessment, noting that "at least initially it (missionary incursions into the region) did not avow or manifest any imperial or colonial ambitions."[20]

For these two reasons the first "area of intersection" suggested by Swanson will not be a critical consideration of this book. However, the other three areas of intersection will. Here is where Said's Orientalist thesis and the critique it represents can serve as important analytical tools to apply to Fisk's developing perspectives of the religious other. I believe, in fact, that Fisk himself might have appreciated Said's reflections on the need to approach the religious other on the basis of a more humanizing narrative. He would understand how important it is to remove any "blinders," "text-based" or otherwise, that might cause the kind of "intimate estrangement" that Said rightly criticizes as an impediment to humanizing relationships. He would understand because his perceived missional purpose could only be fully realized with the kind of relationships Said commends.

## INDIVIDUALISM IN THE MISSIONARY ENTERPRISE

South African missiologist Pieter Pikkert makes reference to David Bosch's observations[21] about the imprint of the Enlightenment on the

18. Makdisi, *Artillery of Heaven*, 88.

19. In Khalaf's words: "I intend to argue here that both in its disparaging views of the 'other' and in its intrusive strategies to undermine and deprive 'native' groups of their spiritual inheritance and cultural identity, Protestant Evangelicalism shares much with all other modes of colonial domination." *Protestant Missionaries in the Levant,*113.

20. Ibid., 133.

21. Pikkert quotes Bosch as saying that "the entire Western missionary movement of the past three centuries emerged from the matrix of the Enlightenment." Pikkert, "Protestant Missionaries to the Middle East," 32.

nineteenth-century western missionary enterprise when he writes: "[E]arly Protestant missionaries [exported] the doctrine of individualism to the Islamic world as if it were a tenet of Christianity."[22] What Pikkert and Bosch attribute to the Enlightenment can also be seen as determinant of the kind of Christianity that shaped Fisk's missiological considerations. Fisk's faith was refined in the fire of an Edwardsian revivalism that demanded discernible marks of an individual conversion experience. This defined both the experience of the evangelical missionaries of this era and what it was they sought to achieve. Jerald Brauer makes note of how critical a conversion experience was to the evangelical mindset of the era.

> There is a sense in which conversion exists for its own sake in Revivalism, solely in relation to the individual to be born again. Though one is to be converted in order to live a godly life, it is the experience of conversion itself which becomes central and all-pervasive. Even the possibility of correct ethical action depends upon a positive answer to the question, "Are you saved?"[23]

That Fisk understood conversion in this way will become apparent in chapter 2. We will see it most readily in his struggle to detect within himself evidence of a regenerative encounter with God apart from which his life had no value.

> I consider the whole of my life till my sixteenth year, as having been one continued course of rebellion against God. Not one holy affection can I find by examination during that whole period. Never did my heart exercise any love for God—never was I willing that God should reign a Sovereign on his throne.[24]

What Fisk saw as his personal need for redemptive grace would also determine how he viewed his non-Christian neighbors. In a long section from a journal he kept during his time at Andover, Fisk meticulously examined the *yeas* and *nays* determining his call to missionary service. As part of this process he declared his desire to be in constant prayer for "Pagans, Mahommedans, Jews, Papists" and even "Protestants"—all those who had not been born again as he had. "Their souls are all precious," he writes, "they are all sinners, and can be saved only by Christ;

---

22. Ibid., 23.

23. Brauer, "Conversion: From Puritanism to Revivalism," 241.

24. Bond, *Memoir of the Rev. Pliny Fisk*, 15.

they are all my *fellow beings*, and objects of Christian benevolence [emphasis added]."[25]

Fisk believed that what he shared with his neighbors as autonomous grace-starved individuals was more important than what divided them. They were *fellow beings*; common objects of Christian benevolence. On that basis we can assume that Fisk would have recognized the importance of meeting the religious other in that contingent space defined by Said's *narrative*, that space where they actually lived as opposed to the imaginary space created for them by Orientalist discourse.

> Underlying all the different units of Orientalist discourse—by which I mean simply the vocabulary employed whenever the Orient is spoken or written about—is a set of representative figures, or tropes. These figures are to the actual Orient . . . as stylized costumes are to characters in a play.[26]

The question this book asks is whether Fisk was able to overcome the orientalizing impulse in order to meet the citizens of the Ottoman Empire as *fellow beings*. There is no doubt that the organization that sent him to the Ottoman Empire operated out of an Orientalist paradigm. The weight of their *vision* may in this case have been too overwhelming to have allowed Fisk to develop a more humanizing *narrative*. Determining whether or not this was the case is the primary analytical purpose of this book.

## TELLING FISK'S STORY

This analytical purpose is foundational to what follows. There is, however, another purpose, which is to tell Fisk's story in a way it hasn't been told before.

Soon after his premature death on the mission field in 1825, Fisk's former Andover classmate, the Rev. Alvan Bond, wrote what was at the time his definitive memoir.[27] Like other memoirs of the era, this was less a critical examination of Fisk's life and ministry than it was an attempt to portray him as a model of selfless missionary service for the purpose of encouraging others to consider similar service. Bond makes this clear in his preface.

---

25. Ibid., 68.
26. Said, *Orientalism*, 71.
27. Bond, *Memoir*.

> If this record of [Fisk's] religious exercises and benevolent works
> may but excite others to emulate his sterling virtues, or inspire
> any one with the holy resolution to gird himself for the perils,
> conflicts, and sacrifices of the same self-denying service, the
> labor of preparing it for the press will not have been in vain.[28]

This memoir was published in 1828. Since that time no scholar has
seen fit to revisit the Fisk oeuvre to give it a less hagiographical, more
critical treatment. This book will be the first to do so in a comprehensive
fashion.

Here the recent work of two scholars needs to be mentioned for
their less comprehensive, yet similarly critical treatment of Fisk's narrative. The first is the work of historian Ussama Makdisi who writes about
Fisk's ministry in two recently published books, *The Artillery of Heaven:
American Missionaries and the Failed Conversion of the Middle East*[29] and
*Faith Misplaced: The Broken Promise of U.S.–Arab Relations: 1820–2001*.[30]
Makdisi used many of the same primary materials I have collected for
this project. His focus, however, is both broader in purpose and narrower
in scope. His broader purpose is to locate Fisk and other early American missionaries to the Middle East in the larger context of an eventful,
sometimes tortured American encounter with Arab culture that would
eventually lead to "a liberalism that can be credited neither to Americans
or Arabs alone but to a transnational history that demands a new kind of
narrative."[31] The narrower scope of his work is its concentration on the
time Fisk spent in the Ottoman Empire.

The second, even more recent work, is that of Samir Khalaf who
writes about Fisk in his book *Protestant Missionaries in the Levant; ungodly Puritans, 1820–1860*. Khalaf's work is more comprehensive than
Makdisi's as he spends more time covering what Khalaf calls the American-based "Nurseries of Piety,"[32] that is, universities and seminaries that
shaped the missionary vision of people like Fisk and Parsons. His interest
in this case is as much with the American evangelical vision that formulated the mission as it is with the mission itself. But, as with Makdisi,
Khalaf examines this foundational narrative in order to examine how it

---

28. Ibid., vi.

29. Makdisi, *Artillery of Heaven.*

30. Makdisi, *Faith Misplaced.*

31. Makdisi, *Artillery of Heaven,* 1.

32. Khalaf, *Protestant Missionaries,* 28.

determined the shape and impact of pioneering missionary discourse on Levant cultures. In his own words:

> I am . . . concerned with exploring the interplay between the religious and secular components, the "Christianizing" and "civilizing" features, or in the idiom of this study, the "godly" and "ungodly" attributes of New England Puritanism as a cultural transplant. More explicitly, it is my hope to demonstrate how the "ungodly" features of Puritanism come to prevail.[33]

For both Makdisi and Khalaf, Fisk is primarily a representative figure; one of many who produced a transformative encounter between American and Middle Eastern cultures. To a certain extent this is also true with what follows. I, too, am interested in locating Fisk in a larger narrative, in this case an historical narrative about the encounter of American missionaries with people of other cultures and faiths. But I am also interested in telling Fisk's story in a way that will allow him to be something more than just a representative figure, as his story is significant in and of itself.

It is significant first of all because he was the first American missionary (one of two) to live and work among the peoples of the Ottoman Empire at a time when only a handful of Americans had made this move at all. This was, as Makdisi puts it, a "foundational encounter between Americans and Arabs."[34] The observations Fisk makes about life in the Ottoman Empire are, in this case, of critical historical value whether or not one is interested in exploring his missiological significance.

It is also significant in that this book will join a growing body of literature[35] that avoids both the extreme of furnishing these early missionaries with halos, as per Bond's hagiographical treatment of Fisk; or condemns them as tools of Western imperialism. Makdisi understands the temptation to do the latter when he writes:

> To denounce missionaries as cultural imperialists is . . . to misunderstand the often ambivalent location missionaries occupied within their own societies as well as in foreign fields. And it is to

33. Ibid., xiv.

34. Makdisi, *Artillery of Heaven*, 7.

35. This includes the work of secular historians, some of which has recently been published in a book edited by Dogan and Starkey entitled *American Missionaries and the Middle East*. The topics covered in this book indicate a desire to move beyond the romantic stereotypes that have been created by hagiographies on the one side and accusations of cultural imperialism on the other.

ignore the polyvalent registers of native worlds and the deliber-
ate choice made by many individuals such as As'ad Shidyaq to
associate with foreign missionaries.[36]

It is hoped that the person who emerges out of the pages of this
book will help counter missionary stereotypes of either extreme. Pliny
Fisk, like every other missionary who went to their chosen field of service
in the early decades of the nineteenth century, was a complex individual
whose perceptions were shaped by an interplay between his unique psychological and social profile and an eclectic, often contradictory blend of
religious and culturally determined sub-texts that shaped the New England Calvinism that served as his spiritual home. We will see in particular
in Fisk's story the tension that existed between Enlightenment rationality
and evangelical piety, a tension that was never fully resolved. We will find
in him contradictory impulses that make it difficult to over- generalize
developments in his character and attitudes. And that may be the most
significant reason for re-visiting his story. Just as orientalist scholarship
has made it difficult for Westerners fully to understand their Middle
Eastern neighbors as neighbors, so hagiographical memoirs on the one
side and post-colonial critiques of these early American missionaries on
the other, have made it difficult to recognize the complexities of their
personality profiles and missional visions. There is a contingent *narrative*
that needs to be heard here, as well. The second purpose of this book is
best understood in this way; as an attempt to allow that *narrative* to be
heard in the story of one of the first Americans to make a significant missionary journey across cultural barriers.

## A NOTE ABOUT SOURCES

When Kenneth Cracknell writes about the complexity involved in analyzing changes in missionaries' perceptions of those among whom they
lived and worked, he also notes how this complexity is compounded by
the fact that few of these mission practitioners were "creatures of libraries" or well published authors. Thus

. . . [t]o reach an accurate assessment of their theological struggles requires patient attention to their diaries and journals, their
speeches at missionary conferences, their correspondence with

---

36. As'ad Shidyaq was the first celebrated convert of this early missionary venture.
His tragic story forms the basis for the primary narrative of Makdisi's book *Artillery
of Heaven*, 10.

their home boards, their replies to questionnaires and, when they are available, their published works.[37]

Cracknell's *Justice, Courtesy and Love* was focused on missionaries who went out with well established organizations following in the wake of pioneers who were in some cases basing their work as much on instinct as on solid missiological principles. Fisk was one of these pioneers, for while he was a keen collector of information that he believed would help him and others become effective missionaries, he was not overly concerned with theoretical reflection. This was so largely because there wasn't a well developed body of missiological research upon which to base his mission. The American Protestant missionary movement was still in its birthing stages. It was also so because this was a movement driven by pragmatic concerns. It was about getting things done for God. As Andover Professor of Pulpit Eloquence, Edward Dorr Griffin, would say in one of many sermons turn-of-the-century New England pastors would preach to urge support for this new venture:

> Do not our hearts throb with desire to be *instrumental* in giving Christ the heathen for his inheritance, and the uttermost parts of the earth for his possession [emphasis added]?[38]

This doesn't mean that these early pioneers didn't engage in serious reflection on the missionary task. As we shall see in our examination of Fisk's years at Andover Seminary, students like Fisk, who were hoping to be sent to various parts of the globe under ABCFM auspices, put a lot of thought and effort into studying both the practical and theoretical ramifications of global missions. They debated the best way to approach people of other faiths. They pondered where these other faiths fit into God's providential pattern. But their focus was primarily on methodology; figuring out the best way to *do* missions rather than the proper way to think about them.

What this means is that what Cracknell identifies as the challenge of discerning the thought processes of missionaries in a later era based on a lack of solid resources, proves to be even more challenging with Fisk, particularly after he made the move to the Ottoman Empire. All we have in this case are what might best be described as the kind of observations and personal reflections one might expect to find in the diaries and

---

37. Cracknell, *Justice, Courtesy and Love*, 2.

38. Quoted in Andrew, *Rebuilding the Christian Commonwealth*, 72.

journals of travelers. Fisk gave no speeches at missionary conferences because there were no missionary conferences to attend. He didn't write articles or books. Excerpts from his letters and journals were published by the board for promotional purposes, but no more than that. Trying to discern what Fisk thought about the religious other in this case means paying careful attention to flashes of insight he shared in the midst of his more mundane observations about life in the Ottoman Empire. The fact that he tended to be more concerned with giving details about the cities and ruins he visited than the people he met along the way adds another challenging twist to the task.

Trying to discern and analyze the development of Fisk's thought on the basis of scattered thoughts contained in his correspondence and journals is one of the challenges posed by the subject matter of this work. Another arises from the unique nature of missionary correspondence.

### Missionary Correspondence

Missionaries write for different audiences each requiring an alternative voice. Letters written to family members, for instance, will take on a different tone than letters written to supporters. This is also true in some cases for diaries and journals that missionaries keep, especially if they are written with the thought of sharing observations with the home board. This was certainly the case with Fisk. He not only kept a daily account of his thoughts and activities in a personal diary, he also jointly authored a journal with his colleague, Levi Parsons, which they prepared for the ABCFM and their supporters. There is no doubt that Fisk and Parsons were aware that what they wrote in this case would be under scrutiny. They knew that the theological stalwarts who ran the affairs of the AB-CFM would be carefully sifting through this material, alert to evidence of dissension from the evangelical/orthodox line. Their supporters would be doing the same. They were also aware that what they wrote would be used for promotional purposes. Missions in this case were a product that Fisk and Parsons needed to help sell to a public that was just being introduced to the idea of a global mission enterprise. Their ability to do what they did depended on it. Based on this, what we can assume is that the journal entries made by Fisk and Parsons for public consumption would take on some of the characteristics of promotional literature with its tendency to fall short of full disclosure if full disclosure carried the risk of losing support.

A quick comparison of contrasting entries Fisk made in his personal diary and official journal while he was on board ship on the journey to the Ottoman Empire will suffice to illustrate the point.

*Entries for December 7, 1819:*

*Personal Diary:* Rose at 9:00 to see land. It is Cape St. Vincent, the S.W. port of Portugal. After day light appeared the view was clear & plain. . . . Hitherto our progress has been rather slow. Most of the time the wind has been easterly—rather unpleasant, more or less rain almost every day with disagreeable wind & seas. I have been much troubled with sea sickness & am not yet entirely free from it.

*Journal:* Early this morning we were called up on the deck to see Land—the southern shores of Portugal. The sun shone clearly, & the view of the Cape St. Vincent and of the mountains of Spain was very distinct, & delightful.[39]

What is notable here is the absence in the journal entry of any reference to Fisk's seasickness or grumbling about the weather. What he wanted the public to hear is that after a long journey from Boston harbor they were finally in sight of Land (the underlining is his) on a delightfully sunny day. Why Fisk found it necessary to exclude the more unpleasant reality of his wretched stomach and sour disposition is hard to know. What is clear is that he made an editorial decision not to include it for public consumption.

What this underscores is the reason why, whenever possible, the primary source for my assessment of Fisk's changing perspectives (if, indeed, there are any changes) will be his personal diary and correspondence. Fortunately, this approach has been made more possible through the recent discovery of the first and fourth volumes of Fisk's personal diaries that have been purchased and made available to the public by the Burke Library archives of Columbia University at Union Theological Seminary in New York City. Volumes 2 and 3 have long been resident in the special collections archives of the Davis Family Library at Middlebury College in Vermont where Fisk did his undergraduate studies. The two volumes now available at Columbia were thought to have been lost. The fact that they are now available makes it more possible to do a reasonable job of determining what was on Fisk's mind during his short but eventful sojourn in the Ottoman Empire.

39. *Pliny Fisk Diary and Journal, Volume 1,* MRL 2: Pliny Fisk Papers, box 1, BLA.

There is one final note to make about the sources. While Bond's memoir can best be described as a hagiography, he, at the same time, felt compelled to include copious verbatim excerpts from Fisk's personal correspondence, sometimes page after page of excerpts from letters that are no longer available. In this case we are being given access to a large amount of material that Fisk did not intend for public consumption; thoughts and observations for the eyes of those who were closest to him. Bond made his own kind of editorial decisions in choosing these excerpts. In this case they may hide as much as they reveal. But their very length suggests that in the end Bond was committed to allowing Fisk's voice to be heard. For this reason, Bond's memoir is a valuable primary source.

## FISK'S STORY

Recent publications that make mention of Fisk and Parson's missionary endeavor, like the aforementioned books by Ussama Makdisi and Samir Khalaf,[40] put these two pioneers in the context of a larger narrative. For Makdisi this is a narrative that gives definition to the unfolding drama of US-Arab relations. For Khalaf it is the narrative of an "ungodly" impact on Levant cultures. This book will also place Fisk and Parsons in the context of a larger narrative, in this case the narrative of the eventful and sometimes tortured encounter between American missionaries and people of other cultures and religions. But it will also pay careful attention to matters that may not fit that larger narrative, as it is concerned with entering as much as possible into the complexities of Fisk's developing character and thought; his passions and prejudices; his hopes and fears; the development of his unique perception of the missionary relationship with the religious other. As a project related to mission history there is a hope that what unfolds in this book will fit like a missing puzzle piece into the larger narrative of the earliest American Protestant global mission effort. There is an even greater hope that it will be true to the person who is its subject matter.

This is the story of Pliny Fisk, first Protestant American missionary to the Middle East.

---

40. Two other notable books in this regard would be Marr's *The Cultural Roots of American Islamicism*; and Oren's *Power, Faith and Fantasy.*

# PART ONE

## In America

Do not our hearts throb with desire to be instrumental in giving Christ the heathen for his inheritance, and the uttermost parts of the earth for his possession?

REV. EDWARD DORR GRIFFITH,
QUOTED IN ANDREW III,
*REBUILDING THE CHRISTIAN COMMONWEALTH*, 72.

# 2

## The Early Years

### MAKING COVENANT

ON AUGUST 21, 1808, sixteen-year-old Pliny Fisk carefully transcribed every word of his congregation's "covenant"[1] into his student's notebook. Today such an assignment might be dismissed as a meaningless rote exercise. But given what it represented we can assume that it was a deeply meaningful exercise to Fisk. He did it to mark his new birth.

The covenant Fisk transcribed was a standard doctrinal statement for an orthodox New England Congregational church of that era. It began with an affirmation of God's Trinitarian nature, "one God only subsisting in three adorable persons" who is "unchangeable in his being, perfect in his attributes, and universal in his Government." It declared that scripture is given "by the inspiration of God" as "the only perfect rule of faith & practice." Human nature is "entirely depraved," our only hope being the "complete atonement by Jesus Christ & the consequent offer of life to sinners on gracious terms." Doctrines of "special grace, regeneration, personal election, the saints' perseverance" echoed the themes of classic Calvinism, as did its strong affirmation of biblical authority, as the Bible alone contains the "only lawful terms of admission to the chh." To these doctrines were added a pledge to "practice secret prayer and family devotion, to keep the Sabbath & support a gospel ministry, to attend public worship and the sacrament of the Lord's Supper" and to train children

1. Fisk, *Chh.Covenant*, ANTS.

"in the nurture & admonition of the Lord" as the faithful anticipated "the resurrection of the dead" and "the absolute eternity of future rewards."

Fisk's pledge to express his faith through the doctrinal and ethical dictates of his congregation's covenant was the capstone to a transformative process that had brought about a dramatic reorientation of his life, so dramatic that he would later describe the years previous as a time of pointless spiritual bankruptcy.

> I consider the whole of my life till my sixteenth year, as having been one continued course of rebellion against God. Not one holy affection can I find by examination during that whole period. Never did my heart exercise any love for God—never was I willing that God should reign a Sovereign on his throne.[2]

Christians who were part of the evangelical[3] revivalist tradition in New England in the eighteenth and early nineteenth centuries[4] would have understood what Fisk was describing. It was a conversion experience that had become for evangelical Congregationalists the only legitimate ("lawful") entry point into an authentic Christian life. The radical before and after experience Fisk described was one of its signature characteristics. One wonders , however, how radical it was, particularly when it becomes clear that the covenant to which the adolescent Fisk gave his assent had been an elemental factor in his life from the day he was born. He was a child of the covenant. It was the faith in which he had been raised.

---

2. Bond, *Memoir*, 15.

3. The term "evangelical" will be used in this chapter in the way Noll defines it in his article, "Common Sense Tradition and American Evangelical Thought," 216–38, applied in this case primarily to early nineteenth-century New England Congregationalists: "[E]vangelical" designates both a cluster of religious convictions (a high view of the Bible, stress on the need for experiencing God's grace, and a commitment to the divine nature of Christ's saving work) and the groups in American history that have been most vocal in promoting them."

4. Edwards notes, in his *A Faithful Narrative* that Deerfield, which at the time included the hamlet of Shelburne, was one of the first communities outside of Northfield to experience the revival that became the Great Awakening. The tradition would continue into Fisk's era. Edwards, *A Faithful Narrative*, 41.

## A RADICAL CONVERSION?

Pliny Fisk was born in the hamlet of Shelburne, Massachusetts[5] on June 24, 1792, one of four sons of Ebenezer and Sarah Barnard Fisk whom Fisk's biographer, Alvan Bond, describes as living in "moderate circumstances."[6] Bond says very little else about Fisk's parents, other than to note that they "exhibited evidence of humble piety" and were committed to raising their children "in the nurture and admonition of the Lord." Pliny himself was a "faithful, dutiful and affectionate" child eager to please his parents.[7] We can assume from this that family devotions and regular worship attendance were seamlessly incorporated into the rhythm of his life. And nothing in what Bond intimated suggests that young Pliny was ever openly rebellious. Indeed, the impression gained from the few words Bond devoted to this part of Fisk's life is that of a boy who should have moved effortlessly from a youthful piety to a more mature expression of the faith. "The Christian example and counsel of pious parents," wrote Bond, "made, at an early period, such deep impressions on his mind, as were favorable to the suceptibility of the stronger convictions of religious truth."[8]

The question here is why Fisk would use such dramatic language to describe what happened to him in his sixteenth year, the kind of language one might better expect from the testimony of a recovered drug addict or convert from another religion. The answer is found in the critical role played by the conversion experience in the revivalist paradigm that determined the shape of evangelical Congregational Christianity in New England during Fisk's formative years. This was a paradigm that drew its inspiration from the writings of Jonathan Edwards.

Bill Leonard and Jerald C. Brauer, in separate studies of the role of conversion in early American Protestantism,[9] make the observation that Edwards and his disciples considered the conversion experience to

5. Dwight notes that there were 169 houses in Shelburne in 1790 with a population of 1,183. Ten years later the number had dropped to 1,079. Dwight, *Travels in New England and New York*, 245. What is not known is whether Fisk lived in Shelburne proper or on a nearby farm. Bond doesn't say.

6. Bond, *Memoir*, 13.

7. Ibid., 14.

8. Ibid.

9. Leonard, "Getting Saved in America," 111–27; and Brauer, "Conversion: From Puritanism to Revivalism," 227–43.

be the foundational factor of an authentic Christian existence. It was an inheritance from their Pilgrim forebearers.

> [F]or early English Puritans, a specific conversion experience was at first rarely regarded as normative or necessary, though it might well serve as assurance that election had been received. Gradually, however, often out of pastoral care for those seeking full assurance, these Nonconforming Puritans in the Church of England came increasingly to regard a specific experience of regeneration as an essential sign of election. Thus a particular type of conversion experience and the recounting thereof became in New England a normative requirement for those who would claim both Christian faith and local membership.[10]

Jonathan Edwards' personal experience, coupled with what he observed in the transformative experiences of parishioners and others caught up in the spirit of the revivals that swept through New England under his watch, made this a "normative requirement."[11] His conviction on this account was so foundational that he was willling to give up his prized Northampton pulpit to uphold it.[12]

Conversion as the entry point into a genuine Christian life was, to Edwards, "the honorable badge of Christianity."[13] It became that, as well, to those who considered themselves Edwards' most faithful interpreters, the "New Divinity" men who filled most of the Congregational pulpits in western Massachusetts during Fisk's formative years. In the words of Richard Rabinowitz:

> [I]n western Massachusetts and Connecticut, the dominant party was Edwardsean, variously called New Lights, New Divinity men or Consistent Calvinists. Hating the self-serving strivings of "unregenerate" people for their own reformation, they called upon their parishioners to enact the Calvinist drama of

---

10. Leonard, "Getting Saved in America," 114.

11. Hart, "Jonathan Edwards and the Origins of Experimental Calvinism," 165.

12. Edwards was dismissed from his charge at the Northampton Church when he insisted that evidence of religious affections linked to a conversionary experience was a necessary requisite to be admitted to the Lord's Table, thus overturning his father-in-law, Solomon Stoddard's more lenient approach in admitting those who professed faith, but couldn't show evidence of a conversion experience. Stoddard was the pastor at Northampton just before Edwards. See Marsden: *Jonathan Edwards*, 352.

13. Ibid., 355.

reconciling God's absolute sovereignty with man's infinite sinfulness through an experience of "new birth.[14]

## THE "NEW DIVINITY"

"New Divinity" was a term initially applied in a derisive manner to the group of clergy who clustered around the teaching of Edwards' brother-in-law, Samuel Hopkins, in the years following Edwards' death.[15] The critics who coined it considered Hopkins' theology too extreme. What Hopkins taught was not, they insisted, "consistent Calvinism," which is the term Hopkins and his revivalist colleagues used, nor was it true to Edwards' teaching. It was a "*New* Divinity." Particularly disturbing to these critics was what they considered to be Hopkins' strict interpretation of Edwards' teaching on regeneration, going so far as to claim that "an unregenerate but awakened sinner who used the means of grace appeared more guilty in God's eyes than an unawakened sinner who remained unconcerned with his spiritual state."[16]

What this underscores is the uncompromising position of the Consistent Calvinists with regard to the necessity of regenerative experience for church membership. This was the dividing line between "saved" and "unsaved;" those who were "in" and those who were "out." One of these consistent Calvinists, the Rev. Moses Hallock (who would play a decisive role in Fisk's early theological education),[17] showed how critical, yet existentially complex, this consideration was to these clergymen. He did so in a letter he wrote to his two boys during the time they were together at college.

> Your case gives me much tender concern. The Lord teach you your sinful state, cause you to feel your sins, and your obligation to repent and believe, in Christ ... Depend not on even the best exterior. You cannot be saved *without a change of heart.* The nature of things is against it. The word of God is against it.[18]

14. Rabinowitz, *Spiritual Self in Everyday Life,* 6.

15. Holifield, *Theology in America,* 136.

16. Conforti, *Samuel Hopkins and the New Divinity,* 4.

17. Bond, *Memoir,* 18.

18. Yale, *The Godly Pastor,* 345.

Here, in simple terms, is the crux of the matter: "You cannot be saved without a change of heart." And this change of heart demanded evidentiary proof.

Evidentiary proof was what Fisk was seeking through a process of spiritual discernment that began in the summer of 1807 and culminated with his confession of faith in August of 1808. In this case it didn't matter that he had been a "faithful, dutiful, affectionate child" who did all he could to please his parents. It didn't matter that he had spent many hours in worship and prayer and Bible study. None of what had come before mattered. This was a *new birth*, regeneration from darkness to light. And while some parents might have been dismayed to hear their son speaking of his early years as a spiritual wasteland after working so hard to instill piety in him, in this case one can assume that Ebenezar and Sarah were pleased by their son's testimony. This is what they would have been praying for; that he have this conversion experience. There was no hope for him without it.

## EVANGELICALS AND CHILDHOOD

Philip Greven's study of early American childhood and adolescence helps explain the Fisks' perspective on their son's conversion.[19] The Fisks were among those Greven labels as "self suppressed" evangelicals. Such households were characterized by "an intensely religious family background" where children like Fisk received "early religious training by very pious parents" in an authoritarian setting tempered by doting parental affection.[20] The diaries that have survived from this era (seventeenth to early nineteenth centuries) show that children who were raised this way for the most part appreciated the spiritual foundation it gave them. Typical is Susanna Anthony, a Quaker who converted to Congregationalism during the first Great Awakening, who remembered with fondness that she was "early taught to love, fear and serve the Lord. My dear mother took great pains to form my mind for God."[21]

The critical need to "form" their childrens' minds for God was based at least in part on one of the tenets of the Shelburne church covenant; the one that declared human nature to be "entirely depraved." Greven writes of the angst created by this belief among evangelical families, as it taught

19. Greven, *The Protestant Temperament.*

20. Ibid., 22.

21. Quoted in ibid., 24.

them to be wary of the children they loved, fearful of what they might become if their depraved natures were not kept under careful check. In a reference to an article written by an anonymous writer for a "staunchly Calvinist magazine" in the early nineteenth century, Greven notes that at least to some evangelical Calvinists

> infants . . . seemed to be dangerous little animals, bent upon the aggrandizement of their own wills and their own gratification. All they lacked was power to make themselves truly frightening . . . When asked the question "from what can such a disposition proceed," the answer to any Calvinist was clear—"the most deep-rooted depravity."[22]

Greven tempers this observation with the acknowledgement that parental love, particularly maternal love, often provided a check on the more extreme expressions of this dogma as there was also an appreciation of childhood innocence.[23] Official dogma, in other words, was not the sole determinant of parental attitudes and practices. But it couldn't be entirely set aside by those who attemped to live the Calvinist faith they confessed.

There is no way to determine how Fisk's parents dealt with the paradox created by this clash between dogma and parental affection. Bond wrote so little about this phase of Fisk's life that what can be read between the lines is barely decipherable. What we can assume is that Ebenezar and Sarah agreed, as all devoutly pious "New Divinity" Calvinists of this era agreed, that the most loving thing they could do for their innocent, yet potentially dangerous child, was to raise him in such a way that a spiritual foundation would be laid for the day for which they fervently prayed, the day of Pliny's second birth.

> [Evangelicals] both loved their infant children and feared for their souls. Indeed, it was because they did love their children so much that they cared so intensely about what became of them not only in this life but, even more, in the life to come. Infancy was only the beginning of a long process of training and

---

22. Ibid., 29.

23. Edwards criticized parents for not taking their Calvinist theology seriously enough: "As innocent as children seem to be to us, yet if they are out of Christ, they are not so in God's sight, but are young vipers, and are infinitely more hateful than vipers, and are in a most miserable condition, as well as grown persons; and they are naturally very senseless and stupid . . . and need much to awaken them. Why should we conceal the truth from them?" Ibid., 31.

experience which ultimately could result in regeneration and the second birth.[24]

## HUMAN OR DIVINE AGENCY?

Unknowingly, perhaps, Greven raises an issue here that not only opens a window on this phase of Fisk's life but anticipates a decisive element of his later missiological reflection. The issue is the role of human agency in effecting spiritual transformation. Greven seems unaware of the nature of the issue when he infers (wrongly) that evangelical parents believed that their involvement in the "long process of training and experience" that would shape their child's life "ultimately *could result* in regeneration and the second birth." The "could" here would not have been a strong enough qualifier for the Consistent Calvinists. They would have found this to be bordering on the presumptuous as it was their belief that human effort is of no avail in the act of regeneration. Nothing parents or pastors or anyone else did or didn't do could be said to have any effectual bearing on spiritual re-birth. It might improve a child's behaivor. It might make her more obedient and even better prepared to receive regenerative grace. But it had no effect on the ultimate outcome. Regeneration was God's work.

## FISK ON REGENERATION

This is what Fisk himself believed. The evidence is found in a sermon he preached (one of his first) in the Shelburne church in December of 1814.[25] In this sermon he laid out his own understanding of the conversion process in an expository treatment of John 3:7: "Ye must be born again." According to Fisk this verse causes us to make two inquiries: "Why is regeneration necessary?" and "What is it?"

Fisk answered the first question with reference to human nature. It is necessary, "obviously" said Fisk, because of "the complete native depravity of man" that immediately casts doubt on human agency. Regeneration is raising the dead to life. No human being could possibly accomplish that.

24. Ibid.

25. These sermons are found in the Merrill Department of Rare Books and Special Collections of the Franklin Trace Library at Andover Newton Theological School. Fifteen have survived out of at least thirty-three with each being numbered in sequence. This is sermon number three.

The second question: "What is it?" compelled Fisk to offer its negative. What it is *not*, insisted Fisk, is "water baptism," nor is it merely "professing religion." The addresses in Revelation to the seven churches should immediately put that thought to rest. It is also not an "external reformation" as human nature is too weak to resist the temptation to return to that from which it was reformed. The "Dog return(s) to his vomit," said Fisk. It is also not a "change of sentiment or improvement in knowledge." "The infidel & the heretic may be convinced of the truth," continued Fisk, "but still not love it, still be unrenewed." So what is it? It is "properly denominated *a change of heart, a change of moral character.*"

In the next part of the sermon Fisk developed this theme further by contrasting the regenerate and unregenerate life as he noted the essential nature of regeneration to a salvific relationship with God.

> Being born again is the cause of all holy affections, of all true obedience, of all spiritual life among men. It is a change from sin to holiness, a resurrection from the dead, a new creation, the implantation of holiness in the soul.[26]

Fisk concluded the sermon by making it clear that the process that leads to new birth is brought about solely by divine agency.

> Sinners are dependant on the special favor of God for regeneration. It is a change which nothing but his immediate agency can effect. All creature exertions are of no avail, they cannot make the least approximation towards the great work. They can use no means that will effect it. If God interpose they will be saved. If not they perish.[27]

What we are hearing here is the voice of an aspiring young preacher reflecting back to his pastor and fellow parishioners a comfortably familiar theology. But it was more than that. Fisk was also speaking about something that touched on his own experience. This was Fisk giving doctrinal shape to his personal encounter with divine agency.

## "DOCTRINALIST" CHRISTIANITY

According to Richard Rabinowitz one of the ways revivalist Christians of this era constructed their "spiritual selves" was to give doctrinal definition to spiritual experience as Fisk was doing here. This is a perspective

26. Fisk Sermon No. 3, ANTS.

27. Ibid.

Rabinowitz describes as "doctrinalist" which is one of three fluid categories he uses to describe how revivalists of the era defined themselves:
doctrinalist, moralist, and devotionalist.[28] What characterized the "doctrinalists" was the way they doctrinally legitimized spiritual experience.[29]
According to Rabinowitz this was a discernable difference between the
First and Second Great Awakenings: the way participants in the Second
Great Awakening intellectualized their experience.[30] Regeneration was
defined by a change of heart and moral character, as Fisk said in this sermon. But that experience only took on the meaning it demanded when it
was filtered through an intellectually satisfying doctrinal paradigm.

> The evangelical's understanding/conscience was more than a
> perceiving machine, a sense receptor, or the stimulus part of a
> stimulus-response reflex arc in the mind. This understanding/
> conscience was more like an instant translator, converting mis-
> cellaneous sensations into a set of logically coherent statements
> about the nature of things. Working properly, in the moral per-
> son, it could make instantaneous connections between worldly
> moments and heavenly eternity.[31]

## AN EDWARDSEAN MORPHOLOGY OF CONVERSION

The interpretive grid Fisk would have used to make sense out of his
conversion experience, even before he was able to put it in its proper
doctrinal framework, was a well-worn pattern used by New England
Congregationalists based on hundreds of conversion narratives rooted
in the Puritan experience.[32] Jonathan Edwards gave the pattern its classic
formulation both in his interpretive treatment of the First Great Awakening in his *Faithful Narrative* and in his creative use of missionary David
Brainerd's diary, shaping the narrative in such a way that Brainerd's life
would become a model for a proper evangelical conversion experience.[33]

---

28. Rabinowitz, *Spiritual Self in Everyday Life*, 6.

29. See Part One of Rabinowitz's book where he discusses the doctrinalist position
in great detail.

30. Ibid., 24.

31. Ibid.

32. See Brauer, "Conversion"; and Leonard, "Getting Saved in America," both of
which give extensive treatment to the Puritan roots of this teaching.

33. See Pettit, *The Heart Renewed*, 123–25, which makes a strong case for Edward's
use of Brainerd's diary to give shape to the conversion narrative.

And while Edwards stressed that no two conversion accounts were the same, he found enough similarities to detect a common pattern:

> [H]ere there is a vast variety; perhaps as manifold as the subjects of the operation; but yet, in many things there is a great analogy in all.[34]

Brauer observes that the "analogy" to which Edwards referred would over the years evolve into a morphology of conversion that would more or less follow a seven-fold scheme:

1. A "period of inattentiveness or indifference—and in some cases an open hostility—to religious matters" the first signs of "dissastisfaction" along with an "awareness of shortcomings, failures, sinfulness."

2. A "new level of understanding under the guidance of the Holy Spirit" which led to an increased interest in pursuing spiritual matters and attitudinal change that led to a belief that conversion had occurred, even though, in many cases it had not.

3. A sudden conversion *experience* where, "led by the Holy Spirit, the person sees the full depth of his alienation from God and enmity toward him, toward his fellow human beings and toward himself."

4. The sense that the believer has now become an entirely new person. "Where there was disunity and terror, there is now unity and sweetness."

5. The person now enters the "path of transformation" of both self and society.

6. Regeneration is followed by sanctification.[35]

Sermons and table talk would have introduced this pattern to Fisk at an early age. He might have read some of the conversion narratives himself when he learned to read, or met converts who told their stories in a compelling way. The Rev. Moses Hallock, who would later become Fisk's theological mentor, led a number of dramatic revivals in the nearby church of Plainfield in the years before Fisk had his own conversion experience. One of the men converted during an early revival in Hallock's church became well known enough to have his story published by the

---

34. Edwards, *A Faithful Narrative*, 48–49.

35. Brauer, 227.

American Tract Society.[36] Fisk was almost certainly aware that he was walking a well trodden path when he began to sense what he would have described as the stirring of the Spirit in his life. Julius H. Rubin suggests that such accounts were so widely distributed and read that it would have been hard for someone like Fisk not to have been influenced by them.

> The ubiquitous published conversion narratives of the early New England revivals represent exemplars of the expected, authentic spiritual exercises of successful converts. Readers of the popular religious press could not fail to encounter these didactic accounts when seeking guidance in their lives. The exemplars simultaneously validated their own experiences and constituted a prescriptive conversion model.[37]

Bond helpfully included Fisk's own account of his conversion in his memoir. The fact that he recorded it verbatim with a fuller treatment than any other event in Fisk's early life shows how critical Bond considered this event to be in shaping Fisk's life and career. This occurred, says Bond, "about two years after he began to hope that he was a Christian."[38]

## Fisk's Conversion Narrative

Fisk's conversion narrative opens with Fisk confessing to an early fear of death rooted in an anxiety over his eternal destiny. It was a fear that arose out of family conversations.

> As I was educated in a religious family, and heard much conversation about the things of religion, I often felt alarmed at the prospect of dying in my sins, and going down to destruction. Such fears, however, though frequent, were of short duration.[39]

The fear of death began the process, but, it was not enough to make him seek what was needed to remove the anxiety. For the most part Fisk lived as most young people live: torn between a desire to throw off parental retraints and a fear of the consequences.

> I was busily employed in plans of vain amusement and restraints of parental authority, that I might feel more free to pursue my career of youthful folly;—and yet I wished to avoid all those

36. Hallock, *The Mountain Miller*.
37. Rubin, *Religious Melancholy and Protestant Experience in America*, 130.
38. Bond, *Memoir*, 15. What follows is taken from pages 15–18.
39. Ibid.

appearances that would lower me in the estimation of the sober part of society.[40]

About this time, some of Fisk's peers who had already been granted the gift of regeneration ("Zion's friends") started a regular prayer meeting "for the cause of religion and the souls of sinners." Fisk began attending. It was at one of these meetings, in January of 1808, that he met a friend who challenged him to give more serious consideration to his status with God.

> "Remember," said this friend, "you have an immortal soul that must exist beyond the grave either in happiness or woe!"

It was a wake up call for Fisk, who, "after much reluctance, and many hard struggles for a few days" made a determined effort to "seek religion."

> I endeavored carefully to keep my mind on religious subjects, I read much, prayed often, and frequently attended religious meetings. I began to conclude that I was a subject of genuine conviction and should soon be converted.[41]

This was the critical "in-between" stage where Fisk found religion, but didn't find God. And it was a "trying time" for him, as he faced the frustration of actively seeking what he could not attain through his own efforts. All he could do is hope that he would soon "be converted" even while it appeared that it would never happen.

> I did not feel, as I had expected I should. I therefore began to fear that my expectations of being converted were delusive.[42]

This began a short time of disquiet as Fisk engaged in a silent, simmering protest against the injustice of a God who failed to respond positively to his earnest religiosity.

> I was vexed that a just God possessed all power, and would do his pleasure, without regard to the dictates of his creatures.[43]

And then regeneration happened; not, according to Fisk, because of his new-found commitment to religious activities, but because God

---

40. Ibid., 16.
41. Ibid.
42. Ibid.
43. Ibid., 17.

decided for no reason beyond his own will to act redemptively in Fisk's behalf.

> I am fully persuaded that I should have continued in my sins, and rejected the Saviour, and grieved away the Spirit, had not God, of his own good pleasure, applied to my heart the washing of regeneration and the renewing of the Holy Spirit.[44]

Interestingly, Fisk didn't actually describe what it was he experienced at this life-altering moment. All we know from his testimony is that something happened to effect a radical transformation from a self-serving to a Jesus-serving lifestyle.

> O how sweet the joys of believing in Jesus! What pleasures didst thou my soul realize, when the light of God's countenance first shone upon thee? What can compare with the joy and peace of believing in Jesus? "Give me 'affliction with the people of God,' rather than 'the pleasures of sin for a season.' Let the Lord be my God, and may I never be unfaithful in his cause. I devote myself, O Lord, to thee. . . . Cleanse me from my sins—save me from stupidity—keep me humble—prepare me for thy service, and make me an instrument of good in the world."[45]

## MAKING SENSE OF REGENERATION

This is where Pliny Fisk's missiological journey began: with this regenerative experience, as it would become both the initiating motivation for the journey and the framework within which it would unfold. In this case the experience itself was less important than the implications Fisk drew from it.

The most critical implication Fisk took from this experience was what it said to him about the need for his own personal involvement in an evangelical mission to those who were on the wrong side of the regenerative divide. "Make me an instrument of good in the world," he prayed, and like many evangelicals then and today "good" was defined primarily if not exclusively in terms of a persuasive evangelical proclamation that would (by God's grace) evoke faith responses.

44. Ibid.
45. Ibid., 18.

"From this time," wrote Bond, "[Fisk] manifested a deep solicitude for the salvation of sinners, and often exhorted, and affectionately urged them to immediate repentance."[46]

## DISINTERESTED BENEVOLENCE

Fisk's "deep solicitude for the salvation of sinners" gives evidence of the influence of a critical New Divinity teaching related to what Samuel Hopkins described as "disinterested benevolence," which was an interpretive twist on Jonathan Edwards' theology of regeneration. Both Edwards and Hopkins believed that the conversion experience was rooted in the will. This (the will) is what changed when the Spirit infused a person's life with regenerative grace allowing a selfish person to become a self-*less* person.[47]

The twist Hopkins made to Edwards' teaching was related to the form selflessness took in the regenerated sinner. In his work, *The Nature of True Virtue*, Edwards had defined the virtue obtained through regeneration as "benevolence to Being in general."[48] Hopkins felt this was too esoterically ill-defined to issue in the kind of Christian action he felt to be necessary for an authentic Christian life.

> In Hopkins' view, the quietistic emphasis of *True Virtue* made Edwards vulnerable to the charge that he had involved practical religion in a cloud. Edwards' detailed descriptions of the subjective nature of regeneration, when combined with the mystical quality of his concept of Being in general, enouraged passive contemplation and rapt otherworldliness.[49]

Hopkins' solution was to redefine "Being in general" to "God and our neighbors," thus giving concrete definition to what Edwards had left indistinct. This proved to be a critical shift for the Consistent Calvinists, as it activated them for transformational mission. David W. Kling explains it this way:

> Samuel Hopkins ... furnished an explicit theological rationale for missions by revising Edwards' aesthetic concept of 'disinterested benevolence' into a practical one of self-denial

---

46. Ibid.

47. Conforti, *Jonathan Edwards, Religious Tradition & American Culture*, 130.

48. Edwards, *The Nature of True Virtue*, 3.

49. Conforti, *Samuel Hopkins and the New Divinity*, 112.

for the greater glory of God's kingdom and the betterment of humankind.[50]

When Fisk prayed "make me an instrument of good in the world," this is what he had in mind.

## THE INFLUENCE OF FISK'S PASTOR

Fisk's pastor recognized immediately what a valuable asset this spiritually-charged young man could be to his own revivalist ministry, as his congregation, like most other congregations in the region, drew their vitality from the spiritual energy emanating from youthful conversions.[51] This is verified in the fact that immediately after making public confession of faith Fisk "was requested," presumably by Packard, "to assist in the services of private religious meetings" where his evangelical fervor could be showcased. "Many will long remember," said Bond, "how on such occasions he warned them with entreaties and tears to be reconciled to God."[52]

Fisk would have learned to interpret his conversion experience through a doctrinalist lens under Packard's influence. It was the lens Packard used to interpret his own calling. As one of Packard's ministerial colleagues said of him: "He was more intellectual and metaphysical than most of his brethren and never faltered in defence of his doctrinal views, which were strictly Calvinistic."[53] Packard also had a rhetorician's flair for doctrinal debate which is an approach Fisk would later employ as his primary means of evangelism in the Ottoman Empire. This is what a colleague said about him:

> Dr. Packard's mode of debate was deliberate, clear, demonstrative, and in perfect good temper ... He carefully traced every effect to its cause. Admit his premises and there was no way of avoiding his conclusions. In conversational discussion, in which he took great delight, he was fond of the socratic method

50. Kling, "The New Divinity and the Origins of the ABCFM," 12.

51. One of Packard's colleagues noted that Packard "ever felt a deep interest and took an active part in the revivals of the era. He enjoyed many such seasons in his own congregation, during his long ministry" (Sprague, *Annals*, 411). That the Second Great Awakening was overwhelmingly directed to and energized by youth (a fluid category ranging from age fourteen to twenty-five) is affirmed in chapter three of Kett's book, *Rites of Passage: Adolescence in America*.

52. Sprague, *Annals*, 411.

53. Ibid.

of asking questions, concerning points nearly self-evident, and thus advancing step by step, until, in the result, you must yield the point, or contradict your first admission.[54]

The manuscripts of four of Packard's sermons have been preserved: one he preached just before the time of Fisk's conversion, two just after and one during Fisk's junior year at Middlebury. Of most interest are two he preached on a Sunday when Fisk was in the throes of his conversion experience.[55] Almost certainly Fisk was there to hear them. Even more certainly (given his heightened awareness of spiritual realities) Fisk would have been unusually attentive to what his pastor had to say.

What Fisk heard that Sunday were two sermons focused on the reasonable nature of biblical doctrine related to the person and nature of Jesus Christ. "It is rational to conclude," said Packard at the beginning of the first sermon, "that his *true character* is plainly revealed and clearly distinguished in the sacred volume," which he then proceeded to prove using deductive reasoning more conducive to a theological lecture than a sermon. From Packard's standpoint the case for Christ's divinity was so rationally compelling that any reasonable person would accept it. "What man," he asked, "can upon any principle of just and sober reasoning, deny the Divinity of character which Christ claimed?"[56]

The second sermon was along the same lines as the first: a reasoned exposition of Christological doctrine.

> Having endeavored in the previous discourse to exhibit the evidence in favor of the essential Divinity of our Lord Jesus Christ, we proceed to a number of remarks and inferences which may serve further to illustrate the subject and shew its importance.[57]

Having proved to his satisfaction the reasonable nature of orthodox Calvinist doctrine regarding Christ's divinity, Packard went on to critique the unreasonable attitude of those who didn't accept it. Of particular interest is Packard's inclusion of two of the religious groups who would figure most prominently in Fisk's future mission: Muslims and Jews. They weren't Packard's primary targets. His primary targets were those who claimed to be following the dictates of reason and nature—"modern free thinkers and latitudinarians"—who trafficked in "the inventions of men."

54. Ibid., 409.

55. Packard, *Two Sermons Delivered in Shelburne*.

56. Ibid., 8.

57. Ibid., 11.

But the fact that he included them at all may suggest that the roots of what would later become Fisk's negative conceptualizations of Muslims and Jews in the preaching and teaching of his boyhood pastor.

> The divinity of Christ is important, because it is a designating truth of that genuine religion of the Gospel, which is infinitely superior to every other. This, altho' it may contain many things in common with other religions, which have prevailed in the world, still has certain things peculiar to itself, certain discriminating doctrines, which characterize it; among which the *Divinity* of Christ holds a preeminent rank. This distinguishes it from the religion of Mahomet, which has spread dark delusion over a great portion of the East. This distinguishes it from the religion of the Jews, who are given up of God to judicial blindness, and scattered among the nations. This distinguishes it from the religion of ancient moralists and heathen philosophers, modern free-thinkers and latitudinarians.—In short, this distinguishes the true and genuine religion of the Bible from the religion of corrupted christianity, and the *religion* of reason and the light of nature, *both* of which, though flattering and popular, are false and dangerous to the souls of men. Therefore, to deny the Divinity of Christ, is to corrupt christianity, and to confound the true religion of the Gospel with the inventions of men.[58]

It is difficult to know exactly what impression this sermon made on Fisk, but we can assume that the dogmatic certainty it represented did impact his thinking, particularly at this time of heightened spiritual apprehension. Under Packard's guidance Fisk would begin to define his regenerative experience with a doctrinal certainly ascribing to Christianity a superiority to all other religions and philosophies. Fisk's conversion had brought him spiritual enlightenment. Now it would lead to dogmatic certainty. Under Packard's guidance Fisk would soon be caught up in the spirit of doctrinalism.

> In 1800 words never failed. Because the doctrines of orthodoxy perfectly expressed a view of the world as a consistent whole, anything that contradicted orthodoxy was senseless and unacceptable. God simply did not appear outside his laws, and the laws were available for human inspection in his inspired Scriptures. The Bible caught the entirety of God's breath for man. Incomplete testimonies were valuable only as parts of a more thorough account like Hopkin's *The System of Doctrines,*

---

58. Ibid., 22.

*Contained in Divine Revelation, Explained and Defended. Show-
ing their Connection with Each Other.*[59]

## A CONTROVERSY IN DEERFIELD

Doctrinalism figured large in a controversy in which Packard played a
role the year before he preached these two sermons. Fisk almost certainly
would have been aware of it as controversies can rarely be kept quiet in
small, rural communities. It would have been an important conversation
topic around the Fisk table.

The incident in question took place against the backdrop of a long-
running ideological battle that New England Calvinists had been having
first with deists then with Unitarians who denied the essentials of Calvinist doctrine. Edwards had sparked the battle with a near obsessive fixation
on deism in his writings. According to Gerald R. McDermott, Edwards
believed deism to have been the *greatest* existential threat to orthodox
Christianity, evidenced by the large number of references Edwards made
to it in his voluminous work, always in a highly critical vein.[60]

> Jonathan Edwards recognized, perhaps more accutely than any
> other American thinker in the eighteenth century, that if Chris-
> tian thinking seriously entertained the most elemental deist
> presuppositions, the Reformed faith would collapse.[61]

This fear resurfaced in a different form among Edwards' disciples in
the 1790s particularly after the publication of Thomas Paine's vituperative
attack on dogmatic Christianity, *Age of Reason; Being an Investigation of
True and Fabulous Theology* (1794), coming as it did at a time of growing
disillusionment with the French Revolution which had now entered its
violent anti-clerical phase.[62] The radical nature of Paine's attack accompanied by the anti-Christian tenor of the French revolutionaries signaled
to many Americans, evangelical or otherwise, the rise of a dangerous

---

59. Rabinowitz, *Spiritual Self in Everyday Life*, 24.

60. McDermott, *Jonathan Edwards Confronts the Gods*, 38–39.

61. Ibid., 34.

62. "The great fear of deism arose in the mid-1790s and centered on "The Age of
Reason." Then, but not before, deism or infidelity, became the main surrogate for every
sort of clerical fear." May, *The Enlightenment in America*, 185.

religious and moral "infidelity."[63] This, they believed, threatened not only the Christian faith, but the foundations of a Christian society.[64]

One of the founders of Andover Seminary and a prominent figure in mission circles, Nathanael Emmons, indicated how seriously evangelical clerics regarded this threat in a series of sermons he preached in 1803 and 1804 in the hope of keeping young people like Fisk from falling prey to the insidious seductions of infidel philosophy. In one of these sermons, "Caution Against Bad Company," Emmons warned young Christians to avoid the company of those who

> wrest the scriptures to serve an hypothesis. The denial of them is but an easy transition. And the next step is to take the seat of the scoffer. When the belief of a future life, and the superintendency of an all-wise and just Ruler of the world, the rewarder of right and the revenger of wrong; and faith in a Redeemer, and the influence of his Spirit, and of his doctrines, are no longer suffered to check the passions, regulate the desires, and restrain the will of such fallen and degenerate creatures as we became by sin, what must man be to man ?[65]

Emmons was drawing a firm line between what was acceptable and unacceptable to evangelical Christians. It was a thin line that, once crossed, became a slippery slope.

> Beware . . . of such as seek to enslave your souls, to strip you of the true riches, to blot out your name from the book of life, and destroy your title to an eternal crown—would bring on you a

---

63. Late eighteenth-century Harvard theology professor David Tappan called infidelity a "system of ideas . . . which considers all religious principles, observance and instructors, as the remains of monkish ignorance, superstition and bigotry, or the antiquated offspring of worldly policy begotten in the early and cruder stages of society; but which are wholly unsuitable and useless, if not a heavy tax upon the public, in this more enlightened, and mature period of human affairs." Phillips, *Jedidiah Morse and New England*, 65–66.

64. The extent to which this continued to be a theme of the Consistent Calvinists throughout the early nineteenth century is seen in an article published in the *Panoplist and Missionary United Magazine* in 1815 that linked Boston-based Unitarianism to "the lowest degrees of Socianism, and to the very borders of infidelity" brought out by a Deistic preaching that was "totally at variance with the Gospel." This led to a flurry of charges and counter charges that flew back and forth in the *Panoplist* between the Consistent Calvinists and the Boston clergy who denied the charges of deism or Socianism. "Reviews: American Unitarianism."

65. Emmons, "Sermon XV: Caution Against Bad Company," 234.

spiritual disease, the end of which is the second death, everlasting contempt, and the chains of the bottomless pit.[66]

This fear of the slippery slope provided the backdrop for an incident
that would bring home to Fisk the importance of defining his conversion experience within the boundaries of an acceptable (and reasonable)
orthodoxy. It happened in the spring and fall of 1807 when the Congregational church in the nearby village of Deerfield initiated a call to a recent seminary graduate with unitarian leanings named Samuel Willard.[67]
Willard began his work before his ordination, preaching his first sermon
at the Deerfield church in March of that year.

A council drawn from the regional clergy association, which included Packard who served as its clerk, met in August to review Willard's
credentials in preparation for his ordination and installation. What they
heard was not at all pleasing to their Consistent Calvinist ears.

> A long and searching examination of the candidate was made,
> during which his confession of faith was laid before it. At the
> adjornment of the council it became evident that ordination was
> to be refused Mr. Willard and a great excitement followed.[68]

The "excitement" was created by the members of the Deerfield congregation who violently disagreed with this decision, in at least one case
literally, as a group of boys from the congregation expressed their opinion by "bowling stones at the shins of the members of the council" when
they left the meeting where the decision had been made.

The next day the congregation met to draft a crudely written, yet
impassioned plea for the council to reconsider their decision. Already,
they said, "attachments" to their pastor "have been formed, and affection excited the cords of which cannot be severed without a Struggle
little Inferior to the Pangs of Dissolving nature." In response the council
met a second time with Willard, this time asking him to prepare a more
detailed confession of faith (which is included verbatim in Sheldon's account). What is most striking about Willard's confession was its apparent
agreement with the spirit if not the substance of orthodox Calvinism. But
it was not good enough for the Consistent Calvinists.

---

66. Ibid., 235.

67. This incident is recorded in Sheldon's *A History of Deerfield, MA*.

68. Ibid., 786.

> After a long and patient investigation, *the Council did not discover in him that belief of the true and essential Divinity of our Lord Jesus Christ* nor those sentiments respecting the entire moral depravity of fallen men, while in a state of unregenerancy, nor of supernatural, special and effectual influence of the holy spirit, nor of the sovereign gracious election of God in choosing believers to everlasting life, nor of the certain perseverance of all true believers in faith and holiness thro' the influence of the spirit and promises of the covenant of grace, which doctrines they seriously and deliberately believe to be contained in the Gospel of Christ, and to be not only important but necessary to be believed and taught for the ingathering of souls to the great Shepherd and Bishop of souls [emphasis added].[69]

The decision of the council did not prevent Willard's ordination as the Deerfield church chose to subvert their decision by choosing, with the blessing of the town council, a more sympathetic council to oversee the process. This council ordained and installed Willard as the pastor of the Deerfield church on September 23, 1807, making it, in essence, the first Unitarian Congregational church in the region. Packard was notably absent from the ordination service.

## AN ANALYTICAL MIND

This controversy brings to the forefront the most striking characteristic of the doctrinalist position among New England Congregationalists. Fearing infidelity if even one element of their doctrinal scaffolding were removed, these Calvinists created a rigid demarkation line between insiders and outsiders. Theirs, they believed, was the only reasonable theological system, which meant that if Fisk wanted to be among the insiders he would have to adopt the same reasoning himself.

Actually, taking a reasoned approach to a doctrinally defined faith would not have been difficult for Fisk, given a trait of his character that we can deduce from one of the few things Bond intimated about him in his pre-conversion days. Fisk, according to Bond, had a "taste for mathematical science."

> His predilection for this science was such, even in childhood, that it was thought advisable for him to defer attention to it, till he had made competent proficiency in the other elementary branches. He obtained permission, however, to devote his

---

69. Ibid., 790.

evenings during a winter quarter to the study of arithmetic, and at the close of the term, he had acquired a good knowledge of the principal rules.[70]

We can assume from this that Fisk had an analytical mind, which, had he pursued his more natural inclinations, might have led him into a career as an accountant or bookkeeper. Knowing that all things fit together in a systematically coherent system of doctrine would have given him great satisfaction.

## CALL TO MINISTRY

Soon after he had confirmed his conversion with a public confession of faith Fisk came to believe that he was being called to propagate his doctrinalist faith through "the service of his Divine Master" in "the work of the ministry."[71] When he told his parents his intentions they were pleased. This was in contrast to how they had reacted earlier when he expressed his intension to pursue his secondary studies in a public school, as at that time they had been hoping that Pliny would stay home to carry on the family business. "[H]e was the one whom they fondly hoped to retain with them," writes Bond, "to be the staff and solace of their declining years."[72] That was when they were still praying for his eternal salvation. Now, perhaps seeing his call to ministry as a superadded answer to prayer, they gave him their blessing, "promising him whatever assistance, it was in their power to render."[73]

Fisk now began his preparations for formal pastoral ministry. What this meant for him is what it had meant for many aspiring "New Divinity" ministerial candidates of this era. It would begin with tutelage under an older, more established pastor, in this case Packard's good friend, Moses Hallock, who was in charge of a Congregational church in the nearby hamlet of Plainfield,[74] followed by four years at an evangelical college (Middlebury College) and post-graduate work at the newly established Andover Theological Seminary (1805) in Massachusetts.

Initiating theological education under the mentorship of an evangelical minister was a tradition going back to the time of Jonathan Edwards.

70. Bond, *Memoir*, 3.

71. Ibid., 18.

72. Ibid., 14.

73. Ibid., 18.

74. Ibid.

Edwards believed it was necessary for aspiring ministerial candidates whose faith had been awakened in revivalist fires to be trained for ministry by pastors who had felt the fire themselves.[75] What this meant was having established revivalist clergy offer their homes as training sites for clergy candidates, in many cases taking these candidates in as boarders. These "Schools of the Prophets" did not necessarily replace a university education, but supplemented it as a way of assuring that new clergy were suitably grounded in Consistent Calvinist theology as a defense against those who adhered to contrary beliefs. As Robert L. Ferm says of these schools at the time of the Second Great Awakening:

> [M]ost ministers who had a "school" were part of the New Divinity tradition and had been supporters, in varying degrees, of the "enthusiasms" of the revivals. These teachers sought to guide carefully the doctrinal development of their students, to nurture their individual religious fervor, to instill in them the need to be concerned about the state of the souls of their future congregations, and to make them vigilant about the currents of heresy infiltrating the Connecticut Valley—namely Arianism, Arminianism, and Deism.[76]

Schools of the Prophets were still in session during Fisk's era. Most of the Consistent Calvinists who occupied the pulpits of Congregational churches in western Massachusetts and Litchfield County, Connecticutt, including both Moses Hallock and Theophilus Packard, received ministerial training this way.[77] It was natural for Packard to suggest the same for Fisk.

Hallock's temperament was a contrast to Packard's, as he was more atuned to the devotional, pastoral side of ministry. Packard himself acknowledged as such in a tribute he wrote for his friend in the *Annals of the American Pulpit*:

> There was a simplicity and godly sincerity pervading his whole conversation, that showed clearly that the prevailing motives of his conduct were derived from the invisible and the future. "Thou God seest me," seemed to be impressed upon every action of his life.[78]

75. Conforti, *Samuel Hopkins and the New Divinity Movemen*, 24.

76. Ferm, "Seth Storrs, Congregationalism and the Founding of Middlebury College," 257.

77. Sprague, *Annals*, 310 (Hallock) and 408 (Packard).

78. Ibid., 313.

Under Hallock's guidance Fisk would have been encouraged to develop the devotional side of his spiritual life as a balance to intellectual pursuits. Hallock also would have impressed upon Fisk what Fisk had drawn from his own experience: the need to be constantly alert to signs of God's regenerative presence in his life. Excerpts from Hallock's correspondence with members of his family show how critical this ministry focus was to him.

> It has been my favored lot to see several awakenings before, but the present displays of divine power and grace in Plainfield far exceed, in my opinion, what I ever before saw. In this little place there are at least fifty persons hopefully born of God within a few months.
>
> — from a letter to his brother, Jeremiah, June 3, 1798[79]

> My very dear Brother:—I have the happiness to inform you that an awakening has begun in the eastern part of this place. He that appeared to Joshua as Captain of the Lord's host has come. Do read the two last verses of the fifth chapter of Joshua. Some seem to feel as that solemnized man did when he fell on his face, and loosed his shoes. Christians have wonderfully waked up, and I hope some few persons are lately born again that we could praise the Lord of victory.
>
> — from a letter to his brother, January 1, 1808[80]

> Very, DEAR Brother and Sister—An awakening appears to have begun here. One of my scholars . . . a step-son of Elisha Billings, Esq. of Conway, was hopefully born again three weeks ago.
>
> — from a letter to his brother and sister, April 25, 1814[81]

While we don't have any letters from Fisk indicating what he studied under Hallock's mentorship, we do have part of a letter he wrote to his brother (unnamed) from Plainfield dated September 8, 1810, that gives clear indication of his continued conversionary fervor. In this letter Fisk urged his brother to deepen his commitment to "the Redeemer's cause." The letter also gives what Bond called early evidence of an "interest in the missionary cause."[82] That it was written just ten days before the Ameri-

---

79. Yale, *The Godly Pastor*, 333.
80. Ibid., 337.
81. Ibid., 338.
82. Bond, *Memoir*, 20.

can Board of Commissioners for Foreign Missions (ABCFM) held their first organizational meeting in nearby Worcester, Massachusetts[83] may have been coincidental, but the self-sacrificing spirit that would drive Fisk and others to leave home and country for "the Redeemer's cause" under the auspices of this board is unmistakable.

> Dear Brother—We have publicly renounced the world, and avouched the Lord to be our God. Do we feel the importance of living according to our holy profession? What will it avail us, that we have been with Christians here, that we have set down with them at the table of the Lord, unless our hearts are true to the Redeemer's cause? If we would be disciples of Christ, we must deny ourselves, take up the cross, and follow him. We cannot serve Mammon, and at the same time render acceptable service to God. Our great business must be, *to act for God*.[84]

The sentiment expressed here throws into question the sometimes stark differentiation Rabinowitz makes between those he labels doctrinalists and those he labels moralists as a way of understanding the "spiritual self" among evangelicals in early nineteenth century New England. We have already seen evidence in one of Fisk's sermons of a decidedly "doctinalist" approach to his faith, something that will be reinforced when we examine several other of his early sermons at the end of this chapter. This was the interpretive grid through which Fisk gave definition to his experience of regeneration. Yet in this letter to his brother Fisk's focus was on *action* as the defining motif of an authentic Christian life which, according to Rabinowitz, would have put him in the moralist camp. For Rabinowitz the two were mutually exclusive.

> In the first quarter of the nineteenth century many evangelicals turned away from the privation, passivity, and void of orthodoxy toward a more active religious life. These moralists could not tolerate the unrelieved absence of human emotionality and, even more, the obscure place of personal responsibility in the orderly orthodox universe.[85]

Rabinowitz does recognize that there were transitional figures, people like the influential president of Yale University, Timothy Dwight, who held these two positions in a creative tension. But Rabinowitz believes

---

83. Tracy, *History of American Missions*, 27.

84. Bond, *Memoir*, 19.

85. Rabinowitz, *Spiritual Self in Everyday Life*, 86.

that Dwight had moved decisively into the "moralist" camp near the end of his life. This, suggests Rabinowitz, is most apparent in the way Dwight came to interpret scripture:

> For the orthodox, biblical texts were used largely to verify the theological or theoretical structure of the revealed plan of redemption. The passages were instructive but only if interpreted as proof-texts for Calvinism. For Dwight and the moralists who learned at his knee, Scripture was instead an endlessly entertaining collection of instructive tales, literally a compendium recounting the actions of God, Jesus, kings, prophets, saints and sinners, each tale richly and individually informative. The Bible was more like a father's storytelling than an alchemists's mysterious formula. It was not useful merely in exemplifying principles that could be stated most clearly in the dogmatic theology of Calvin or Edwards. Literal believers in Scripture could discover positive tenets and exact directions for everyday life.[86]

It's possible that Fisk was a transitional figure like Dwight, showing evidence of both emphases in his writing. But it is more probable that Fisk was one of many Consistent Calvinists who held these two positions in a creative tension. He was, in other words, not a transitional figure, but rather one of many of his era who operated with a foot in both camps. Without abandoning Rabinowitz's categories altogether we might label Fisk a doctrinal moralist, or moral doctrinalist, at least at this point in his development. The question is whether that would still be the case after he had completed his studies at Middlebury College in Middlebury, Vermont.

## THE MIDDLEBURY YEARS

In the fall of 1811 Pliny traveled through the hills of northwest Massachusetts and southwest Vermont to Middlebury College "unaccompanied by friend or acquaintance."[87] He was going to a college that had only recently celebrated its first decade of existence.[88]

Middlebury College was the pride of the town both for the educational opportunities it offered and as a way of attracting business. The entrepeneurs who built it, says Middlebury's historian, David Stameshkin,

---

86. Ibid., 89.

87. Bond, *Memoir*, 20.

88. Stameshkin, *The Town's College*, 1.

did so with the hope of attracting new settlers to the area, "thereby raising land values and making the town a likely regional center."[89]

There was a business angle to Middlebury's founding, but the principles upon which it was founded and for which it drew the support of the larger community had more to do with faith than profit. Those who founded Middlebury College, as well as those who gave it their support, were Congregationalists, many of whom had come to the area in the mid to late eighteenth century from the heart of New Divinity territory in Litchfield County, Connecticut.[90] Many of its first professors, presidents and board members were New Divinity men, or at least Edwardsean in their leanings.[91] What Robert L. Ferm writes about Williams College at this time could also be said of Middlebury:

> From the highest reaches of the presidency and board of trustees to the student body, [Jonathan] Edwards' second,third, and fourth generation disciples shaped the religious character of Williams College. For forty years, they read New Divinity works, taught New Divinity theology, discoursed in New Divinity language,behaved in New Divinity ways, and promoted New Divinity revivals.[92]

This, almost certainly, explains why Fisk chose to attend Middlebury as it was neither the only institutional option open to him nor the closest to home. He chose it because his pastoral mentors, Theophilus Packard and Moses Hallock, would have recommended it to him as a place that would reinforce their own teaching, or at least not contradict it in ways that would lead Fisk to stray too far from his theological bearings. They also knew that Fisk would find companions for his spiritual journey there in a community of like-minded Christians whose own regenerative experience would match his own.

Fisk met his Ottoman traveling companion, Levi Parsons at Middlebury whom he would later describe as his "dearest earthly friend"[93] during the time they would spend together as a missionary team. We have no indication when or how they met, although we can assume that

89. Ibid., 3.

90. Ibid.

91. Ferm, "Seth Storrs, Congregationalism and the Founding of Middlebury College," 258.

92. Ibid.

93. *Fisk Diary*, Vol. I. DFL, 120. Fisk wrote this about Parsons the day Parsons died.

their common passion for revivalist-centered mission, as well as shared conversion experiences, would have drawn them together early on in their years at Middlebury.

Parsons' revivalist fervor was more pronounced than Fisk's. He was also more demonstratively pious given alternatively to flights of millennial ecstacy and troughs of spiritual despair, something that we find occasionally in Fisk's writing, but rarely with Parsons' emotional *élan*. We see this when we set Parsons' conversion narrative alongside Fisk's. Both follow similar contours, both lead to the same end, but Parsons' has a dramatic flourish that is absent in Fisk's more analytical account. This is evident in Parsons' description of something he experienced during a revival on Middlebury's campus in November of 1811; three years after he had made public confession of faith.

> Wearied and distressed I sat down upon a log, and contemplated the miseries of hell. My thoughts were thus; "your doom is now certain, you did hope for heaven, but you will hope no more. Your sentence is just. O miserable hell! God commands you to repent; but your heart is too hard, it will not relent." At this moment, I was directed to Jesus, as an all-sufficient Saviour. Then my heart acquiesced in his atonement, and in his dealings with such a vile sinner, as I saw myself to be; and my soul reposed itself on the arm of everlasting love. I felt the chain break; O it was the bondage of sin! I opened the Bible, and read these words, "For this cause, I bow my knees to the God, and Father of our Lord Jesus Christ." It will never be in my power to give an adequate description of my feelings in view of this passage. There was a beauty, majesty, and sweetness in it, which are indescribable. I dwelt upon it until my heart was in a flame of love.[94]

### Revivalism at Middlebury

The revival that sparked Parsons' conversion[95] was one of several that would sweep through Middlebury's campus during the time Fisk was there. Parsons' account mentions a revival that happened in the fall of 1811, another took place the following year. This one was notable enough to have been written up in the popular evangelical publication, *The Pano-*

94. Morton, *Memoir of Rev. Levi Parsons*, 11.

95. Morton suggests that Parsons after "more mature reflection" would look back on this incident and question whether it really was a conversion. "[H]e was on the whole rather inclined to think otherwise," 13.

*plist and Missionary Magazine United*. What we learn from this article is that about half of the student body of 135 were "exemplary professors of religion," that is, able to give testimony to an experience of regeneration.[96]

David F. Allmendinger observes that revivals like these not only had the blessing of college authorities, but were often led by them, at least partly because of the way they fostered the maintenance of order and discipline on campus.[97] The transformation that regeneration effected was seen in this case not only as a way that people made peace with God, but also as a means of moral transformation. Parsons himself made note of this, remarking to his sister in a letter he wrote in March of 1812 that "the revival of religion has cured our class of that unbounded jealousy which formerly reigned."[98] Other students at other colleges noticed the same thing. Moral revival almost always accompanied religious revival.

> Before the Williams College revival of 1812, Albert Hopkins reported, 'it became a trial to live in college, especially in the building occupied by the two lower classes.' Then came a revival, and with revival change came.
>
> The results were permanent. Those various petty mischiefs and tricks which had been so common before, entirely disappeared, and during the three years which followed, the students pursued their appropriate pursuits, in an atmosphere quiet and tranquil, congenial to mental improvement as well as growth in divine things.[99]

Fisk understood moral transformation to be a critical element of the regenerative experience. We heard it in his sermon when he defined such an experience as: "a change of heart, a change of moral character ... a change from sin to holiness, a resurrection from the dead, a new creation, the implantation of holiness in the soul."[100] To the evangelical mind, then and now, this is how colleges and communities and nations are transformed for the better; one regenerated soul at a time.

96. "Revival of Religion at Middlebury College," *The Panoplist and Missionary Magazine United for the Year Ending July 1, 1812*, Vol. IV, New Series, 380.

97. Allmendinger Jr., *Paupers and Scholars*, 119.

98. *Letter from Levi Parsons to Mrs. Lucretia Parsons* dated March, 1812. DFL.

99. Allmendinger Jr., *Paupers and Scholars*, 120.

100. See note 25 [X-REF].

## Passionate Revivalist; PoorScholar

Fisk not only participated in revivals on Middlebury's campus, he was fixated on them. This is clear from one of the few criticisms Bond leveled against Fisk at any time of his life. His critique was that Fisk's revivalist fixation led him to neglect his studies. Bond offered this critique through the words of one of Fisk's professors at Middlebury who said this of Fisk's academic performance:

> His talents were highly respectable; though as a *scholar* he never greatly distinguished himself. He had an aversion to the study of the ancient languages. Owing to his reluctance to apply himself closely to the investigation of difficult passages, the knowledge he acquired of these languages, was somewhat imperfect. The branches of science which belonged to my department—the mathematics and natural philosophy—he pursued with more eagerness and greater success. But even here he was *good,* rather than *excellent.*[101]

Bond's own critique is heard in his insistence that Fisk's lack of academic prowess was not due to a lack of ability, but rather to "the mistaken notion that vigorous and persevering application to the sciences was necessarily unfavorable to the cultivation of the religious affections."[102] Fisk himself acknowledged at a later date that this was his attitude at Middlebury, but rejected the critique. This, he insisted, was a proper Christian perspective. What mattered for the believer was not the development of the intellect, but the development of moral character, which called for more attention being given to spiritual matters than academic studies. The fact that Fisk said this in a letter he wrote to his brother, Joel, just a year before his death in Beirut, shows how tenaciously Fisk held to this belief over time.

> God has given us intellect, that we cultivate it and use it in his service. But in order to become what ministers should be, I am persuaded that we have much more need of *moral* than of *intellectual* cultivation, and I believe as the millennium approaches, there will be a change in the whole system of education; and it will be conducted more as if it were intended to raise up men for the service of Christ, *and for holy action.*[103]

101. Bond, *Memoir,* 21.

102. Ibid., 22.

103. Quoted in Stameshkin, *Town's College,* 89.

There is little else we learn from Bond's memoir about Fisk's time at Middlebury that gives insight into the workings of his mind, which is unfortunate as this is the only source of information for this period of his life. However, Bond did include a commendation from a classmate who praised Fisk's Christian "*zeal*" and "*promptitude* in seizing opportunities for promoting the spiritual interest of others."[104] He also made a point of quoting the same professor who had questioned Fisk's scholarship saying that "he brought with him to the college a religious character of inestimable value" that "never slumbered nor slept, . . . always alive, always bright."[105]

Fisk's time at Middlebury was focused as much on promoting revivalist causes as cracking books. But given the evangelical emphasis of a Middlebury education this was a commendable flaw. In the end it is what gained him the admiration of faculty and students alike, such as the student who wrote this commendation giving reference to the impact Fisk made at Middlebury during the revival of 1812:

> In the year 1812, the hearts of Christians were cheered with a revival of religion in the college. It was not so powerful as has, at some other times, been experienced, still it was enough to warm the hearts, and engage the energies of all the officers and students who loved to witness the advancement of the Redeemer's kingdom. In this happy company Mr. Fisk stood in the foremost rank. The influence he exerted on his fellow students was most salutary. The pious were animated, and stimulated to duty by his example. Sinners, even the vilest, listened to his pathetic admonitions, for they all believed "That he was *honest* in the sacred cause."[106]

## A Missionary Interest

What is notably absent in what Bond wrote about Fisk's years at Middlebury is any reference to Fisk's growing interest in and attachment to an American evangelical missionary venture that went global the year before he began his studies. We know from the records that he was a member of the secretive[107] Brethren Society, which came to Middlebury from

104. Bond, *Memoir*, 24.

105. Ibid., 23.

106. Ibid.

107. Which included the use of a secret code they used to keep records of their

Williams College in 1810,[108] and remained active in this organization throughout the years of his graduate studies. The sole purpose of this society, according to its constitution, was "to effect, in the persons of its members, a mission, or missions to the heathens."[109] And admission to membership was strictly regulated, reserved solely for those who could show both a personal commitment to missionary service and the proper evangelical credentials. The constitution of the society made this clear.

> The utmost care shall be exercised in admitting members. All the information shall be acquired of the character and situation of a candidate which is practicable. No person shall be admitted, who is under an engagement of any kind which shall be incompatible with going on a mission to the Heathen. No person shall be admitted until he express a firm belief in those distinguishing doctrines commonly denominated evangelical.[110]

Fisk's involvement was more than casual.[111] He wrote the history of the organization. He decoded their documents when they felt secrecy was no longer necessary nor appropriate.[112] So why the silence from Bond about Fisk's involvement in this organization?

The answer lies in the secretive nature of the Brethren which all members swore to uphold. One can only guess at the reason for this, although the little we have by way of explanation indicates that it may have had to do with the fearful respect these students had for authority and public scrutiny. This is how one of the founding members of the Brethren[113] explained the secrecy:

> The reason for secrecy was the possibility of failure in the enterprise, public opinion then being opposed to us; in accordance

---

activities.

108. *The Historical Sketch of the Society*, which was written by Fisk during his time at Andover, notes that Ezra Fisk (no relation) was sent to Middlebury from Williams College by its founding members two or three years after its establishment in 1808 "to promote the good object there." The membership list in the Andover-Newton archives has Fisk joining this organization in 1810, which he affirms in *The Historical Sketch*. This is puzzling given the fact that he only became a student in 1811. Whatever the case, his involvement came early on during his time at Middlebury.

109. ANTS, *Constitution of a Society of Brethren*.

110. Ibid.

111. ANTS, *Brethren Journal*, 37.

112. Ibid.

113. Ezra Fisk.

with which good men often said, the enterprise of a foreign mission, of which we talked, was the result of overheated zeal, and would be soon forgotten; there was enough to do at home, etc. Under these circumstances, *modesty* required us to conceal our association, lest we should be throught rashly imprudent, and so should injure the cause we wished to promote [emphasis added].[114]

This is why Bond said so little about Fisk's interest in missions during his Middlebury years. Fisk, like all other members of the secretive Brethren, said little about it himself. Fisk admitted as such in a letter he wrote to his professors at Andover Seminary in 1817.

Knowing that I was liable to misjudge, that my resolution might fail, that Providence might defeat my purpose, I said but little, except to particular friends. My conviction of duty and desire to perform it increased, till I left college. This single object, a mission to the heathen, was almost invariably before me. And this was the principle thing that led me to this Seminary.[115]

This same letter indicated what it was that sparked Fisk's interest in missions.

Early in life I professed religion, and soon desired the work of the Gospel ministry. About this time I read Horne and Buchanan on the subject of missions. The subject deeply interested my feelings more than a year, and for a few months engrossed a large share of my attention. The result was a conviction that it was my duty, and an earnest desire, to be a missionary to the heathen.[116]

The work to which Fisk referred is *Christian Researches in Asia* by Claudius Buchanan which in its first edition included a sermon preached in London by the Rev. Melville Horne on the subject of missions.[117] Both were British clergymen speaking and writing to fellow British clergymen. But what they said inspired Fisk to develop a keen interest in missions as it did for many others of his generation.

Buchanan's book was in the form of a voyeuristic travelogue offering colorfully lurid eyewitness accounts of the religious practices of various

114. Quoted in Worchester, *The Life and Labors of the Rev. Samuel Worcester, D.D*, 85.

115. Bond, *Memoir*, 41.

116. Ibid.

117. Buchanan, *Christian Researches in Asia.*

communities in India, China and Malaysia, including indigenous Christian communities. These were countries that British evangelicals had targeted for missionary service. It was Buchanan's hope that the information he provided from his travels throughout Asia would both spur those involved to an even greater effort and inspire new legions of missionaries. What he saw in Asia convinced him of the need, a need derived from what he perceived to be the vile, sometimes criminal practices of those who practiced non-Christian religions. Hinduism was the worst, particularly their worship of a god Buchanan identified as the "Juggernaut."[118]

> [N]o record of ancient or modem history can give, I think, an adequate idea of this valley of death; it may be truly compared with the valley of Hinnom. The idol called Juggernaut, has been considered as the Moloch of the present age; and he is justly so named, for the sacrifices offered up to him by self-devotement, are not less criminal, perhaps not less numerous, than those recorded of the Moloch of Canaan.[119]

The overall effect of Buchanan's account was to evoke disgust and pity from his readers, leading them, he hoped, to the same conclusion he had reached, which was the need to preach the gospel to those who were caught in the grip of idolatrous worship and practice. Citing the example of King Nebachadnezzer's testimony to the miraculous power of God in Daniel chapter four, Buchanan urged his fellow citizens to participate in an evangelical missionary effort to bring liberation and happiness to the people of China and Malaysia and India:

> It (Nebachadnezzar's testimony in Daniel 4) reminds us of the last charge of HIM "who ascended up on high:" Go, TEACH ALL NATIONS. It discovers to us the new and extended benevolence, greatness of mind, and pure and heavenly charity, which distinguish that man, whose heart has been impressed by THE GRACE OF GOD . . . Let Great Britain imitate the example of the Chaldean King; and send forth to all the world HER testimony concerning the TRUE GOD.[120]

---

118. "The form of Krishna worshiped in Puri, Orissa, where in the annual festival his image is dragged through the streets on a heavy chariot; devotees are said formerly to have thrown themselves under its wheels. Also called Jagannatha." Oxford Dictionaries, http://oxforddictionaries.com/definition/Juggernaut?region=us&rskey=ZdYHn 8&result=1 (accessed July 8, 2016).

119. Buchanan, *Christian Researches in Asia*, 29.

120. Ibid., 152.

Horne went further than Buchanan in urging his fellow citizens to become fervent about missions. The image he used to make his case was that of millions of people living in darkness who were desperately grop- ing for the light and blessings that belonged to those who were citizens of God's Kingdom.

> I plead for the millions, rational, immortal as yourselves; the meanest of whose souls is more prized by their Redeemer, than the fabric of their material system. By me they sue; not to be instructed in our European arts, not to be freed from the iron bondage of the worldly oppressor, nor to be admitted to the participation of the civil rights and liberties of Britons; no, my brethren, they sue for nobler things. By the tender mercies of Christ, by the blood of his cross, by the promises of truth, by the hope of the Gospel, they sue to be admitted into the peaceful Church of Jesus, to be associated with the privileges and honor of the Christian name; and that inheritance in the heavens, incorruptible, undefiled, and that faded not away, which is the Christian's lot. This, they solicit, they demand, in the name of their Lord and ours; who hath *asked*, and received *the heathen for his inheritance, and the uttermost parts of the earth for his possession.*[121]

After reading this it would have been difficult for Fisk with his re- vivalist faith informed by a "disinterested benevolence" to resist the call to spiritual arms. What Buchanan and Horne were laying before him was an evangelistic task with global significance. Just as the people of Shel- burne and Plainfield and Wilmington needed God's regenerative power, so did the heathen. It was all God's work, and Fisk was God's servant.

This is a speculative estimation of how Fisk might have been influ- enced by this work, as he didn't indicate specifically how it impacted his thought. But it is reasonable to assume that Horne's plea for the "millions . . . prized by their Redeemer" suing for admission into the "peaceful Church of Jesus" would have made this kind of impression on him. A conversation Bond recorded Fisk having with a fellow Andover seminar- ian a few years later suggests this to be the case. "How little we feel," said Fisk to his friend, "that probably now there are 500,000,000 of people entirely ignorant of the Saviour!"[122]

---

121. Ibid., 233.

122. Bond, *Memoir*, 37.

We hear this same thought expressed with more detail by Levi Parsons in a letter he wrote in 1815 to the man who would become his posthumous biographer, Daniel O. Morton. As Fisk had been inspired by Buchanan and Horne, so Parsons had been inspired by a sermon he had just heard on the primary thesis put forward in Buchanan and Horne's work.

> Could you have been there & heard the wretched state of pagan Asia described, you would have said to me, go with them & by the assistance of God, break their iron fetters, liberate their enslaved minds & proclaim the freedom of the Gospel. I doubt not, that it was the language of every pious heart, "O that I would give them the bread of life." . . . Let me ask you, my brother, does [sic] not the cries of the perishing millions around the world often prompt you to greater exertions in your own sphere? Does not the unwearied zeal of many of our brethren, for the souls of the heathen quicken your spirit in the discharge of your ministerial duties? I ask for no other evidence of the propriety of foreign missions.[123]

Both Fisk and Parsons were expressing a motivation for mission widely held among the evangelicals of their era. It was the motivation of pity felt for an amorphous mass of nameless, faceless people who were living outside the boundaries of Christian grace and morality; "500,000,000 of people entirely ignorant of the Saviour!" What we can assume from this is that Fisk would have been focused less on determining who these people were than how he might be used by God to help these poor people experience the regenerative grace that had transformed his life. Just as he was lost without that grace, so it was with the 500,000,000. In the words of a New Divinity contemporary who echoed this thought:

> Their gods cannot save them; their wise men will not, cannot direct their feet into the way of peace; their religion does not satisfy the heart or the life; does not bring them to the blood which cleanseth from sin,—does not shew them a redeeming God, does not fit them for the mansions of immortal light and purity,—does not dissipate the darkness which heavily broods over them, thickening into the blackness of eternal night![124]

---

123. *Letter from Levi Parsons to Rev. Daniel Morton dated June 21, 1815.* DFL.

124. A quote from Fisk's contemporary, Samuel Worchester, who was one of the founding members of the ABCFM. This quote from a piece he wrote in 1815, is cited in Hutchinson, *Errand to the World*, 48.

## PREACHING IN VERMONT

While Fisk thrived spiritually at Middlebury he had a much more difficult time taking care of his immediate needs. He suffered, says Bond, from "pecuniary embarrassment" brought on particularly by the "protracted illness of his father."[125] As a result when he graduated from Middlebury he found himself in the same situation as many of today's students. He was loaded with debt. This forced a change in his plans. Rather than going directly to Andover Seminary as he had hoped, he took a year off to begin paying off his loans. And his pastor, Theophilus Packard, convinced him that the best way to spend this year was in the pulpit.

Fisk graduated from Middlebury in August of 1814. By September he was back in Shelburne under Packard's mentorship preparing to convince his local Congregational association that he was qualified to be licensed for ministry.[126] It was a humbling moment for Fisk, as he was well aware of his youth and inexperience. "I feel that I am very inadequate . . . ," he said, "My help must come from God." It was this help he sought in a prayer he recorded that reveals both sides of his nature—analytical and pious.

> Almighty Saviour, to thee I look for assistance in discharging the important duties which now devolve upon me. Thou knowest my weakness, ignorance, want of experience, and the temptations to which I shall be exposed. Do thou strengthen, instruct, and support me. I pray for assistance in the choice of texts, in studying and preparing sermons. Teach me the true meaning of thy word. Let me never adopt sentiments, or form determinations hastily. Enable me to resist the influence of all unhallowed motives; give me a spirit of devotion; make me studious and faithful. May I be prudent and zealous, humble and dedicated, conciliatory and consistent. Give me health of body and soundness of mind. Let my preaching be solemn and interesting, doctrinal, experimental, or practical, as the occasion may require. O my God, enable me to preach "in demonstration of the spirit, and with power," and wilt thou give the word an efficient influence, that it may reach the hearts of men.[127]

The Franklin Association of Congregational ministers granted Fisk the ministerial license he sought in January of 1815. By the first of March

---

125. Bond, *Memoir*, 22.

126. Ibid., 26.

127. Ibid., 27.

he accepted an offer to preach for a year at the Congregational church in Wilmington, Vermont, where tension existed over the dismissal of the former pastor. "[P]arty animosities," wrote Bond, "were excited in consequence of the dismission of their pastor."[128] It was a difficult situation for a novice preacher, but Fisk made the best of it. "Meetings for prayer and conference were frequent, and well attended" under his pastoral leadership "and it was evident that the Holy Spirit had come down with power to revive his work."[129]

Fifteen of the sermons Fisk preached during this time have been preserved in the archives of Andover Newton Theological School. Meticulously hand written, numbered and dated, these sermons offer us the best opportunity to ascertain where Fisk was at this stage of his mental and spiritual development. What follows is a synopsis of the primary themes found in these sermons.

## *The Sermons*

The format of these sermons is expository preaching revolving around a series of rhetorical questions that Fisk answered with what he apparently considered to be biblically and rationally airtight arguments. It was the Socratic method without the complicating counterpoint of an oppositional voice. This was true even with a funeral sermon he preached, which took on the flavor of an intellectual discourse on death.

> The term usually, in scripture, & in common discourse, relates to the death of the body, otherwise called natural death or temporal death. To this allusion is evidently had in our text (Job 14:10) concerning the nature of this we are enquiring.[130]

The style here is less important than what it reveals about Fisk's analytical nature. This is someone who read the Bible and interpreted its teachings with a dispassionate empiricism, engaging in biblical exegesis as though he were reading an operational manual for a complex machine. This was also the way he interpreted the structure of the universe. Creation was to Fisk a well ordered, perfectly functioning machine doing exactly what its creator intended it to do.

128. Ibid., 28.
129. Ibid.
130. *Fisk Sermon*, May, 1815, No. 27, ANTS.

> The hand of God guides alike the revolving planet & floating
> atom; alike the revolutions of nations & the motions of insects;
> alike the common & the miraculous events which the world has
> witnessed; alike the formation, the continuance & the change of
> moral characters . . . In the government of them all, God wills
> that, vast & complicated as the machine is, he can manage all its
> parts & move the whole according to his pleasure.[131]

This belief in a providentially ordered universe was a theme Fisk
would return to several times in these sermons. It was important for him
to know that God was in charge of all that occurred, including those elements of existence that would cause others to doubt providence.

> If God is almighty then he will dole out pain or pleasure to his
> creatures *as he* chooses. He is under no necessity of making
> them happy, except what arises from his own benevolent dispo-
> sition. . . . Diseases are all his servants. The avenues and sources
> of pain are all under his control. He can send such disappoint-
> ments & inflict such evils as he pleases on his creatures.[132]

Fisk's certainty about God's providential determination paralleled
his conviction that Christianity was the only reasonable religious option
for human kind. This is what common sense confirmed: Christian belief.

> Christianity exhibits the most rational scheme of doctrine ever
> yet promulgated. This scheme, though incomprehensible, con-
> tains no absurdities, no contradictions.[133]

Fisk was preaching familiar themes to his Wilmington congregation. But they weren't his only audience. He was also looking beyond this
congregation to the Unitarians and deists and rationalists who accused
Calvinists like Fisk of perpetuating irrational beliefs. In Fisk's mind they
were the irrational ones.

> With all their boasting they are resisting *the plainest dictates
> of common sense* & discarding the most obvious principles of
> right reason . . . Let everything that militates against the divine
> authority of sacred scripture be considered and avoided as dan-
> gerous poison [emphasis added].[134]

131. *Fisk Sermon*, April, 1815. No. 18, ANTS.

132. Ibid.

133. Ibid.

134. Ibid.

## Scottish Common Sense Realism

The basis for Fisk's certainty about the rationality of his doctrinalist faith was a pedogogical epistemology utilized by Middlebury College and other evangelical insitutions of the era. This was an epistemology alternatively called "Common Sense Realism" or "Scottish Common Sense Realism," given its origins in the work of Scottish moral philosophers, particularly the work of Thomas Reid and Dugald Stewart.[135] According to Mark Noll this was the most prominent philosophical tradition in American colleges (including Middlebury)[136] in the era "dominated by the American Revolution" (1763–1815).[137] This era, says Noll, "witnessed the triumph of Common Sense in American intellectual life."[138]

We can see the influence of this philosophy in the first sentence of the Declaration of Independence: "We declare these truths to be *self evident*." Truths that matter are "self evident," able to be grasped naturally with divinely-gifted *common sense*. This is so because the One who endowed humanity with common sense built these truths into the structure of a divinely-created universe.

> His [Thomas Reid's] answer to the problem of knowledge was a concept of the mind as not merely an empty receptor for sense impressions, but as something already furnished with active, self-evident principles. These principles included overwhelming belief in the existence of God, an orderly universe and our own selves; in the realiability of perception; and in the reality of causality and other principles. As Levi Hedge of Harvard explained, such propositions as "I know that I exist," "Everything that happens has a cause," and "The events I remember really happened," are self-evident truths that we know by intuition; they are the foundation for all other knowledge, and one cannot go beneath them in an endless regression of doubt.[139]

Evangelical educators extended the range of self evident truths to include truths drawn from the biblical account by a Protestant hermeneutic.

135. See Ahlstrom, *The Scottish Philosophy and American Theology*, 257–72.

136. "[T]he president's lectures were often considered the most important academic experience in the undergraduate's career. Bates, whose specialty was metaphysics, presented a mixture of Lockean empiricism, *Scottish common sense philosophy*, [emphasis added] and orthodox Calvinism." Stameshkin, *Town's College*, 71.

137. Noll, *Common Sense Tradition and American Evangelical Thought*, 218.

138. Ibid.

139. Matthews, *Toward a New Society: American Thought and Culture*, 38.

There was in this case little of the tension that exists in many people's minds today between science and religion as the two disciplines were held together by their mutual affirmation of God's providential governance of the universe. "God's handiwork was everywhere apparent to Middlebury faculty," says Stameshkin, "in history, literature, and the laws of science and mathematics."[140]

Fisk learned his lessons well at Middlebury. In one way or another this emphasis on the reasonable nature of the Christian faith came across in nearly every sermon he preached in Wilmington, including one he preached in January of 1815.

> [W]hat history has more evidence of its truth than this? What doctrines are in themselves more reasonable, what requirement more proper than these? What facts ever were better attested than the Christian miracles? What system can be introduced in lieu of the Bible, more harmonious in itself, more rational & consistent, more favorable in its tendency or more beneficial in its effects?[141]

All of this underscores why Fisk could make the confident assertion in the same sermon that "Mahometan & different systems of Pagan religion" were the "inventions of men."[142] What these "systems" lacked was the confirmation of common sense. They were not congruent with divine logic. The proof was found in the fruit they produced.

> Compare your situation with that of those who do not enjoy these instructions. Go visit yonder Hottentots. See these thousands who have never thought of a God or any spiritual being. They live & die from generation to generation in this wretched state of ignorance. Visit other heathen countries. Ask their wise men concerning God. By some you will be directed to the sun, by some to a golden or silver or a wooden god. By others a long list of imaginary gods & goddesses will be exhibited attended perhaps by an equal number of demi gods, and heroes diefied. These modes of ignorant superstitious worship need not be mentioned. They are such as might be expected from such theories as theirs, verily they live in darkness & the shadow of death. But around us the light of truth shines.[143]

140. Stameshkin, *Town's College*, 75.

141. Fisk Sermon, January 1815, No. 7, ANTS.

142. Ibid.

143. Ibid.

## SUMMING UP AND LOOKING AHEAD

The picture that emerges from this phase of Fisk's life, as he followed a trajectory leading to a ministerial vocation, was of someone whose analytical nature warmed to a common sense epistemology that drew a stark contrast between those who grasped the inherent logic of the evangelical world view and those who didn't. This perception, combined with a "disinterested benevolence" that fostered active engagement in evangelical witness in a world increasingly bereft of the salutary influence of the pure gospel, found Fisk being drawn (as others like him were being drawn) towards the consideration of cross-cultural mission service.

What began as a vocational exploration at Middlebury would become a full blown calling at the next educational institution Fisk would attend. This was Andover Theological Seminary, whose origins lay in a controversy raised by the kind of dogmatic certainty Fisk exhibited in his sermons at Wilmington. Understanding these origins is critical to determining how Andover shaped Fisk's thought as he prepared for a missionary career. An exploration of these origins will be the subject matter of chapter three.

# 3

## Building the Orthodox Fortress

### JEDIDIAH MORSE AND THE ILLUMINATI CONSPIRACY

JEDIDIAH MORSE WAS ONE of many American pastors who, in May of 1798, embraced John Adams' call for a day of "solemn humiliation, fasting and prayer"[1] occasioned by the possibility of war with the French over American trade with Britain. The impetus was what many Americans perceived to be the humiliating treatment of peace commissioners sent to France by Adams in March of 1797.

When Morse prepared his sermon for this "solemn" occasion he was drawing on several years of growing alarm among Americans in general, but orthodox clergy[2] in particular, over the radical secularization of the French Revolution in its violent anti-clerical phase. This was a reversal of earlier orthodox assessments of the Revolution. Morse himself had given ringing endorsement to the Revolution as late as February of 1795.

> [T]he rejection of the Christian Religion in France is less to
> be wondered at, when we consider, in how unamicable and

1. Morse, *A Sermon Delivered at the New North Church in Boston.*

2. Although the term evangelical was used in the previous chapter to describe more conservative Calvinists who were, in one way or another, influenced by the revivalist orientation of Jonathan Edwards, orthodox is being used here and throughout this chapter as a way of underlining their emphasis on doctrinal purity. It is also the term they used to describe themselves. The two terms are nearly synonymous, but not entirely, as "evangelical" stresses the missional nature of their belief system, while "orthodox" focuses on their self-image as defenders of what they believed to be the primitive Christian faith revived by the Reformation.

disgusting a point of view it has been there exhibited, under the hierarchy of Rome. When peace and a free government shall be established, and the people have liberty and leisure to examine for themselves, we anticipate, by means of the effusions of the Holy Spirit, a glorious revival and prevalence of pure, unadulterated Christianity.[3]

What Morse and others soon realized is that the anti-clerical turn of the Revolution was not just directed against Catholicism, but Christianity in general. By 1798 what had previously been perceived as a divinely inspired eruption of liberty was cast in more sinister terms. Now the Revolution was perceived as a threat to what the orthodox understood to be the necessary Christian foundation of a righteous republic. Most disturbing to Morse, and the subject of his Fast Day sermon, was what he considered to be evidence that a conspiracy was afoot to infect the American public with the French- inspired poison of radical secularism.

> Have we not reason to suspect that there is some secret plan in operation, hostile to true liberty and religion, which requires to be aided by these vile slanders? Are they not intended to bring into contempt those civil and religious institutions founded by our venerable forefathers, and to prostrate those principles and habits formed under them, which are the barriers of our freedom and happiness, and which have contributed essentially to promote both; and thus to prepare the way among us, for the spread of those disorganizing opinions, and the atheistical philosophy, which are deluging the Old World in misery and blood?
>
> We have reason, my brethren, to fear that this preparatory work is already begun, and made progress among us; and that it is a part of a deep laid and extensive plan, which has for many years been in operation in Europe. To this plan, as to its source, we may trace that torrent of irreligion, and abuse of everything good and praise-worthy, which, at the present time, threatens to overwhelm the world. This plan is now unveiled.[4]

What precipitated this accusation was what Morse had recently read in a book written by John Robison who was a professor of "Natural

3. Nash notes that "among the 'publishing clergy,' those ecclesiastics whose pulpit oratory was committed to print, such views were held with virtual unanimity during the first five years of the Revolution." "The American Clergy and the French Revolution," 393.

4. Jedidiah Morse, *Sermon Delivered at New North Church*, 20.

Philosophy and Secretary to the Royal Society of Edinburgh."[5] This book, entitled *Proofs of a Conspiracy against all the Religions and Governments of Europe*, outlined the alleged attempt of a secret society known as the Illuminati (which Morse transcribes as "the ILLUMINATED") to "root out and abolish Christianity, and overturn all civil government." Most disturbing, according to Morse, was evidence that the conspiracy had "secretly extended its branches . . . even into America"[6] via the machinations of the French.[7] Clearly it was time to sound the alarm.

> As Christians we ought to be alarmed for the safety of the church; to be vigilant in resisting the open and secret attempts to bring into disrepute and to prostrate our religious institutions. If these foundations be destroyed, and infidelity and atheism prevail, what will the righteous do?[8]

The historian whose work serves as the foundational text for the study of this alleged conspiracy, Vernon Stauffer, notes that while the Illuminati was, as Morse indicated, a secret society whose aim was to promote a secularized utopian vision of human freedom in line with the radical thrust of the French Revolution, it was neither the inspiration for the French Revolution nor the threat Morse perceived it to be.[9] At its height the order boasted at most two or three thousand members, most located in Germany. And by the time Morse wrote this sermon, the group had essentially been eliminated by the Bavarian government who issued a series of edicts aimed at their suppression between 1784 and 1787.[10] Even more to the point, there was never any evidence apart from Robison's speculative imagination that the order had migrated to America. This, however, didn't stop Morse from continuing to push the conspiracy

5. Ibid., 21.

6. Ibid.

7. "There is great reason to believe that the French revolution was kindled by the *Illuminati*; and that it has been cherished and inflamed by their principles." Ibid., 23.

8. Ibid., 28.

9. Stauffer notes this:

> "The meagerness of his [Morse's] resources is perhaps best illustrated in his treatment of the conspiracy which he assumed underlay the French revolution. Such proofs as he made use of in this connection amounted to little more than the political manifestoes of certain secret lodges and clubs, fugitive revolutionary documents which chanced to blow across his path, current historical conjecture and gossip, etc." (Stauffer, *New England and the Bavarian Illuminati*, 202)

10. Ibid., 183.

theory in the face of withering criticism in the local papers even when he was unable to find any proof that such a conspiracy existed.[11]

A year later Morse preached another sermon on the subject to his congregation in Charlestown, Massachusetts, this time claiming to have found the proof that his critics demanded. This proof included the names of primarily French immigrants connected to a Masonic order with branches in Virginia and New York. But the accusation that these were agents of the Illuminati conspiracy proved to be groundless, as a Virginia senator who knew the alleged conspirators insisted that "they were honest and industrious men" attached to a lodge which was "entirely harmless as far as fomenting hostility to the institutions of the country were concerned."[12] Apparently Morse was speechless after this. No reply or apology was ever published.

> Morse . . . came to the conclusion that there was no further action he could take in the case, and his advocacy of the idea of an Illuminati conspiracy against religion and the government ceased.[13]

## A SIEGE MENTALITY

What appears here is a characteristic that is evident in many of the sermons and writings of the orthodox clergy of the era, both in America and the United Kingdom. It was a siege mentality that magnified the threat of real or perceived enemies to the Christian values they determined to be essential to the realization of a righteous republic. The Illuminati represented one such threat,[14] but there were many more subsumed for the most part under the rubric "infidelity." What was at stake was made clear in a sermon preached by Robert Hall at a Baptist church in London in 1801, which Leonard Woods would later recommend to his theology

---

11. Morse, *A Sermon Exhibiting the Present Dangers and Consequent Duties of the Citizens of the United States of America.*

12. Stauffer, *New England and the Bavarian Illuminati*, 319.

13. Ibid., 321.

14. Dwight located the Illuminati in an apocalyptic narrative soon after Morse delivered his Fast Day sermon, noting that the rise of this society was evidence that they were entering into days characterized by "unclean teachers, or teachers of unclean doctrines," which "will spread through the world, to unite mankind against God." Dwight, *The Duty of Americans, at the Present Crisis*, 12.

students at Andover Theological Seminary during the time Fisk was a student there.[15]

> Modern infidelity not only tends to corrupt the moral taste; it also promotes the growth of those vices which are the most hostile to social happiness. Of all the vices incident to human nature, the most destructive to society are vanity, ferocity, and unbridled sensuality; and these are precisely the vices which infidelity is calculated to cherish.[16]

This characteristic of orthodoxy was an influential element in Fisk's educational experience both at Middlebury and Andover. It was particularly prominent at Andover, where it served as the *sine qua non* of the educational system. Andover was founded as an educational bulwark against the encroachments of liberalism and infidelity in church and society. And Morse would be a primary moving force behind its establishment.

## THE SPARK THAT LIT THE FLAME: HENRY WARE

One of the champions of Calvinist orthodoxy, David Tappan, held the prestigious Hollis chair of theology at Harvard University from 1792 until his untimely death in 1803.[17] In the summer of 1798 he, too, raised the alarm about the Illuminati threat in a discourse he delivered to Harvard's graduating seniors. Beginning with a laudatory expression of appreciation for "that unfettered liberty of thought, which is eminently the boast of this enlightened and liberal age,"[18] Tappan at the same time warned his students against those who abuse this liberty by introducing "wrong opinions" to easily perverted young minds. Among the most sinister were the secretive members of the Illuminati who Tappan, like Morse, believed to have infiltrated American society through French agents. Quoting at great length from Robison's work, Tappan alerted his students

15. Andover Theological Seminary, *Outline of the Course of Study in the Department of Christian Theology*, 3.

16. Hall, *Modern Infidelity Considered with Respect to its Influence on Society*, 21.

17. Interestingly, Harvard liberals considered Tappan a "moderate," whose views were not as offensive to them as other more rigid Calvinists. "His Calvinism was of the moderate kind," said one of Tappan's contemporaries characterized as "liberal" by Wright, "and though he was firmly fixed in his own opinions, far from being dogmatical or pertinacious, he was desirous of correcting his own errors, and was willing, that others should enjoy their sentiments." Wright, *The Unitarian Controversy*, 3.

18. Ibid., 5.

to the enormity of the threat, then warned them what might happen if the Illuminati had their way. What happened in France could happen in America, as well.

> Behold France converted by it [infidelity] into one great theatre of falsehood and perjury, of cruelty and ferocity, of robbery and piracy, of anarchy and despotism, of fornication and adultery, and of course reduced to a state of unspeakable degradation and misery. Compare this picture with the existing character and state of our own country; with the unsullied purity of its public administration, and the general order, refinement and happiness of its citizens; and then say, which is most friendly to the human character and condition, the atheistical system of France, or the Christian institutions of America? Does not the comparison force a conviction, that infidelity is the mortal foe, and Christianity the guardian angel both of personal worth and public felicity?[19]

As long as Tappan was resident in the Hollis chair Morse and his orthodox compatriots could look with favor on the theological education their sons were receiving at Harvard. Morse's endorsement was particularly critical as he was a member of the Corporation, the board that, along with the Board of Overseers, governed Harvard's affairs. But then Tappan died and those trustees, along with other Boston-based clergy and educators who were increasingly critical of the doctrinal rigidity of orthodox Calvinism, recognized the opportunity to introduce to Harvard a more theologically liberal perspective. This happened with the appointment of Henry Ware[20] as Tappan's replacement, over the strong objections of Morse and others who interpreted it as a liberal coup. It was that and much more, as it also provided the spark that led to a decisive fissure in the Congregational ranks with the Boston liberals (who would later embrace the label "Unitarian"[21]) on one side and the more provincial orthodox (which included not only the New Divinity clergy, but those labeled Old Calvinists as well) on the other.

19. Ibid., 23.

20. Henry Ware was by all accounts a gentle and reasonable man, who had been serving a Congregational Church in Hingham, MA, for seventeen years. His liberal sensibilities were well known, but he was a man of "spotless reputation" who "afforded no opening for attack on personal grounds." Ibid., 9.

21. The word "liberal" covered a wide range of perspectives united in opposition to the kind of doctrinal dogmatism represented by Morse and his orthodox compatriots. Only later would they embrace the label "Unitarian." See Noll, 284.

Soon after Ware's appointment, Morse published a pamphlet giving his perspective on the turn of events at Harvard.[22] What the Corporation and the Board of Overseers did was improper, he said, as Ware's views were not in keeping with the orthodoxy of the man who established the chair. Even more it was improper because it opened the door to infidelity in the church. The threat wasn't on the same level as that posed by the French radicals and the Illuminati, but it was a threat nonetheless.

> God forbid, that this change should be injurious and ruinous; that in consequence, the faith of our church should become less pure, their discipline less strict, the standard of Christian morality lowered, the difference lessened between those, who professedly serve God, and those who avowedly serve him not; till at length the spirit and power of our religion shall have evaporated, and its very forms be abolished.[23]

## BUILDING THE ORTHODOX FORTRESS

### The Panoplist

Morse and others who were disturbed by what transpired at Harvard soon put in motion a series of steps aimed at constructing an institutional apparatus to keep liberalism and infidelity at bay. The first order of business was to establish a literary mouthpiece for orthodoxy, a periodical that could serve as counterpoint to the material issued from the pens of the Boston liberals and French infidels. New England at that time was a culture defined by the written and spoken word, and the liberal establishment in Boston excelled at it.[24] Even before the Ware appointment Morse had been working with other prominent orthodox clergy to counteract their literary influence. In 1800 Timothy Dwight and the Federalist leader Oliver Wolcott had urged Morse to unite with them in the creation of a newspaper that would challenge the liberal paradigm.[25] But the urgency of the enterprise was even greater now. Working with soon-

---

22. Morse, *The True Reasons*.

23. Ibid., 28.

24. Miller speaks about the liberal-orthodox controversy engendered by the Ware appointment as "a critical moment in the transformation of New England's print culture and of the public Christianity of New England's Congregational clergy" as each side vied for the right to determine the "cultural project" of the new nation. Miller, "Proper Subjects for Public Inquiry," 102.

25. Morse, *Jedidiah Morse: A Champion of New England Orthodoxy*, 73.

to-be Andover theology professor Leonard Woods, chosen not only for his literary and theological acumen, but also his ties to the New Divinity clerics,[26] Morse managed to get all sides in the orthodox camp to back his effort to publish what might best be described as a literary broadside in the increasingly strident liberal-orthodox ideological skirmish.[27] It was a monthly magazine he and Woods called the *Panoplist,* appropriately subtitled "the Christian's Armour."

The first issue of the *Panoplist* went public on June 1, 1805. Soon after its launch Samuel Worchester, who would become a prominent figure in the missionary society that would send Fisk to the Middle East, described its purpose.

> The Panoplist rises to counteract prevailing evils and to prevent their increase; to stem the torrent of vice & etc. Its aim is, to detect the corruptions of modern literature; to unfold the subtleties and absurdities of what is called rational Christianity, to strip learned pride and impiety of every fair disguise, and to promote the theoretical knowledge and practical influence of sound divinity.[28]

A quick perusal of the contents of the first edition gives a good sense of Morse's literary battle plan. While doctrinal themes are explored ("Predestination," "God, character of"), more prominent are human interest stories illustrating orthodox piety and morality as counterpoint to the perceived impiety and vices of the infidels. There are memoirs of pious clergy and laity ("Life of Mrs. Savage," "Memoirs of Rev. Archibald Maclaine"), letters and reports from mission societies ("Account of the Hampshire Missionary Society," "Missionary Station in South Africa") as well as conversion stories, including one that would have warmed Morse's orthodox heart: "Conversion of Deist."[29] All spoke to the transformative power of the orthodox message. Doctrine receded into the background

---

26. Morse himself was aligned with the Old or "moderate" Calvinists.

27. "[T]he editors of the Panoplist feel it incumbent on them, to cooperate with the conductors of similar periodical works, both at home and abroad, in detecting the corruptions of modern literature, in opposing the progress of dangerous principles, in stripping skepticism and imposture of their artful disguise, and in exposing libertinism and impiety, in all their deformity, to deserved contempt and abhorrence." "Preface," *Panoplist,* iii.

28. Worchester, *The Life and Labors of Rev. Samuel Worcester, D.D.,* 58.

29. *The Panoplist,* i.

in favor of a principled narrative; orthodoxy as the only secure foundation of a moral life and a moral society.

The defense of orthodoxy was the primary purpose of the *Panoplist*. It also had a secondary purpose, which was to promote unity among the orthodox. The "professed object" of the publication, wrote Morse and Woods in the preface, was, among other things, "to soften the rancor of party spirit."[30]

One of Morse's biographers, Joseph W. Phillips, believes that this focus on unity among the orthodox was a predominant theme in Morse's ministry from the outset. It was, he says, a "tactical dimension" of what Morse set out to do, a necessary foundation for the institutional response Morse saw as necessary to counteract the insidious influence of infidelity on church and society.

> From the outset of his ministry Morse dreamed of a vigorous, inclusive American church, of an informal orthodox union that would embrace New England Congregationalism and the prestigious Calvinistic denominations to the south: Presbyterians, Associate Presbyterians, and Dutch Reformed. Such a union, Morse and his friends in these denominations believed would strengthen Christianity and enable it to keep pace with the development of the United States.[31]

## *The Founding of Andover Theological Seminary*

The *Panoplist* set the stage for a unified orthodox response to the liberal threat,[32] but the *pièce de résistance* of the orthodox battle plan was the establishment of Andover Theological Seminary. This, too, was part of the "tactical dimension" of Morse's project. But in this case the vision was not his alone. It was a shared vision of the leadership of the various

---

30. Ibid., v.

31. Phillips, *Jedidiah Morse and New England Congregationalism*, 130.

32. It should be said here that the unity Morse desired with the publication of the *Panoplist* wasn't fully achieved until 1808 when the *Panoplist* merged with the *Massachusetts Missionary Magazine*, which was a primary literary vehicle for the New Divinity men. The editors of the *MMM* were cold to his entreaties at first. They felt there were too many differences in the two perspectives—New Divinity and Old Calvinist. But Morse was well networked and admired for the work he did on the premier geographical textbook of the era. He was also very persuasive. In 1808 they agreed to the merger. When that happened it proved to be all that Morse hoped it would be. Philips, *Jedidiah Morse and New England Congregationalism*, 138.

groups that made up the as yet un-unified body of orthodox Christians: New Divinity, Old Calvinist and everyone in between. This proved to be a complicating factor.

At issue was the fact that two different clusters of prominent leaders from each camp had come up with the idea at the same time in separate locations. Morse was aware that one of these clusters had been in conversation about the idea as early as April of 1806. "There is considerable said in the circle of a few confidential friends of establishing a Theological Academy at Andover," he wrote to his friend Lyman Beecher in April of 1806.[33] What he was unaware of at the time is that a group led by the charismatic New Divinity minister, Samuel Spring, of Newburyport, was discussing the same thing for the same reason, that is, alarm over the Ware appointment. It was their idea to create a seminary in Newburyport, which would be dedicated to training ministers in New Divinity theology. According to Phillips, Morse became alarmed by this when it became clear that the New Divinity crowd was not in a mood to compromise. His plans for an orthodox defense against liberalism depended on a united front. This was no time, he thought, for the orthodox to "waste their strength in division and jealousy."[34]

Leonard Woods, who was a major player in the negotiations that swirled around these conflicting plans, gave some indication of the tension that existed between the two groups when the negotiations began. "[A]lthough there was a substantial agreement between Calvinists and Hopkinsians (New Divinity), and a real foundation for union," he wrote in his history of Andover Seminary, "there appeared at that time no small tendency to division and separate action."[35]

It is outside the scope of this book to go into any kind of detail about the at times exasperating and exhausting "exertions"[36] made by Morse and others to bring about the compromises that would allow both clusters to agree to establish one seminary at one location.[37] Suffice it to say

33. Quoted in Jedidiah Morse, *A Champion of New England Orthodoxy*, 102.

34. Phillips, *Jedidiah Morse and New England Congregationalism*, 139.

35. Woods, *History of the Andover Theological Seminary*, 42. See chapter 2 for a detailed account of the theological differences that separated the two parties.

36. "Exertion" in its various forms was a favorite word of the orthodox as it is found in nearly all their documentation as a description of an active Christian life. To be a good Christian was to be "exerting" oneself for the cause of Christ.

37. Woods gives a blow-by-blow account in his history, albeit one colored by his own participation in the exertions. It covers a major part of this work. Of particular

that they were able to reach an agreement. The Old Calvinists got the location (Andover), while the New Divinity men got most everything else. They got it mainly by standing their ground in the face of strong pressure to meet the other party half way. What this meant is that in its early years, including the years Fisk was there, Andover would play the New Divinity tune, which, given their emphasis on "disinterested benevolence," meant that Andover would become the premier training center not only for Edwardsean clergy but Edwardsean missionaries as well. This is historian David Kling's contention.

> Andover as well as the first organized American Protestant global missionary effort were heavily influenced by, and reflective of, New Divinity ideology. Though Andover was established upon an Old Calvinist-New Divinity compromise, William Bentley was rightly convinced that "the Calvinists have been made to play into the hands of the Hopkinsians." The seminary was stacked with Edwardsean faculty at its inception and ensured that future faculty remained so with its "Hopkinsian" Associate Creed. From the beginning Andover was *the* training center of the ABCFM's missionaries. During the board's first decade all but one of its missionaries were educated at Andover, and within thirty-eight years 100 students carried the New Divinity message to the ends of the earth.[38]

## An Unwieldy Constitution

One of the consequences of creating an institution on the basis of compromise between two groups heavily invested in doctrinal certainty was an unwieldy constitution. "The Constitution and Associate Statutes" runs to nearly sixty pages in its printed form.[39] What it offers is a glimpse into the shared ideology of the orthodox community, albeit with a New Divinity bias.

---

historical interest is the collection of letters he included, which were exchanged between the various parties in the negotiations. This collection of letters gives the most comprehension picture of the torturous nature of the negotiations.

38. Kling, "The New Divinity and the Origins of the ABCFM," 30.

39. Published by order of the board of trustees soon after the seminary opened, the original copy of which was "signed, sealed, and delivered" in the presence of Samuel Spring and Jedidiah Morse, underscoring here Morse's critical role in making this happen. Andover Theological Seminary, *Constitution and Associate Statutes of the Theological Seminary in Andover; with a sketch of its Rise and Progress*, 68.

The document begins with a "historical sketch" by former Harvard professor and soon to be Andover professor Eliphalet Pearson,[40] which he delivered at the seminary the day it opened, September 28, 1808. It was short sketch that painted an idyllic picture of the events leading up to the founding of the seminary filled with mellifluous praise for those who made it happen. It also expressed how this institution would fit into the orthodox battle plan.

> [A]s the Seminary originated in a conviction of the importance of a *learned* and *evangelical* ministry; so its primary object is to lay such a foundation of sacred literature, as will best support and protect the superstructure of gospel truth against the open assaults and secret machinations of atheism, infidelity, and error. Not the peculiarities of any sect or party, but the great system of revealed truth, contained in the Bible, avowed by the Reformers, embraced by our Fore-fathers, and expressed in the Assembly's catechism;[41] it will be the duty of the Professors to illustrate and maintain; as must be evident from the creed, which they are required to subscribe.[42]

This apologetic purpose is repeated in various forms throughout the document, serving as a foundational principle for the seminary. It would be the duty of professors "to guard against religious error, and to accelerate their acquisition of heavenly wisdom."[43] The professors themselves would be continually checked to make sure that they hadn't embraced "heresies or errors" that conflicted with their pledge to uphold the tenets of the Westminster Shorter Catechism and an "associate creed" that was written primarily to appease the Hopkinsians.[44] And then to ensure that all understood what it was they were combating, a group of "heresies and errors" was listed which included Judaism and Islam, indicating a belief that, to the orthodox, these two faith systems were more akin to heresies than the "ignorant fallacies" of heathenism.

---

40. Despite the fact that Pearson played an instrumental role in the establishment of the seminary, Woods noted, with a degree of sadness, that he "was neither successful nor happy in his labors" at Andover as the first professor of sacred literature. He quit just a year into his assignment. Woods, *History of the Andover Theological Seminary*, 146.

41. The Westminster Shorter Catechism.

42. Andover Theological Seminary, *Constitution and Associate Statutes*, 7.

43. Ibid., 14.

44. Printed out verbatim on ibid., 32–35.

> Every person, therefore, appointed or elected a Professor in this
> Seminary, shall . . . maintain and inculcate the Christian faith, as
> above expressed, together with all the other doctrines and duties
> of our holy religion, so far as may appertain to his office, accord-
> ing to the best light God shall give him, and in opposition, not
> only to Atheists and Infidels, but to Jews, Mahometans, Arians,
> Pelagians, Antinominans, Arminians, Socinians, Unitarians,
> and Universalists, and to all other heresies and errors, ancient
> or modern, which may be opposed to the gospel of Christ, or
> hazardous to the souls of men.[45]

The "Associate Statutes" were prefaced with remarks that gave added emphasis to Andover's apologetic purpose. And the unity sought by Morse was critical to its success.

> Motives to unite the hearts of all devout and orthodox men in
> promoting the interest of the Institution are numerous. The dar-
> ing strides, made at the present day by infidels and other errone-
> ous men; the urgent necessity of a learned and pious ministry, to
> check and countervail their dangerous influence, is no inferior
> motive to combine the efforts of all the faithful.[46]

Most critical in assessing the way Andover shaped Fisk's thought is noting the essential missionary purpose of the institution, thus linking the battle against infidelity to the effort to bring non-Christians into the orthodox fold.

> What benevolent mind, while contemplating the superior ad-
> vantages of the church, does not weep over the millions of igno-
> rant men, who are perishing for lack of vision? What Christian
> does not commiserate the destitute in all sections of the globe,
> and devoutly pray that, agreeably to CHRIST'S injunction, the
> gospel may soon be preached to every creature? How long, alas,
> shall the greatest part of the human race remain unacquainted
> with the gospel! How long shall they continue unbelievers! "But
> how shall they believe in him, of whom they have not heard?
> And how shall they hear without a preacher? And how shall
> they preach, except they be sent?" And how can preachers be
> consistently sent, unless properly qualified?[47]

45. Ibid., 19.

46. Ibid., 46.

47. Ibid., 44.

## A Rational Faith

Although Andover was founded as bulwark against liberal Christianity and infidelity it was by no means anti-intellectual. Both the orthodox and their liberal counterparts were operating out of an Enlightenment paradigm. The orthodox impulse to create Andover Seminary was not in this case so much a reaction against rationalism per se as it was a protest against a certain kind of rationalism that called into question what the orthodox considered to be bedrock doctrines necessary for a reasonable apprehension of reality. Both the orthodox at Andover and the liberal establishment in Boston valued the cultivation of the mind through open inquiry. They both placed high value on a broad-based liberal education. The difference was how they chose to define the term "reasonable discourse." Neil Brody Miller makes this clear in his critique of scholars who have dismissed Morse (and his orthodox counterparts) as "a one-dimensional stereotype of anti-intellectualism and religious bigotry."[48] Morse and his orthodox compatriots, says Miller, were Enlightenment rationalists operating out of a separate, but no less reasonable paradigm from that of the liberals they opposed.

> The moderate Calvinists' faith in the rational outcome of public discourse, and their cultural project of founding periodicals, embracing controversy, and encouraging intra-and interdenominational cooperation among evangelical Protestants manifested a newfound confidence in human agency born of Enlightenment thought. Enlightenment, more specifically eighteenth century Newtonian natural philosophy . . . provided an essential aid to the cause of true religion by experientially confirming the efficacy of revivals, empowering evangelical Protestants as the necessary, secondary agents of Providence, and by expanding the traditional ministerial means of grace to include the latest technologies of print discourse and mass distribution.[49]

In an article that appeared in a 2012 edition of the Dordt College magazine *Pro Rege*, Roger Henderson writes about a term that is in vogue among evangelicals today which may help clarify this. It's the term "worldview," although Henderson chooses to give definition to this term with the more evocative French phrase *esprit d'ensemble*[50] ("spirit of the group").

48. Miller, "Proper Subjects for Public Inquiry," 106.
49. Ibid., 107.
50. Henderson, "Connotations of Worldview," 10–21.

> This French expression . . . is insightful: It says there is some-
> thing that colors and gives flavor to the content of what a person
> or group believes. It implies that such an *esprit* unites all the
> particulars into a consistent whole . . . The *esprit* is an overall
> meaning and impression arising in and through everything . . .
> It is something under, over, and above all the parts as such, a
> shared quality or feel. As such, it denotes *the web-like structure*
> *of human belief(s), the coherence of life as reflected in thought,*
> *the interconnectedness of thought and reality* [emphasis added].[51]

The clash between the orthodox and liberals was a clash of world-
views, with each side looking for the "interconnectedness of thought and
reality" in different places; liberals in an unfettered rationality that appealed to the *literati* of the era, the orthodox in rationality read through
the authoritative lens of biblical revelation.

The ideology that would shape Fisk's perception of the religious
other during this period of his life operated within the boundaries set
by the orthodox *esprit d'ensemble,* a "web-like structure" of beliefs that
had its own coherent rationality. Andover was created to promote it; its
professors were committed to ensuring that its students stayed within its
bounds. This was not a protest against Enlightenment rationality. This
was an attempt on the part of the orthodox establishment to set the parameters within which rational discourse would occur.

This explains what might otherwise be seen as a contradiction to the
apologetic thrust of an Andover education in a lecture Leonard Woods
used as an introduction to his theology course. Here Woods urged his
students to adopt a posture of open inquiry.

> When any proposition is laid down, inquire with an *unbiased*
> mind, what can be offered for it, and what against it. Let no prej-
> udice render you inattentive to the reasoning of your opponent.
> Let no wish for the confutation of his scheme render you unjust
> or partial. Acknowledge frankly the strength of his objections
> against your opinions, and of his arguments in favor of his own
> . . . Prize every ray of light cast on the subject of inquiry, from
> whatever quarter it may come, and to whatever result it may lead
> . . . Disdain, therefore, the narrowness of mind, which would
> deprive you of any important advantage, and give yourselves to
> a fair and thorough examination, not only of those authors who
> exhibit the theology of the Bible, but of those also, who teach
> the various systems of error both ancient and modern, always

51. Ibid., 10–11.

keeping your mind open for the reception of truth, even though it may proceed from the pen of a heretic.[52]

What appears puzzling on the surface—Woods encouraging a free, open inquiry in the face of rationalist attacks on orthodox Christianity—is less so in light of the confidence the orthodox invested in their worldview as they believed that all such inquiry would ultimately lead to an affirmation of the truth as they perceived it. This was the effect of Scottish Common Sense Realism on the orthodox mind. In the words of Jean Matthews:

> Belief in the truth of Christianity as revealed in the Scriptures provided a fundamental paradigm within which all other knowledge was interpreted; since facts could never contradict the word of God rightly understood, people would never get into trouble as long as they stuck to empirical investigation. What was feared was not scholarship, but "speculation," the mind unfettered by acceptance of fundamental "truths" and the minutiae of empirical research.[53]

## SUMMING UP AND LOOKING AHEAD

This is the pedagogical milieu into which Fisk would enter in the fall of 1815 when he began his studies at Andover Theological Seminary. The ideological emphases of this institution would in many ways reinforce what he had learned up to this point, as Andover was created for Consistent Calvinists like him with an experience of and passion for revivalist Christianity. But it would also draw him into new ways of thinking that would nurture his growing missionary convictions and lead him to give greater emphasis to what Rabinowitz characterizes as a moralist perspective on his ministerial calling.[54] Here his analytical nature would find a home among like-minded scholars seeking the knowledge and skills that would allow them to defend the orthodox faith in what they perceived to be an increasingly hostile world. Whether it would be good preparation for the task that he would face in the Ottoman Empire is a matter yet to be determined.

---

52. Woods, *The Works of Leonard Woods*, 1:25.

53. Matthews, *Toward a New Society: American Thought and Culture*, 37.

54. Rabinowitz, *Spiritual Self in Everyday Life*, 86.

# 4

## The Andover Years

### MAKING THE MOVE TO ANDOVER

FISK'S ORIGINAL PLAN HAD been to go to Andover immediately after his graduation from Middlebury. That plan had been put on hold so he could pay off college debt. But in the fall of 1815, after a year of parish ministry, Fisk determined that it was time to make the move.

A letter Parsons wrote to Fisk from Andover in December of 1814 suggests that it may have taken some persuading to convince Fisk to do this:

> Br. Richards & Bardwell frequently enquire where is Br. Fisk? Has he forgotten that millions of souls are perishing in India for want of Christian instruction? Has he concluded that 4 or 5 missionaries are sufficient to Christianize the eastern world? No, it cannot be. The same zeal for souls which he once manifested, he manifests still.[1]

What this letter confirms is not only Parsons' gift of persuasion, but also the role Andover had of attracting students who, like Fisk and Parsons, were considering missionary careers. To consider such a career had only recently become feasible, as America's first global missionary organization, the ABCFM, had been established four years prior with Andover as its launching pad.[2]

1. Letter from Levi Parsons to Pliny Fisk ( December 30, 1814), ANTS.

2. There are several primary sources for information about this organization. Of primary interest are those that were written by early participants or their biographers.

Andover's role in the establishment of America's first global mission venture is clear. It was Andover students who proposed the idea of a global mission organization to the founding body, the General Association of Congregational Clergy in Massachusetts.[3] Andover founders and faculty were also its most enthusiastic supporters, including Jedidiah Morse who would serve as one of the early board members. There is also evidence to suggest that Morse and other key orthodox leaders, including seminary professors, played a primary role in the students' proposal. Andover's celebrated professor of sacred literature, Moses Stuart, opened his home to the students who made the proposal. He may have joined them on occasion.[4] The proposal itself was only made after the students had consulted with Congregational leaders.[5]

Another connection to Andover was through a major donor, an entrepreneurial philanthropist named John Norris. Norris donated considerable funds to launch the seminary with the hope that Andover might one day serve as a center for an American-based global mission effort. This is what Norris intimated in conversations with Samuel Worchester several years before either Andover or the ABCFM came into existence. Worchester's son characterized the conversations this way:

> It was of foreign missions that they often spoke to each other, impatient for the day when it could be said of the American churches, that they had their own missionaries in Asia, Africa,

This includes Samuel Worcester's biography [see below] as well as the work of Rufus Anderson who served the Board in an administrative capacity for forty-four years. His account of the founding and early years of the ABCFM can be found in the memorial volume he wrote on the board's behalf in 1862: Anderson, *Memorial Volume of the First Fifty Years of the American Board of Commissioners for Foreign Missions.*

3. "On June 27, 1810, in the village of Bradford, Massachusetts, four students from Andover Theological Seminary —or Divinity College as it was then called— appeared at a meeting of the General Association to present a brief petition to the assembled Congregational clergy ... The action of these young men provided the immediate stimulus for the inauguration of American missions abroad." C. Phillips, *Protestant America and the Pagan World,* 20, 22.

4. DeJong notes that Stuart invited several prominent New Divinity clergy, including Andover founder, Samuel Spring, to his home to study the proposal the students would make to the Association just before the proposal was made. What he doesn't mention is the fact that this may indicate that Stuart had a greater hand in the formulation of the proposal than is normally acknowledged. DeJong, *As the Waters Cover the Sea,* 223.

5. Worcester, *The life and Labors of Rev. Samuel Worcester,* 59.

and the island of the sea . . . "My great object," said he [Norris],
is the foreign missionary enterprise."[6]

There is no doubt that Andover served not only as the primary institution for the preparation of orthodox clergy, but orthodox missionaries, as well. Pastoral ministry and global mission were inseparable at Andover. This is what drew Fisk to Andover as he himself acknowledged:

> This single object, a mission to the heathen, was almost invariably before me. And this was the principal thing that led me to this Seminary.[7]

## SETTLING IN

As part of his attempt to convince Fisk to attend Andover, Parsons (in the aforementioned letter) gave Fisk a brief glimpse of what it was like to be there. Parsons was one of a class of twenty-two students, "most of them young men of the most brilliant talents & most ardent piety." And while theological studies were "interesting," the subjects discussed "as thoroughly as I have ever heard them," what was of more interest to Parsons was what the seminary did to cultivate an active piety. On Wednesday evenings students met together with professors "for the express purpose of promoting their growth in grace." Thursday evenings were set aside for prayer, where "the brethren are generally very free to converse on practical subjects." And while the professors treated the students "as gentlemen," they, at the same time, "exercise the tenderness of parents." It was a picture of a community of pious scholars with the emphasis on *pious* and *community*. And that, apparently, is what Fisk found most attractive about the school, as we discover in a letter he wrote to his parents in November of 1815; several weeks after his arrival at the seminary.

In this letter Fisk first mentioned the journey he took through the hills of northern Massachusetts to get to the seminary. What today is a leisurely two hour drive through a scenic landscape was back then an arduous two day journey on foot and horseback. Nonetheless, wrote Fisk, "the journey was pleasant & I arrived in good health & good spirits."[8]

---

6. Ibid.

7. Bond, *Memoir*, 41.

8. *Letter from Pliny Fisk to Ebenezer Fisk sent to Shelburne, MA from Andover,* Nov. 17, 1815, HLH.

Fisk next wrote with some enthusiasm about what he found most stimulating about this new experience. It wasn't his studies that excited his imagination, of which he said nothing. It was the meetings Parsons mentioned in his letter where students and faculty came together as a community for spiritual refreshment.[9]

> Last Wednesday evening the Professors met according to custom in conference with the students. The subject of their remarks was the care of the heart. They exhibited our obligations to be holy in heart, to grow in spiritual mindedness and live near to God. This obligation they inferred from the pure nature and benevolent design of Christianity, from the holiness of the heavens it offers, from the immaculate character of Christ, his gracious advent and atonement the design of which was to redeem his people from sin, from the precepts of scripture enjoining so frequently inward purity, spirituality of affection, practical Godliness and hearty conformity to Christ, from the necessity of eminent holiness in order to advance our own spiritual comfort, peace and blessedness and from the absolute necessity of having our hearts in heaven in order to be extensively useful upon earth.[10]

Fisk also expressed his continued enthusiasm for revivals mentioning "different brethren" giving "an account of awakenings" during a Saturday night worship service. He followed this with a detailed account of awakenings breaking out in various parts of New England. Finally he told his father about articles and reports that piqued his interest which were almost certainly *not* assigned to him by his professors.

> I am now reading a report of a Missionary tour through the western part of the U.S. by Samuel J. Mills and Daniel Smith. From information herein contained, it appears that in the state of Ohio there is not more than one bible to five families, that 13,000 bibles are wanting in order that there may be one to a family . . .
>
> Have just started reading the reports of the prudential committee to the American Board of Commissioners for foreign

9. Woods devotes several pages of his history to these meetings, noting that it was woven into the fabric of the community's life together. "But while we attached high importance to literary acquisitions, we gave a still higher place to spiritual improvement. We strove to make the impression upon those who became members of the Seminary, that spiritual religion and growth in grace should be their paramount object." Woods, *History of the Andover Theological Seminary*, 163–64.

10. Letter from Pliny Fisk to Ebenezer Fisk.

missions. They have made enquiry about the western Indians. It
is ascertained that there are about 240,000 within the territories
of the U.S. in about 70 tribes. Nearly 100,000 this side of the
river Mississippi the rest beyond. The four tribes Creeks, Choc-
taws, Chichasanes [*sic*] & the Cherokees include about 70,000.
To these tribes the eye of missions is now directed.[11]

Fisk concluded this letter with a note of appreciation for the com-
munal bonds he experienced at Andover, the "dear delights of friendship"
and the "union of Souls" before launching into a sermonic reflection on
Disinterested Benevolence which put all he had written in its proper missiological context.

There is an affection of which the human mind is susceptible
which has universal existence as the object of its love & the
complete prevalence of holiness & happiness as the object of
its drive. If this divine principle actuates us we shall not stop
in our thanksgivings at the national favor we have received . . .
How many causes have we then to give thanks, to the name of
the Lord! Do we love the church? She is breaking forth on the
right hand and on the left. The Lord is appearing on her behalf,
the spirit is found out, the gospel is spreading, and the nations
are turning to the Lord. Who has a heart so hard as not to be
moved by such appearances? O my dear Friends may we all be
interested heartily and deeply interested in this cause which so
much engages the attentions of Christendom.[12]

## Formal Studies

Fisk was drawn to Andover because it was a revivalist and missionary-
friendly learning environment. But he also had to attend to his formal
studies. That wouldn't have been easy given his other interests. The course
of study laid out at Andover was time consuming and taxing.

Students at Andover were instructed in five general areas fixed by
the constitution: 1) Natural Theology 2) Sacred Literature 3) Ecclesiastical History 4) Christian Theology and 5) Pulpit Eloquence.[13] The constitution also outlined in some detail the expected content of each.

11. Ibid.

12. Ibid.

13. Andover Theological Seminary, *Constitution and Associate Statutes,* 14
(quotes and information in this section are taken from pp. 14–17).

Studies in Natural Theology focused on the nature of God and humanity discoverable both by reason and "the necessity and utility of a divine revelation." Sacred Literature included "lectures on the formation, preservation, and transmission of the sacred volume." Students also studied Greek and Hebrew to be able to read scripture in its original languages.

Ecclesiastical History began with "Jewish antiquities" and progressed through to the modern era, making certain that students understood "the rise and progress of popery and mahometanism" and "the corruptions of the church of Rome." They were also to become well versed in "the state and prevalence of paganism in our world; and on the effect, which idolatry, mahometanism, and Christianity have respectively produced on individual and national character," the wording of which suggests the way those subjects were taught.

Christian Theology received the most detailed description in the constitution, as would be expected given the doctrinal concerns that led to Andover's founding. Here students learned about the nature of divine revelation "as proved by miracles, internal evidence, fulfillment of prophecies, and historic facts." They also studied "the great doctrines and duties of our holy Christian religion, together with the objections made to them by unbelievers, and the refutation of such objections" particularly related to those doctrines most cherished by the orthodox such as the Trinity, human depravity, the atonement, "the nature and necessity of true virtue or gospel holiness," the immortality of the soul, the "nature, interpretation and use of prophecy" and "the eternity of future rewards and punishments," with the insistence that each lecture be "preceded and followed by prayer." Finally, students studied rhetoric under the rubric of Pulpit Eloquence which along with theology served as one of the two cornerstones of an Andover education following the example of "the most eminent Divines and the best models for imitation."[14]

What this mandated curriculum indicates is what was noted earlier about the central role of apologetics to the pedagogical purpose of the institution. It is seen in the underlying assumptions built into this course of study. Students studied Natural Theology in order to answer those who challenged the role of revelation in determining truth. They studied

14. "The study of rhetoric—along with, of course, theology—was at the center of Andover's curriculum, and many articles on rhetorical history and practice would fill the pages of *Bibliotheca Sacra*" (the academic journal of the seminary). Fehler, *Calvinist Rhetoric in Nineteenth Century America*, 37.

Sacred Literature to ground themselves in an orthodox interpretation of the Bible as a defense against those who challenged that interpretation on the basis of liberal scholarship. They studied theology so that they could defend orthodoxy against the attacks of infidels and atheists. They studied Ecclesiastical History to help them understand their primary role in God's providential ordering of human society over against "popery and mahometanism" and other historical aberrations of the Truth. And, as Brian Fehler points out in his study of early nineteenth-century rhetoric, Andover excelled in the study of rhetoric (Pulpit Eloquence) not for the sake of eloquence itself, but to ensure that those who studied there would be able to "to reach and affect the human mind and heart" with the orthodox message.[15] Apologetics required not only an assurance of being on the side of Truth, but the persuasive gifts needed to convince others of the Truth, as well.

## The Pursuit of Active Piety

What Fisk would have gained from this pedagogical approach is hard to assess with any degree of certainty. It can be assumed given his analytical proclivities that he took well to Andover's emphasis on the development of a rationally conceived apologetic. But apparently Fisk did not excel academically. Bond, who was not only his biographer, but classmate at Andover, made no attempt to hide this fact.

> In respect to his intellectual features nothing very brilliant or striking was developed. The creations of a fertile and glowing imagination were not found among the productions of his mind. Nor was he distinguished for boldness and vividness of conception.[16]

At issue here was not Fisk's lack of ability, as "[t]he power of analysis he possessed in a high degree."[17] The issue was where he focused his thought and energy, which was on what Bond characterized as the pursuit of "active piety."

> With an ardent thirst for sacred knowledge he entered the rich fields which opened to his view, and which produced powerful inducements for laborious research. Here [at Andover] he

---

15. Ibid., 173.
16. Bond, *Memoir*, 9.
17. Ibid.

found materials for "the feast of reason," though he had been but moderately interested with the enchantments of classic ground. Lest, however, the richness of the intellectual banquet might impair his relish for devotion and holy living he united with diligent and close attention to study habits of active piety.[18]

## Self Examination

Fisk's attention to "active piety" can be seen in an entry he made in his journal on July 4, 1816. Here he mentioned reading the eighth chapter of *Baxter's Saint's Rest*,[19] a devotional book written by a British non-conformist in the seventeenth century whose theme was the Christian journey to heaven.[20] This is a book to which Fisk would make frequent reference in his Ottoman journals. It was one of his primary devotional manuals.

The chapter Fisk read in *Baxter's Rest* urged Christians to adopt the discipline of self examination to check for evidence of elective grace. Calvinists of that era believed that Christians could not simply assume that they were in God's good graces even if they had had a proper conversion experience. There must be evidentiary proof discoverable through what Baxter described as "the serious and diligent trying of a man's heart and state by the rule of scripture."[21] After reading this chapter, Fisk dedicated himself to this purpose. For several months he made daily journal entries related to it. "Was my heart ever renewed?" he asked. "What evidence of piety can I obtain from my subsequent religious exercises?" "What is my faith in the Holy Spirit?" These questions and others like them consumed Fisk as he sought evidentiary proof that his conversion had been genuine. Unfortunately what he discovered was inconclusive.

> I have not that evidence which removes all doubt. It will take me all my life to *prove* my adoption, and make my "calling and election sure."[22]

---

18. Ibid., 32.

19. Ibid., 45.

20. Baxter, *The Saints Everlasting Rest*, 2. This is a later abridged reprint of the book containing a short biography of the author. Fisk would have read an earlier edition.

21. Ibid.

22. Bond, *Memoir*, 57.

This constant search for empirically verifiable proof of regenerative grace was not unique to Fisk. It was a common characteristic of young evangelicals of the era, particularly those who committed themselves to missionary service. Baxter urged it upon them. So did the eighteenth century missionary icon David Brainerd, or at least the David Brainerd Jonathan Edwards created as a "nearly perfect case study of genuine religious affections"[23] with his carefully edited version of Brainerd's diary.[24] The book was Edward's *Life of Brainerd* that was widely read in orthodox circles. Missionaries found it particularly compelling, leading to a near idolization of Brainerd for his self-sacrificial lifestyle providing the perfect model for a missionary life shaped by the imperative of disinterested benevolence.[25]

Establishing Brainerd as a revivalist role model was one of the primary reasons Edwards wrote Brainerd's memoir. It was also the reason why he didn't simply transcribe Brainerd's diaries, choosing instead to edit them in such a way that only those parts that illustrated Edward's revivalist ideals remained. This editing, however, did not distort Brainerd's character, as by all accounts he was as the memoir characterizes him: a self-sacrificing missionary leaving behind the comforts of home to pursue an evangelistic ministry among embattled first nation tribal peoples. Despite rounding off "some of the sharper and less orthodox edges of Brainerd's life," says the most recent scholarly study of Brainerd's life (or better, "lives"), "the essential message [Edwards] conveyed in the *Life of Brainerd* was true to its subject."[26]

> God's dealings towards me," Brainerd noted, had prepared him for "a life of solitariness and hardship; it appeared to me I had nothing to lose, nothing to do with earth, and consequently nothing to lose by a total renunciation of it.[27]

This is the example ABCFM missionaries had before them as they engaged in their own missionary service. And an obsessive spiritual and

23. Conforti, *Jonathan Edwards*, 194.

24. Edwards, *An Account of the Life of the late Reverend Mr. David Brainerd*. It is notable that the most recent book written on the legacy of David Brainerd is entitled *The Lives of David Brainerd: The Making of an American Evangelical Icon.* Edwards was not the only one who wove Brainerd's life into a proper evangelical pattern. See Grigg, *The Lives of David Brainerd*.

25. Ibid., 197.

26. Ibid., 136.

27. Ibid.

moral self-examination was its handmaiden. Joseph Conforti, in his assessment of the impact of the *Life of Brainerd* on early nineteenth-century missionaries, goes so far as to say that this, even more than a passion for souls, was their primary motivation for missionary service.

> For young men inspired by Edward's thought and Brainerd's example, missionary life came to be viewed as a spiritual trial—a personal test of their commitment to disinterested benevolence. Thus, like Brainerd, missionaries often seemed disproportionately concerned with their own spiritual lives and quests for sanctification and only secondarily concerned with the salvation of non-Christians.[28]

Conforti may overstate the case, but what he says is helpful in understanding what drove these young men to make the kind of sacrifices they did to embrace the missionary calling. It certainly helps explain what might otherwise be perceived as a bizarre death wish found in a letter Parsons wrote to Fisk in January of 1818, when it was still uncertain which mission field they would enter. Persia was Parsons first choice, even though he realized that decisions about placements were made by the Board. But given a choice, that's where he would go. He had said so in an earlier letter to Fisk dated October 23, 1817, which apparently was based on a conversation he and Fisk had had about this possibility.

> As to the question you last proposed, shall we engage in a mission to Persia? I have thought much of it, till further information is obtained. I am rather inclined to call Persia my home with the permission of providence.[29]

Now, in January of 1818, Parsons was not only convinced that this would be the field to which God and the Board would call them, he was passionately anticipating the possibility. The prompt was a journal entry he had just read in the *Panoplist* written by one of the ABCFM missionaries in India urging the Board to open a new mission station in Persia.

> This, I said, is the answer to my prayer. Is not the door open? Can we not go & thro. Christ who strengtheneth us, erect there the standard of the Cross? . . . The Lord hastens that joyful day, when we may be in Persia proclaiming salvation by the Cross. O what happiness to go to heaven from Persia after wearing out for Him who gave his life for us . . .What if we are Martyrs to

28. Ibid., 200.

29. *Letter from Levi Parsons to Pliny Fisk* (October 23, 1817), ANTS.

the cause! It is the path in which multitudes have gone to glory. They found it, if we may believe their dying testimony, a pleasant and triumphant passage.[30]

Fisk's response to this letter is not available to us. We don't know if he shared Parson's enthusiasm for martyrdom. But we can assume that his commitment to self examination flowed out of a similar impulse to follow the selfless example of David Brainerd. That this was the case can be seen in the constant reverential references Fisk made to *Life of Brainerd* in his Ottoman journals which would both inspire him and cause him to doubt the level of his commitment to the missionary vocation.

## Questioning his missionary calling

Fisk's self-examination at Andover extended to another area of his life: his missionary calling, or what he believed to be his missionary calling. This is apparent in copious excerpts Bond included in his memoir from Fisk's journal entries on this subject during his time at Andover.

When he first came to Andover, Fisk's passion for a missionary vocation was intense, more so than it had been at Middlebury. Bond indicates just how intense it was:

> When he thought that there were any movements to detain one in America, whose heart felt as his did for the heathen, his soul at times would almost take fire. I have seen his countenance kindle with vivid expression, while speaking on this subject.[31]

Fisk was passionate about missions, but his time at Andover also led him to ask difficult questions about the level of his commitment. This became grist for an intense season of self-examination that occupied Fisk for the whole of his second year at Andover. What he asked himself during this time is whether he had what it took to become a missionary.[32] His earliest thoughts on the subject led him to doubt whether he did.

> I was young, only eighteen, when I first resolved on being a missionary. Much that is unholy has been mixed with my feelings on this subject. Many unholy motives may induce a man to desire this work. In pursuing this inquiry, I desire to have no regard to private interest, personal convenience or suffering,

---

30. *Letter from Levi Parsons to Pliny Fisk* (January, 1818), ANTS.
31. Bond, *Memoir*, 67.
32. Ibid.

reputation, natural attachments, advice or wishes of friends, any farther than it may conduce to the good of souls.[33]

Fisk's analytical nature worked overtime in the year-long process of self examination he underwent to discover the answer to his doubts as the process he used resembled that of an investigative journalist. The inquiry was formulated around nine categories: "one's age, health, talents, habits, feelings, connexions in life, reputation, the leadings of Providence, and the teachings of the Holy Spirit."[34] These are the measures Fisk used to determine his suitability for missionary service.

As for *age* Fisk determined that, while older people can make good missionaries, it was better to enter into service at a younger age because "new languages are to be acquired, new habits formed, and new modes of living adopted." Fisk was twenty-four. He qualified. "No objection, therefore, can be raised from this source against my being a missionary," he said.

*Health* was a critical consideration given the "privations, the sufferings and the labors, connected with the missionary life." From Fisk's perspective a missionary needed to be in good health simply to survive on the field as he believed the heathen lived in unhealthy environs. That was not a deterrent for Fisk as he was relatively healthy. "[M]y strength remains firm," he said, "my sight, hearing, voice, and lungs are unimpaired; and my whole constitution seems fitted for the fatigues of a mission."

The missionary, said Fisk, should also have "superior *talents*" even though this wasn't absolutely necessary as scripture itself affirms that God "employs the weak things of the world to confound the things that are mighty." At the same time Fisk noted that the apostle Paul's example showed that God chooses those who have natural talents and education to work among the heathen with "much prudence and skill." So, asked Fisk, do I have the requisite talents? This was hard to determine, as "it is exceedingly difficult for one to form a correct opinion of his own talents." At the very least, said Fisk, "my talents are . . . of the *ready* kind, and this, I hope, would be favorable for the missionary work."

Fisk proceeded in this manner for all nine categories, checking his accomplishments and character over against the list in the hope of finding a rationally determined assurance for his calling. By the time he finished he concluded that he was qualified, trusting that God would help

33. Ibid., 71.

34. Quotes in this section are taken from Bond, *Memoir*, 71–86.

him overcome those areas of weakness that didn't make him a perfect fit for the vocation.

> When I have most sensible communion with God, and experi-
> ence most sensibly the influences of the Holy Spirit, then I feel
> most anxious to go among the heathen. May I not call this an
> indication that this Heavenly Guide approves of my purpose to
> go? May I not hope, that it is his influence which has made a life
> of trial look so pleasant, and weaned me thus from the society of
> friends I naturally love so much?[35]

This long process of self examination set aside Fisk's earlier doubts. But those doubts were resurrected when his professors raised questions about his suitability for missionary service, at least missionary service outside the United States.

> My respected Instructors have given me to understand, that
> they think me better qualified to aid the cause of the Redeemer
> in this country, as an agent in behalf of charitable objects, and as
> a domestic missionary, than to labor among pagans. So others
> have thought before.[36]

One can only wonder what it was that led the professors to come to this conclusion. Was it Fisk's lack of intellectual vigor, their ideal being the missionary scholar? Or perhaps something related to his personality? We don't know what it was, as neither Fisk nor Bond gave any clue what this was about. What we can determine is that the professors' critique came as a heavy blow to Fisk, replacing a confidence in his calling with a tormented uncertainty.

> I feel that my happiness and usefulness are deeply concerned.
> I tremble at the thought of relinquishing the object, after hav-
> ing so often consecrated myself to it, and had such comfort-
> able evidence that I ought to engage in it . . . I know not how
> to understand the language of Providence. Is this to forbid my
> laboring among the heathen? Or it is only to test my resolution,
> my patience, and my love for the work? Why have I been led to
> think and feel so much on this subject? Was it to prepare me for
> Foreign Service, or was it to prepare me to be disappointed and

---

35. Ibid., 79.
36. Ibid., 83.

labor at home? . . . O my Saviour I give myself to thee. Do with me as thou wilt.[37]

Interestingly, and perhaps tellingly, Bond mentioned nothing about what it was that brought a resolution to the dilemma the professors' doubts caused. The only hint Bond gave came in a footnote he included in his account, making reference to a letter Fisk wrote to his professors in which he made his case for foreign missionary service with cloying deference to their authority: "Though the result of my examination has, on the whole, been such as to lead me to conclude, it would be right to offer myself for the service of Christ among the heathen, still my views may have been wrong."[38] What we do know is that Fisk's professors eventually endorsed his calling. We know this from a letter Eliphalet Pearson and Leonard Woods wrote on behalf of the faculty to the Prudential Committee of the ABCFM in August of 1817 recommending Fisk and Parsons and several other Andover students for missionary service.[39]

Clearly Fisk's time at Andover offered him an opportunity for spiritual and vocational self-assessment. It also offered him what it was he sought from an Andover education: the information and tools needed for a career in cross-cultural missions.

## A NEW MISSION SOCIETY

Given the apparent passion Andover's founders and professors exhibited for global missions it is striking that the mandated curriculum offered nothing in terms of courses dedicated to the history and theology of Christian missions. Other than the study of world religions as it intersected with church history or conflicted with orthodox theology, Andover students were given little in terms of what it was many of them came to Andover to study. In this subject they were largely self-taught, which may be another reason why Fisk didn't apply himself to his formal studies as well as he should have. When he wasn't working through his spiritual profile he was poring over missionary correspondence in the *Panoplist* and other periodicals and books dedicated to Christian missions, particularly those written out of an evangelical paradigm. Here his involvement with the Brethren, which moved its activities to Andover when its founders advanced their studies to the post-graduate level in

37. Ibid., 80.
38. Ibid., 41.
39. ABC: box no. 6 v. 1, HLH.

1808, and the newer and more influential Society of Inquiry, founded by these same students, came to dominate his thoughts and time. The fact that he became president of the Society and was given the task of writing its short history during his senior year[40] is an indication that his involvement was more than casual. This is where Fisk would have developed his missiological insights, making a study of the documentation of this student society a critical imperative for understanding the state of his mind prior to his departure for the Ottoman Empire. The fact that several of the documents that have survived were authored by Fisk himself gives such a study even more significance. This will be the focus of what follows.

## THE SOCIETY OF INQUIRY: ORIGINS AND OBJECTIVES

At a meeting of the Brethren at Andover on January 8, 1811, eight students, including the co-founder of the organization, Samuel J. Mills, made the decision to form "the Society of Inquiry on the subject of Missions,"[41] which, unlike the Brethren, operated in the open. The object of this society, according to the constitution drawn up by these students, was "to inquire into the state of the Heathen; the duty and importance of missionary labors, the best manner of conducting missions, and the most eligible place for their establishment."[42] What this indicates is that Andover students were taking upon themselves the responsibility of helping the ABCFM determine the where and how of missionary service. They apparently did so with the enthusiastic endorsement of the Board. Soon after they went public with their plans, the board's Prudential Committee published a letter indicating their desire to help them stock their library.

> One object of the above named Society is to furnish its members suitable means of information. And for this purpose they have established a Library denominated "The Missionary Library." This Library, being recently established contains few books of importance. To the pious generosity of those, who, anxiously desire the salvation of the Heathen, in the name of the Society of Inquiry, we make an appeal.[43]

40. Fisk, *Historical Sketch of the Society.*

41. Beaver, ed., *Pioneers in Mission*, 26.

42. Ibid.

43. Ibid., 27–28 (this letter was recorded in the records of the Society).

## A Parallel, Yet Complementary Educational Experience

One way of understanding the purpose that these students envisioned for the Society is to think of it as an alternative, yet complementary, educational experience to what was formally provided by the seminary. The students had their own meetings (*sans* professors) during which they would take turns delivering papers called "dissertations." These papers, some of which required extensive research, were prepared outside the required curriculum using resources housed in their own separate library. The Society functioned, in other words, not only as a body dedicated to fostering a missionary spirit among the students but also as a self-educating mission society.

What needs to be recognized here is how new the missionary venture was to the orthodox. Mission work among first nation tribes had been going on for some time, as evidenced in the example of Brainerd who was a contemporary (and aspiring son-in-law) of Jonathan Edwards. But Protestant mission efforts with a global emphasis were still in their infancy. Even British mission societies, which provided the inspiration and model for American missions, had only been in operation since the later part of the eighteenth century.[44] What this meant is that there was very little experience upon which these students could draw for instruction. There was even less in-depth missiological reflection. "American missions to the world," says Charles W. Forman, "began with a minimum of theory and a maximum of practice. There were no long treatises, major studies or extensive research programs at the beginnings of the world missionary movement."[45]

When it came to missiological reflection, students who belonged to the Society of Inquiry at Andover Seminary were the closest thing

44. Chaney traces the roots of an evangelical American impulse for missions to the Puritans, which he calls "Puritan Rib Work" (*The Birth of Missions in America*, chap. 1), but it was this later British effort that is usually credited with being the most definitive source of inspiration for the ABCFM. The first British global mission society was organized by Northamptonshire Baptists the same year Carey published his highly influential, *An Enquiry Into The Obligations Of Christians To Use Means For The Conversion Of The Heathens (1792)*. Several other more prominent societies were organized soon after. The work of these societies provided the inspiration for the students who established the Society of Inquiry. (See Thorne's excellent treatment of the founding and ideological bearings of these British societies in chapter two of her book *Congregational Missions and the Making of an Imperial Culture in Nineteenth-Century England*).

45. Forman, "A History of Foreign Mission Theory in America," 69.

the seminary had to experts in the field. Their passions for missions had driven them to accumulate information from whatever sources they could find, primarily in this case the journals and letters of British and, by Fisk's time, American missionaries. They read whatever books they could find on Islam and Hinduism and other "heathen" religions. They studied world geography and history and met together on a regular basis to discuss what they had learned. They studied missions because they were the ones being called upon to *do* missions. At a time when a Protestant global mission effort was largely a work in progress, the students who formed the Society of Inquiry at Andover seminary were its resident experts. And apparently the faculty affirmed this as they gave their blessings to what was for all intents and purposes a student-led alternative educational experience.

## Comparing Libraries

The difference between these parallel educational experiences can perhaps best be illustrated by comparing the contents of the institutional library with the students' missionary library. The catalogue of the Missionary Library was heavily populated with books giving information about various parts of the world: travelogues and historical and geographical works with titles like *Universal Geography, Discovery of the Northern Coasts of South America, Asiatic Researches, Bigland's View of the World, History of Persia* as well as missionary journals opening windows onto various parts of the world, like Mayhew's *Mission to Indians*, Buchanan's *Researches in Asia* and Edwards' *Life of Brainerd*. There were also complete sets of the *Panoplist* and other missionary periodicals along with missionary memoirs, reports of the various missionary societies (which at this point were mainly British), and collections of sermons with missionary themes. Doctrinal works were also found here (*Essay on the Doctrine of Christ, Baptism* by Jewell) but they constituted a token presence. And notably, nearly all of the library's collection was in the English language.[46]

The seminary library,[47] in contrast, reflected apologetic and biblical/doctrinal concerns, with works not only by those whose writings

46. The works referred to here are only those which would have been published early enough for inclusion in the library during Fisk's time at Andover. This is taken from an undated list found in the archives of the Franklin Trask Library of Andover Newton Theological Library in Newton Center, MA.

47. A complete listing of books for this library is found in Andover Theological Seminary, *Catalogue of the Library* .

represented orthodox theology such as Jonathan Edwards, Dwight Woods and Samuel Hopkins, but the theology and philosophy of their ideological opponents, thinkers like Hume, Priestly and Bolingbroke. It also included a large selection of works in Latin, German and French. Perhaps most interesting for the purpose of this work were the number of books related to the study of Islam, particularly Qur'anic studies. These included several editions of the Qur'an in various translations including Latin (Ludovico Marracci's *Alcorani Textus Universus*, Padua, 1698), French (Andre Du Ryer's *L'Alcoran de Mahomet*, Paris, 1647) and George Sale's English translation (1734) as well as Theodor Hackspan's *Fides et leges Mohammaedis exihibitae ex Alkorani manuscipto duplici*, which was a "grammatical outline of Arabic . . . based entirely on Koranic texts."[48] Other works related to what at the time would have been called "Oriental studies" were found in the library, as well, including books by "Zainoddin Omar Ibn Alwardius of Damascus" and "Nuwairi, Mufti at Cairo."[49]

There were volumes held in common between the two libraries. Prideaux's *Life of Mahomet*, Edward's *Life of Brainerd* and Morse's *Universal Geography* were among them. But in general what we find is a contrast between a library focused on theological apologetics with aspirations of academic respectability,[50] versus a library dedicated to practical research for global missions. Most telling for the purpose of this book is the fact that there is no evidence from the dissertations that the students who wrote them ever made use of the seminary library for their research, certainly not books written in other languages. Andover students caught up in the spirit of global mission unleashed by the formation of the ABCFM had two separate educational experiences. And they were in control of the second.

## A Moral Motivation for Mission

Tucked away in the folder of surviving dissertations is a report Fisk wrote reflecting back on a ministry project in which he was engaged in Salem, Massachusetts in the spring of 1818.[51] This is not a dissertation,

48. "Koran Translations 1543–1800," Warburg Institute Archive, http://warburg-archive.sas.ac.uk/mnemosyne/Quran_trans/List%20of%20Koran%20Translations%201543%20to%201800.docx (accessed July 20, 2016).

49. Andover Theological Seminary, *Catalogue of the Library.*

50. With, perhaps, an eye on Harvard?

51. Fisk, *Copy of a Report of Labors in Salem Performed in the spring Vacation 1818* (Series 7/Dissertations), ANTS.

but serves as an introduction to themes found in the dissertations. More importantly it gives insight into Fisk's thought processes in the last year of his Andover education.

Fisk's summer project was to make pastoral home visits in Salem to "colonized people" which was apparently a term used by Andover students to describe either slaves or freed slaves. Fisk went as a pastoral visitor, but the approach he took had less to do with pastoral care than data collection. In his own words, he was engaged in "research" akin to what Nehemiah did when he surveyed the ruins of Jerusalem. Just as Nehemiah surveyed those ruins, says Fisk, "so the Nehemiahs of this age are surveying the 'old wastes' that they may repair those 'desolations of many generations.'"

> Societies are organized, schools are formed, monies are raised, preachers, catechists & teachers are employed and the moral machinery is in motion which is to elevate this class of our fellow beings to their proper rank and privileges.[52]

What this indicates is a shift in Fisk's ideological emphasis, from a dominant "doctrinalist" perspective to a "moralist" perspective. Both remained part of his intellectual make-up, but a perceptible shift in emphasis had taken place during his Andover years. Where the younger Fisk would have spoken about the need for changed hearts and spiritual revival, the maturing Fisk talks about putting "moral machinery in motion" to "elevate" people living "in a state of very abject degradation." What he wrote in the introductory paragraph of this report brings this home with even more force. It is worth quoting in full.

> It is the object of that "restless benevolence" which characterizes this age, to extend the blessings of literary, moral and religious instruction to all classes of the community. In pursuit of this object it has led many to form institutions, & organize societies various in their immediate object, diversified in their operations, but all tending to the same grand result. The Patrons of these institutions and the members of these societies have been naturally led to investigate with accuracy the real condition of the poor & vicious, to visit, in person, the haunts of vice and the abodes of wretchedness. While a Henderson, a Pinkerton & a Buchanan[53] have been engaged in ascertaining the moral

---

52. Ibid.

53. Buchanan was cited earlier as one of the earliest British missionaries to explore missionary possibilities in India. Ebenezer Henderson and Robert Pinkerton were

wants of nations & exploring the dark places of the earth that are full of the habitations of cruelty, an almost immeasurable multitude have been engaged with the same object & this same spirit in ascertaining the actual conditions of the needy around them. A spirit of Christian vigilance is waked up and every dark corner is to be searched out and every class of the community is to receive attention.[54]

Much is made in contemporary scholarship of the motivational force of millennialism in studies of the early American Protestant mission effort.[55] "The missionary spirit—in common with the whole evangelical movement of the first years of the nineteenth century—was deeply steeped in the millennial ferment of the turn of the century," writes Clifton Jackson Phillips.[56] "The importance of eschatology as a major motivator to missions cannot be overstated," says David W. Kling.[57]

This is certainly true as attested in numerous sermons and reports emanating from evangelical sources during this era.[58] We also see evidence of it in several of the student dissertations. But one would expect to find it more prominently present in the missionary documentation of the era given the importance with which historians have invested it. In fact, it is a relatively minor theme in the Society of Inquiry documentation, taking a back seat to what is most evident in Fisk's report: a *moral* motiva-

early Scottish missionaries who engaged in similar "researches" in Iceland and Russia.

54. Ibid.

55. DeJong notes this to be a consistent thread throughout the entire early history of the Protestant missionary movement which he illustrates with examples drawn from the dawn of the Protestant missionary movement in 1740 to the establishment of the ABCFM in 1810. His book, *As the Waters Cover the Sea:Millennial Expectations in the Rise of Anglo-American Missions, 1640–1810* is the most thorough treatment of the subject, but many others have addressed the subject. See especially the insightful work of Rogers in "'A Bright and New Constellation,'" 39–61, where Rogers correctly, I believe, identifies the narrative function of millennial themes in mission history. "Millennialism," he says, "should not be viewed as an end in itself; rather, it should be studied as a cultural idiom whose meaning shifts based on the reasons for its appropriation and the context of its use. To capture the malleability of millennial discourse, I have chosen to treat it as a form of narrative" (53).

56. Phillips, *Protestant America and the Pagan World*, 7.

57. Kling, "The New Divinity," 26.

58. It is found particularly, as Rogers notes, in publications of sermons and discourses delivered "during missionary society meetings and missionary ordinations" ("'A Bright and New Constellation,'" 39), which may suggest that it was utilized primarily as a promotional narrative. It is found less frequently in the literature produced by missionaries themselves.

tion for missions, the "restless benevolence which characterizes this age."
The overwhelming sense one gets from this and similar literature of the
era is that orthodox missionaries and clerics visualized themselves not as
a vanguard ushering in the Second Coming, but as religious physicians
offering the antidote to the world's spiritual and moral ills. They were
compelled into missionary service not by millennial speculation but by
the belief that they were in possession of what it was that was needed to
elevate humanity to its highest level of fulfillment and achievement. In
the words of an orthodox minister urging Christians to an active engagement with and support of the ABCFM:

> The spiritual privileges we enjoy we have no right to monopo-
> lize; and if we are Christians, we have no disposition to do it.
> Under a sense of their value, we should be in earnest to dis-
> seminate them, among all the benighted beings who now sit in
> darkness, and dwell in the habitations of cruelty. Thus may we
> enjoy the satisfaction of obeying and pleasing our Divine Re-
> deemer, of following in the steps of his holy Apostles, and of
> evincing our attachment to him and his cause. We may have
> the satisfaction of bearing some humble part, in promoting the
> promised triumphs of the gospel, and in terminating the cruel-
> ties and miseries of man.[59]

## The Dissertations: Topics

A moral motivation for missions is one of the more predominant themes
found in the dissertations written by Society of Inquiry students during Fisk's era. Other themes accompany it which, when taken together,
provide the foundation of a nascent evangelical missiology. Among these
themes are those that provide insights into student perceptions of the
religious other, including members of the faith communities whom Fisk
would encounter during his sojourn in the Ottoman Empire.

The Society of Inquiry at Andover met once a month.[60] Each meeting began with prayer followed by the presentation of a dissertation
prepared by different students in rotation. After the meetings the dissertations would be collected and later bound for future reference. Most
have been preserved in the Andover Newton Theological School archives.

59. Pond, *Short Missionary*, 139.

60. Beaver, ed., *Pioneers in Mission*, 28. After 1825 the monthly meetings gave
way to smaller committee meetings and the
presentation of dissertations ended.

Four years' worth of dissertations had already been bound and catalogued when Fisk began his studies at Andover. It's not certain that he read them, although given his thirst for missionary "intelligence," it's probable that he did. Among the titles of these early dissertations were: "Ceylon," "What are the peculiar encouragements for missionaries?," "What exertions have been made, and are now making, by Christians in other countries for introducing the gospel among the heathen?," "On an American Mission to China," "Arguments in favor of attending to missions, drawn from the state of American churches and from some recent events in divine providence" and "Hindooism."

Other than a proclivity for long titles, what we discover here are several types of topics favored by the students. The first were country studies where geographical and historical information was presented along with a social, political and religious profile of the people who lived there. In most cases these details were taken verbatim from Morse's *Universal Geography*[61] or Bigland's *Geographical and Historical View of the World*.[62] The purpose in this case was to assess each country's suitability for missionary service.

The second category had as its subject matter missionary activity already in existence. Notable here was the variety of different mission organizations given favorable treatment by the students, indicating the erosion of a more divisive "doctrinalism." A paper prepared for the Society in 1812 listed seventeen different mission societies operating around the world at that time, including missions undertaken by British Baptists, German Moravians, Dutch Reformed, Danish Lutherans and British Methodists.[63] All were considered valid expressions of the one mission of Christ's Church.

The third category might best be labeled "practical missionary concerns," covering various aspects of the missionary vocation. These were the dissertations with the exceedingly long titles.

Finally there were dissertations dedicated to the study of non-Christian religions or those expressions of Christianity the orthodox considered unacceptable. Most interesting to the subject matter of this book is a dissertation by Fisk's biographer, Alvan Bond, during the time

61. Morse, *The American Universal Geography*.

62. Bigland, *Geographical and Historical View of the World*.

63 *A book of Reference on the Subject of Missionary Societies begun December 1812*, ANTS. "The inclusion of Methodists is especially noteworthy, as the great theological battles fought by earlier Edwardseans was with Arminian Methodists."

Fisk was a member of the Society. What makes it interesting is the topic: "The present state of Mohomedanism," which Bond presented to the Society in December of 1816.[64]

## The Dissertations: Themes

As noted above, a primary theme running through the dissertations was the moral imperative for missionary service. Nearly all either spoke directly to this theme or alluded to it. We hear it, for instance, in what a student named George Calhoun wrote about the "promotion of human happiness" being the reason that Andover students needed to "give special attention to the subject of Missions."

> To the Christian above all is this delightful subject . . . In the cause of Missions he sees the cause of humanity. He views multitudes, who not long since had no bowels of compassion, now taking the burdens from the oppressed, consoling the afflicted, and delivering the benighted from the thraldom [sic] of ignorance and superstition . . . Can he who loves the Saviour who died to reclaim sinners be indifferent in the cause of humanity?[65]

Levi Parsons made a similar case by holding Brainerd up as a model of Christian benevolence. Pity was the motivating force for missions in this case.

> The miserable objects of superstition & wretchedness around [the missionary] call forth every feeling of sympathy, & benevolence. He labors to set them at liberty from a tyranny, the most galling & degrading, & which will retain its baneful influence over the precious souls of its victims, when this transitory scene shall have passed away.[66]

Cyrus Kingsbury, who would go on to a missionary career working among first nation peoples, appealed to "national feelings" as a motivation for missions, in this case urging American Christians to pass on the moral blessings of Christian civilization to their immediate neighbors.

> In no point of view does the high character of the English nation appear so preeminent, as in striving for the improvement

---

64. Bond, *The Present State of Mahomedanism* (Dec 17, 1816), ANTS.

65. Calhoun, *What are the reasons, which should induce the Members of this Seminary to give special attention to the subject of Missions?* (March 1816), ANTS.

66. Parsons, *The Peculiar consolations of a Missionary* (July 2, 1816), ANTS.

of the benighted subjects in India. And the appeal ought to be
made to the national feelings of the U. States, whether they will
behold thousands of uncivilized Heathen, dragging out a miserable existence, without taking any decisive measures to improve
their condition.[67]

Fisk added his own moralist perspective to the mix in a dissertation
weighing the relative merits of mission endeavors in the American West
with those of Asia. In both cases Fisk determined that the motivation was
the same. A student whose converted heart was gripped by disinterested
benevolence "cast his eye over the world and sees multitudes perishing in
ignorance of the gospel and many doors open for useful exertion." That
was just as true in America as in countries outside her borders. "They
are," Fisk asserted, "alike in a state of temporal wretchedness."

> In the east the deluded devotee falls before Juggernaut and dies,
> the widow burns on the funeral pyre and Pilgrims starve by
> thousands. In the west they sometimes offer human sacrifices,
> put their prisoners to death with the most excruciating tortures
> and often suffer all the horrors of famine.[68]

Interestingly and perhaps tellingly, Fisk in this same dissertation alluded to something few other students appeared to recognize. What he
said is that there are "gradations" of religiosity among the various peoples
of the world, even in parts of the world where the gospel has never been
heard.

> Between the state of those who enjoy the greatest degree of
> gospel light and that of those who dwell in the thickest dark-
> ness of paganism *there is a regular gradation in point of religious
> knowledge and religious privileges.* Where there is no vision the
> people perish. But how much light is necessary to salvation we
> are not informed. Faith cometh by hearing. But in what manner
> or how much we must hear in order to embrace that faith which
> is connected with salvation we are unable to decide [emphasis
> added].[69]

67. Kingsbury, *On the Establishment of Mission Schools among the Indians within
the Territory of the United States* (August 1815), ANTS.

68. Fisk, *A Comparative View of the Eastern and Western Missions upon the
American churches* (February 1817), ANTS.

69. Ibid.

It appears from this that even before he left the US for missionary service in the Ottoman Empire Fisk was moving towards a more nuanced understanding of the bifurcation between saved and unsaved. It is a discernible move, but not by any means dominant enough to offset his stronger emphasis on the salvific gap that divided insiders from outsiders, orthodox from everyone else.

> Without pretending to draw the line below which there can be no salvation, I venture to say after comparing their characters with the way of life revealed in the bible we shall be compelled to believe the Hindoos in the east and the Indians in the west are in the road to endless ruin.[70]

What is apparent here is the great moral divide these students believed to have existed between Christians and the Heathen which mirrored a similar divide the orthodox saw between Christians and infidels. While Andover students devoted much of their energy to finding ways to combat the forces of infidelity in American society, those who were members of the Society of Inquiry also saw themselves attending to another battle against the "powers and principalities" that held the world outside the boundaries of Christendom in their death grip. And nowhere, thought these students, were these powers more pervasively and despotically present than in those countries and regions whose people were under the dominion of the noxious system created by the "imposter" Muhammad.

The term "imposter" used as a derisive identifier for the prophet Muhammad was normative for the era. It was, in fact, so ubiquitous in the religious literature of Fisk's era that it would have been difficult for him or anyone else to think of Muhammad any other way. The roots for this essentializing imprecation stretched back to the seventeenth-century work of Anglican cleric Humphrey Prideaux whose book *The True Nature of Imposture Full Displayed in the Life of Mahomet. With a Discourse annex'd, for the Vindicating of Christianity from this Charge; Offered to the Consideration of the Deists of the Present Age* provided American Christians with the "most notable and influential treatment of Islam" from the colonial period through the early part of the nineteenth century.[71] Prideaux believed Muhammad deliberately twisted religious truth to suit his own nefarious purposes, thus the label "imposter." Most interesting

---

70. Ibid.

71. Kidd, *American Christians and Islam*, 6.

given the apologetic thrust of an Andover education is that Prideaux tied this accusation to a defense of Christianity against the attacks of Deists, indicating how closely the battle with infidelity was linked to a Christian assessment of Islam.[72]

## The Dissertations: Assessing Islam

Direct treatment of Islam as a religious phenomenon is found in several of the student dissertations, particularly Bond's. But other dissertations also contain references to it, most notably country studies on Muslim majority countries. Levi Parsons also made reference to Islam in the address he made to the Society as outgoing president. Given that he would travel with Fisk to the Ottoman Empire, Parsons early perceptions of Islam are worth noting.

> We have to contend with a more formidable foe—a more destructive enemy to the christian religion—the empire of MA-HOMEDANISM ... [T]here the Kingdom of Satan is firmly established—favored by the prejudice of the people—strengthened and upheld by the power of Magistrates—by the arts and subtlety of Politicians—guarded by all the power & terrors of the world on the one hand, and by all its pomp and allurement on the other.[73]

It should be noted that Jews and Catholics received much the same treatment from Parsons in this address. Catholics were "a barrier as fatal to the progress of the gospel, as the Mahomedan, and pagan powers." Jews "practice many foolish and abominable superstitions." But the Muslim Empire (as opposed to individual Muslims) is by far "the most formidable foe."

Bond picked up on several of Parsons' themes in the dissertation he put together from the largely anecdotal material at his disposal.[74] What his sources told him was that Islam had begun in 618 ("the 40th year of the Imposter's life") as a religion based on a deliberately distorted in-

---

72. Prideaux, *The True Nature of Imposture Full Displayed in the Life of Mahomet.*

73. Parsons, *Address to Society* (Sept 1817).

74. Bond lists Morse's *Universal Geography,* Buchanan's *Researches,* an article from the Panoplist on the history of missions (Vol. V & XII), and reports of the British and Foreign Bible Society and the London Missionary Society as his sources, in some cases quoting verbatim from these materials. None, apart from Morse's work (which was itself written with an orthodox bias), could be considered scholarly sources, more anecdotal in their treatment of Islam than anything based on original research.

terpretation of Christian scripture. The inspired scriptures of Islam, according to Bond, were the "Pentateuch, the Psalms, the Gospel and the Koran," correctly identifying the Qur'anic affirmation of the biblical texts while failing to understand the Muslim affirmation of the Qur'an's unique authority. He also noted that Muslims acknowledge the divine mission of biblical figures like Adam and Noah and Abraham and Moses, but countered this with a critical estimation of "Mohomed's"[75] mission that brought "new dispensations, which ruinously abrogated the preceding." Bond also made note of the basic division between Sunni and Shi'a, calling Sunnis the "Sect of Omar, who rigidly and scrupulously follow the precepts of Mahomed and Omar" and the other "the Sect of Ali," who were "cool in their attachment to their professed religion and very loose in their practice of principles."

Bond's characterization of the nature of the Sunni-Shi'a division as that between a rigid orthodoxy and "loose" heterodoxy was a common theme of other student dissertations that made reference to Islam. It was a central affirmation of Jesse Stratton's dissertation on "Persia." In Persia, said Stratton, "the prejudices are not so strong as other Mahomedan nations. They adopt the mildest form of Mohamedanism for which they are regarded as heretics by the more superstitious & bigoted Turks."[76]

William Goodell, who would be one of the first Andover graduates to join Fisk in the Ottoman Empire after the death of Parsons, echoed this praise of the Persians in his dissertation on Armenia, in this case adding a note about their perceived openness to Christianity and Bible distribution. "In Persia," he wrote,

> little or no jealousy of Christianity, & no apparent hostility to its professors, have existence. Indeed, portions of the scriptures have already been put into the hands of some of the most distinguished Persians; in various places, encomiums on the gospels are openly uttered; and many of the learned evince an earnestness & mildness of enquiry into the character & mission of the Messiah.[77]

---

75. A curious, yet perhaps telling, characteristic of sermons and documents mentioning Muhammad's name is the fact that there didn't seem to be any agreed upon spelling nor any attempt to transliterate. This may be one more indication of the dismissive, contemptuous attitude held by the orthodox toward Islam.

76. Stratton, *Persia* (Aug. 1816), ANTS.

77. Goodell, *Brief History and Present State of Armenia and as a Mission Field* (Dec. 1818), ANTS.

Bond himself was less interested in Shi'a Islam in Persia than Sunni Islam in the Ottoman Empire where "the fallacious principles of the Arabian imposter" were more strictly followed. As would be expected from strict adherence to a religion created by a spiritual "imposter" the result was a degraded morality. "Licentiousness in its most disgusting forms is common throughout the empire," wrote Bond, even while acknowledging that Muslims in the Arabian provinces of the empire ("the 1st scene of Mahomedan triumph and delusion") include "men of considerable science" who "possess acute geniuses." Unfortunately, their morals were not as elevated as their science. "The general character of this nation," alleged Bond, "is very base."

Although not the political threat it once was, Bond believed that the Islamic empire continued to represent the greatest challenge to Christian missionary work. "It is well known," he said, "that the mantle of delusion, which Mahomed spread upon the intellect of his followers, has seldom been penetrated by the glorious light of the gospel." But this would soon change as the ABCFM garnered its missionary resources to mount a spiritual assault on this stronghold of error. A "new era of christian benevolence and exertion . . . will doubtless prevail, till it has entirely overthrown this extensive empire of error, which has been gaining strength through a long flight of ages." This was not eschatological hope, the Islamic empire falling by an act of apocalyptic vengeance. This was a "moralist" belief in the power of "christian benevolence and exertion" to effect positive change.

William Mitchell's dissertation on "Asia Minor" expanded Bond's contrast between the benevolence of Christianity and the moral poverty of Islam by contrasting the mission of Jesus with the mission of Muhammad. This contrast, in his estimation, was the best argument that could be made for the need to establish a missionary presence in the Muslim majority world.

> The religion of Mahomet, is not the religion of Jesus!—The one sends its followers on a tedious pilgrimage, to worship at the shrine of a departed imposter.—the other teaches its followers to bow the humble knee before an omnipotent Savior—the one fills the mind with delusive hopes—the other cheers the soul with light and life. The contrast need not be carried far to show the importance of establishing Christianity upon the ruins of Mahomedanism.[78]

Mitchell took Bond's theme one step further, stretching the moralist paradigm to its furthest extreme. Sending missionaries to Asia Minor, said Mitchell, would introduce civilization to "the lawless hordes that ravage the country" with "the introduction of agriculture, learning, the arts and sciences, and the blessings of civilized society." The setting was perfect for this civilizing mission because, "from the excellency of its climate & the fertility of its soil" Asia Minor "seems to be designed for the residence of a numerous & happy people." Civilization, happiness, learning, good crops—this was what orthodox missionaries would offer to Asia Minor. With blessings as great as these Mitchell assumed that all could see what he saw: the time had come for "the delusions of the imposter" to "yield to the religion of Jesus."[79]

## The Dissertations: Observations

Several observations need to be made here. The first is to note that Mitchell's characterization of Christian mission almost wholly in terms of its civilizing function represents an extreme that is echoed in few of the other dissertations. It is certainly doubtful that Fisk would have shared this perspective, as Fisk's commitment to a missional expression of Christian benevolence was informed by his revivalist faith. His concern for the "perishing multitudes" arose out of a conviction that they were living in ignorance of the gospel as opposed to the blessings of western civilization, even though the two were closely related. When Fisk spoke in his dissertation about heathen in the East and heathen in the West being "equally the objects of Christian benevolence," what he primarily had in mind was a benevolent witness to the saving grace of the gospel. Civilization in this case was seen as the fruit of evangelization as opposed to its central purpose. To characterize it any other way would have been

---

78. Ibid.

79. Ibid.

to slip into the error of the Boston Liberals who engaged in what Fisk would have determined to be a biblically indefensible reductionism by defining the Christian message solely by its moral dimension.[80]

A second observation is that the students who delivered these dissertations had no experiential reference points over against which they could measure the accuracy of their information. Muslims and Jews and the "heathen" were not living in their neighborhoods. They didn't know them as individuals, which made it easy to believe whatever they were told to believe about them. This is why Fisk and others like him hungrily devoured any news they could get from missionaries on the field. Missionaries had an "experimental" knowledge that made what they wrote more credible than other more theoretical sources. But even this was no guarantee of accuracy, especially because there was so little expertise among Protestant missionaries when it came to scholarly assessments of other cultures and religions. Most of their "intelligence" was anecdotal and incomplete, based on things missionaries or travelers witnessed without necessarily understanding the cultural or religious context. A case in point would be what the oft-quoted Buchanan said about the Hindu "Juggernaut," which was based on a mischaracterization and misunderstanding of a phenomenon he only knew as an uniformed bystander. There was no way for students to judge the validity of this information given their lack of experience. And so they accepted Buchanan's interpretation and passed it on until it became what "imposter" had become for Muhammad: an ideological meme reinforcing an uninformed stereotype.[81]

The final observation is to say that even if the students had had the sources to correct the stereotypes, it's not certain they would have. The severity of their characterizations of the religious other, even when

80. Fisk's theology professor, Leonard Woods, made clear the contrast this set up between the orthodox and liberals in a letter he wrote in 1819 in response to a sermon preached by William Ellery Channing lauding the principles of Unitarianism. "He (Channing) is content that men in Christian and in heathen lands should remain as they are, except what may be done for them by the gradual progress of knowledge, and the arts of civilized life." The orthodox, in contrast, recognized that true "progress of knowledge" only came about by the regenerative power of the gospel. *Letters to Unitarians Occasioned by the Sermon of the Reverend William E. Channing at the Ordination of Rev. J. Sparks*, 3.

81. One wonders what the students made of a remark found in a letter written by the first ABCFM appointed missionary to India, Adoniram Judson: "Dr. Buchanan is rather fanciful in many of his representations, and must, therefore, be read with much caution. In some instances he conveys a false idea." Judson, *Letter to the Society of Inquiry* (1812), FTL.

attempting to offer a more balanced perspective, suggests a dualistic *esprit d'ensemble* that demanded a nemesis representing the starkest possible contrast. This is what makes Fisk's reference to "gradations" of religiosity stand out. It introduced an element of ambiguity into an otherwise starkly contrasted portrait. Heathens, Muslims and Jews all served the same function—to be foils for the Protestant Christians' emphasis on disinterested benevolence; a necessary evil to justify missionary sacrifices. This may be overstated, but it does seem to explain the extreme nature of the caricatures. A moralist faith demanded an immoral other.

## A MISSIONARY VOCATION

Given their interest in Persia, Fisk and Parsons might have been more attuned to what the dissertations had to say about Islam than other students. But this remained a largely theoretical interest until Fisk passed his public examination at Andover on September 18, 1818. That was the day the Board appointed him and Parsons to be their agents for the establishment of a mission to the Ottoman Empire.[82]

82. Bond, *Memoir*, 87.

# 5

## Missionary Calling and Final Preparations

### THE ABCFM APPOINTMENT

THE ABCFM MET IN regular session in Boston on September 15–17, 1819.[1] Jedidiah Morse was there as was Fisk's theology professor Leonard Woods as a new appointee. They joined what could be characterized as an assemblage of the most influential leaders of the orthodox clan, gathering to give direction to an enterprise that was now in its ninth year of existence. One of the agenda items at the meeting was the appointment of Levi Parsons and Pliny Fisk to inaugurate the first ABCFM venture in the Muslim majority world. As was true with the other mission fields occupied at that time by ABCFM missionaries, this mission was perceived as an opportunity to ameliorate the conditions of millions who were living in circumstances of spiritual, moral and physical degradation. The report connected to Fisk and Parsons' appointment left no doubt about the need.

> If the countries of Southern Asia are highly interesting to Christian benevolence, and have strong claims upon Christian commiseration, on account of the hundreds of millions of human beings immersed in the deepest corruption and wretchedness; the countries of Western Asia, though less populous, are

---

1. ABCFM, *First Ten Annual Reports of the American Board of Commissioners for Foreign Mission*, 229–31.

in other respects not less interesting; nor do they present less powerful claims.[2]

What made this appointment unique according to this report was not only its pioneering nature, but its location. Fisk and Parsons were going to the land called Holy, "the scenes of those great transactions and events, which involved the destinies of mankind of all ages and all races," which, tragically, "have since been the scenes of direful changes; and the monuments of all their glory have long lain buried in dismal ruins."[3]

Palestine was the Board's primary target, but the territory they had in mind was much more extensive. It also encompassed Syria, the Provinces of Asia Minor, Armenia, Georgia and Persia. In this case Fisk and Parsons' appointment was conceptualized as the first step towards a much grander purpose. They were pioneers who would operate both as scouts surveying the territory for future ABCFM missionary service and as the initiators of a relational witness that would set the stage for a more all-encompassing mission to the diverse populations of the Ottoman Empire. And their *modus operandi,* at least in this early stage, would be to work primarily with the Christian population.

> It is hoped ... that among the Christians there, of various denominations, some might be found, who are alive in Christ Jesus, and who, were proper means employed for their excitement, improvement, and help, might be roused from their slumbers, become active in doing good, and shine as lights in those darkened regions. It is indeed hoped that no small part of those, who bear the Christian name, would ... do something towards imparting the heavenly treasure, as opportunities should be afforded, to the Jews, Mohammedans, and Pagans; and, dispersed as they are, among the different nations, they might do much; at least might afford many and important facilities and advantages for carrying into effect the expanding desires of benevolence.[4]

The one nod the Board gave to an eschatological purpose for this mission was to mention Jews as a particularly important target of the Board's mission efforts. The time had come, they said, for "[God's] mercy to be displayed" to these people who have "been an awful monument to the world of the sovereignty of God, under the tremendous curse so

2. Ibid., 229.

3. Ibid.

4. Ibid., 230.

terribly imprecated, when the blood of the Lord of life and glory was demanded."[5] But there was no attempt to link this missional purpose with an apocalyptic scenario. This mission, like all other ABCFM missions, was conceived as a moral endeavor, doing God's benevolent work in a world that lived outside the boundaries of God's enlivening grace.

## The Instructions

The moral vision that drove this pioneering mission endeavor was given more clarity in the instructions the Board gave to Fisk and Parsons at a farewell service at the Old South Church in Boston just before they set sail for the Ottoman Empire.[6] These instructions made it clear that the ultimate goal was for them to establish a mission station in Jerusalem, or if that proved to be too difficult, Bethlehem as "a place less infested with jealousies, and of greater salubrity." The Board was aware that it would be a difficult task no matter where they settled, but the importance of the establishment of a mission station in the Holy Land to the larger aims of the ABCFM made it a priority.

> We are sensible that it will be a difficult station: we are not certain that the occupation of it will be found practicable; or, if practicable, on the whole eligible: but we devoutly hope that it will be; and are persuaded, that if you can reside there with safety, the importance of the Station will outweigh many difficulties.[7]

What is important to note here is that the mission commission given to Fisk and Parsons was conceived in the framework of a larger missiological purpose that undergirded all that the ABCFM was doing around the world. It was just one part of an expanding kingdom of benevolence. Simply put, their mission was to do good.

> Your Mission is to be regarded as part of an extended and continually extending system of *benevolent action* for the recovery of the world to God and to happiness . . .
> From the heights of the Holy Land,—from Calvary, from Olivet, and from Zion, you will take an extended view of the

5. Ibid.

6 These instructions are included verbatim in a volume of the magazine that served as the mouthpiece for the London Jews Society: *The Jewish expositor and friend of Israel, Containing Monthly Communication Respecting the Jews and the Proceedings of the London Society* (January 1820), 432–41.

7. Ibid., 434.

widespread desolations, and variegated scenes, presenting themselves on every side to Christian sensibility; and will survey with
earnest attention the various tribes and classes of fellow-beings
who dwell in that land and in the surrounding countries. The
two grand enquiries ever present in your minds will be, *What
good can be done?* and by what means? What can be done for
Jews? What for the Pagans? What for the Mohammedans? What
for the Christians? What for the people of Palestine? What for
those in Egypt,—in Syria,— in Persia,— in Armenia,—in other
countries to which your enquiries may be extended? [emphasis
added][8]

## THE FAREWELL SERMON

Fisk and Parsons were both asked to preach at the farewell service where
they received these instructions. This put them, at least for the moment,
on center stage in the orthodox universe. It was an occasion that called
for their best, most critically examined thoughts.

Fisk chose Acts 20:22 for his text: "And now, behold, I go bound
in the Spirit unto Jerusalem, not knowing the things that shall befall me
there (KJV)" indicative, perhaps, of his own sense of uncertainty about
what lay ahead. The language he used, however, had nothing of uncertainty in it, nor did it have the kind of emotive power one might expect
from a preacher embarking on a life-changing mission. Emulating the
style of his boyhood pastor and mentor, what Fisk presented was more
lecture than sermon.

You are aware, my hearers, that the determination was some
time since formed to attempt a mission to Jerusalem and the
surrounding country. You are also aware, that he, who now addresses you, expects soon to embark, with a colleague, on the
proposed mission. You will not, therefore, deem it unsuitable,
that on this occasion, I should endeavor to explain the design,
and the nature, of the contemplated undertaking.[9]

The "design, and the nature" of this "contemplated undertaking"
was in keeping with the Board's instructions regarding the revival of the
indigenous church. "Important advantages to the Church might be expected from the revival of pure Christianity there," said Fisk. This was the
nature of his mission: to revive the ancient churches. But the place where

8. Ibid., 437.

9. Fisk, *The Holy Land an interesting field of missionary enterprise*, 1.

that revival would happen appeared to be more interesting to Fisk than the mission itself, as he spent a good deal of the sermon giving information about the context in which he would work.

This contextual information included details about the climate and soil conditions of the Mediterranean region ("with a temperate and salubrious climate, a soil naturally luxuriant, producing the greatest abundance the means of support for man and beast"), its link to the Christian narrative ("this land is rendered almost sacred in the eyes of every Christian, by a thousand religious associations"), and its present inhabitants. Judea, said Fisk, was "inhabited by several interesting classes of men," which included "Mahommedans, and Jews; and Roman Catholic, Greek, Armenian and Syrian Christians."[10]

Giving this information led Fisk to ponder the kind of people he would encounter, beginning with those who were seen as most problematical to the aims of the ABCFM mission; "Mahommedans." The Ottoman Empire, said Fisk, was under the control of "the followers of that artful imposter, who arose in Arabia about the commencement of the seventh century."[11] In this he was fully in tune with the essentialist orthodox narrative. But he followed this with an assessment of Islam that was relatively accurate and benign, even to the point of admitting that "they have . . . much of truth in their system."

> Mahommedans believe, that Moses and Jesus were true prophets; that Jesus was the greatest of prophets except Mahommed; that the Pentateuch, the Psalms, the Prophets, and the Gospels were revelations from God, but have been so much corrupted by Jews and Christians, as to deserve but little credit. They assert the unity of God, the immortality of the soul, and future rewards and punishments. They have, indeed, much of truth in their system.[12]

The counter balance to this was what Fisk said next, as despite the fact that there was truth in their system, "their customs, established by the usage of centuries, the despotic nature of their government, the prominent articles of their faith, and the very genius and spirit of their religion, shield the Mahommedans almost impenetrably from the influence of

---

10. Ibid., 2–3.

11. Ibid., 4.

12. Ibid., 5.

Christianity." Thus the need to mount what Fisk himself might have labeled a new spiritual crusade.

> To make spiritual conquests from them will require the most
> vigorous efforts of the Christian church. Let the Gospel prevail
> among them, and some of the strongest fortresses of error and
> sin will be taken.[13]

Fisk next turned his attention to the Jews of the Holy Land. Here, too, his assessment began in a relatively positive way, as he lauded their tenacity through years of suffering and exile allowing them "to retain their ancient language, customs and religion." The requisite critique followed immediately after this as Fisk reminded his listeners that the religion the Jews have tenaciously preserved is not the religion "exhibited in the piety of David, Daniel, and Nehemiah" but rather that of the Jews who "rejected and crucified the Lord Jesus."[14]

In what might be seen as a foretaste of Fisk's troubled relationships with Roman Catholics in the Levant, he saw nothing of redeeming quality in Roman Catholic spirituality. "Though they hold the doctrine of our Savior's divinity and atonement, and many of the fundamental doctrines of Christianity, yet they are extremely ignorant of the true spirit of the Gospel; are almost entirely destitute of the Scriptures; and to what they retain of real Christianity they add many inventions of their own."[15]

Fisk was aware that there were other branches of Catholicism in the Holy Land, less beholden to the Pope's authority. They received better treatment. "The Syrian Christians," said Fisk, "are nominally under the Pope's jurisdiction" but they were closer to the truth as "they are said to pay very little deference to his authority, and are much more inclined than the Catholics to the true doctrines of Christianity, and to the diffusion of them."[16]

Fisk's greatest praise was reserved for the Greeks and Armenians, who, though they "very much resemble the Catholics" had not "by any means departed so far from the simplicity of Gospel truth." But even with this more laudatory appraisal Fisk didn't hesitate to offer a critical assessment. "All these sects, though they call themselves Christians, are still

13. Ibid.

14. Ibid.

15. Ibid., 6.

16. Ibid.

destitute almost entirely of the Scriptures, and deplorably ignorant of real Christianity."[17]

Fisk managed to find one glimmer of light in the religious profile of the region. He found it by contrasting Middle Eastern religiosity with the religiosity of countries populated by the heathen.

> All the inhabitants of the country believe in one God, and the leading facts recorded in the Old Testament. Here are no gods of brass or wood; no temples to Juggernaut, or the Grand Lama; no funeral piles; no altars stained with the blood of human victims. Everywhere you see a faint glimmering of light, through the gross and almost impenetrable darkness.[18]

In his final evaluation of the spiritual status of the peoples he would encounter in his mission Fisk gave voice to what he saw as evidence of an elevated civilization in the Ottoman Empire, making the nature of this missional endeavor much different from other ABCFM projects.

> These people are not sunk in such entire stupidity and such brutal ignorance, as are the Hindoos of India, and the Hottentots of Africa. Here is intellect, enterprise, and some degree of literature and science. Here several classes of men are among the most interesting that dwell on earth, and are worthy of the prayers and the attentions of all those, who desire to see influence, learning, talent, and strength of character consecrated to Christ.[19]

There was a "glimmering of light" in the Ottoman Empire, but it was not enough to overcome the "gross and almost impenetrable darkness" that enveloped the peoples Fisk believed God was calling him to serve. This was why Fisk and Parsons' mission was needed: to allow the much greater light of a pure gospel witness to break through the darkness, first through the revival of moribund eastern churches and then through their witness to those who lived in the much greater darkness of Islam and Judaism. "Who can estimate the effects that may at some future day result from the revival of truth and religion among these people?" queried Fisk.

Even as he raised utopian hopes for what his mission could accomplish Fisk also made it clear that he was aware of the challenges and dangers that lay ahead. The lands in which he and Parsons would work did not have the political freedoms they enjoyed in America. There were

17. Ibid.
18. Ibid., 7.
19. Ibid.

none of the "the rights of conscience" people privileged to live in enlightened Christian countries took for granted. The linguistically polyglot nature of the region would raise challenges of another sort. But perhaps the greatest challenge of all, said Fisk, was the prideful nature of the peoples who spoke those many languages. Unlike what missionaries had found to be true among the "savages" in the American wilderness and the "untutored tribes" of the Pacific Islands who willingly submitted themselves to Christian patronage, what Fisk and Parsons could anticipate was "contempt . . . rather than respect, and a haughty sense of superiority."[20]

Fisk concluded his sermon on a somber note that underscored the price he expected to pay to answer this call. It was the price of familial fellowship. When he got on the ship in Boston harbor to say goodbye to his parents and siblings he believed he would be saying goodbye forever.

> But though we are cheered with animating hopes, yet we go, not knowing the things that shall befall us. Whether we shall be buried in a watery tomb; whether disease shall bring us to an early grave; whether the suspicion of government or the bigotry of false religion, shall shut the door against us; or whether a great and effectual door shall be opened before us, and the word of the Lord have free course and be glorified, as it is with you; whether we shall spend a long life in labors, and die having only sown the seed from which others may reap the harvest; or whether we shall see the truths prevail and die surrounded by converts from error, who may soothe the bed of death and weep over our tomb; these are points to be decided not by human sagacity, but by Him, whose Providence calls us, whom we would cheerfully obey, and in whom we would trust the future.[21]

## FISK'S PERCEPTUAL GRID

What is found in this sermon both reinforces and transcends elements of Fisk's earlier perceptions of the religious other. And since the point has been reached in his narrative that will move him from the theoretical into the existential, it is important to examine more carefully what those elements were.

From Fisk's perspective, the most critical element in his life's story was his conversion experience. This not only defined his personal

---

20. Ibid., 8–9.
21. Ibid., 13.

encounter with redemptive grace, it also convinced him that there was no other way to obtain divine favor. The world's population in this case became differentiated between people who had God's favor through experimental faith, and those who didn't, thus creating a strong bifurcation between insiders and outsiders.

Initially Fisk's post-conversion perception was forged in the fire of what Richard Rabninowitz calls a "doctrinalist economy of experience."[22] To be an insider in this case meant not only having the proper revivalist experience, but the ability to conceptualize that experience in theologically orthodox (Calvinist) terms. Cognitive apprehension of the conversion experience and its aftermath was, in this case, as important as the experience itself to give evidence of redemptive grace. This is how Rabinowitz explains the contours of the doctrinalist perspective:

> I have chosen to call this a doctrinalist or orthodox economy of experience, not because the evangelicals adhered more strongly to religious beliefs but because they felt that the end of experience was to exemplify the truth of the doctrines they espoused. Consequently, the faculty of the mind central to their religious enterprise was the understanding, rather than the will or the feelings; intellectual effort was necessary to determine the relationship between one's particular experience and the doctrinal explanations available from the pulpit, the Bible, or the minister's library.[23]

Later, during Fisk's years at Andover, this doctrinalist position would shift towards what Rabinowitz describes as moralism,[24] even though he would never entirely leave his doctrinalist position behind. Moralism sought evidence of God's favor in character development and good behavior that drew their content from the ethos of revivalist culture.[25]

A third factor that shaped Fisk's perceptual grid may have been even more influential. This was the epistemology of Scottish Common Sense Realism that served as an ideological foundation of his education at both Middlebury and Andover. Scottish Common Sense Realism taught Fisk to regard orthodox belief as an accurate representation of the nature of

22. Rabinowitz, *Spiritual Self in Everyday Life*, xxix.

23. Ibid.

24. Ibid.

25. Defined by such things as keeping the Sabbath, chaste relations with the opposite sex, avoiding public displays of unrestrained mirth, and the denunciation of gaming and swearing.

reality. His more benign sermonic assessment of certain elements of Middle Eastern religions and cultural characteristics needs to be read in this context. Those elements of other cultures and religions that conformed to what Fisk considered a "common sense" apprehension of reality (that is, elements that affirmed truths found within the orthodox world view) could be affirmed as legitimate expressions of the structural reality of the universe. Fisk wasn't afraid, in this sense, to admit that truth could be found in other religious systems. 'Common sense' posited universally available truths. In this case it made sense that other religions would find a certain resonance with what Christianity determined to be true. But in the end the full measure of Truth was the orthodox interpretation of the Christian faith and what that faith affirmed about the essential structure of reality. Thus, while Islam may have reflected some elements of truth accessible to all who used "common sense" to determine the way things are, it, at the same time, represented much that contradicted common sense, enough so that whatever good it might have affirmed was negated by unreasonable, even nonsensical teaching and practices.

There were other factors that shaped Fisk's perception of the religious other. The influence of former pastors was one of them. Another was peer pressure within the tightly knit fellowship of missionary societies to which he belonged. But these three ideological constraints: doctrinalism, moralism and Scottish Common Sense Realism played the most predominant roles in shaping his perspective of the religious other. They would give Fisk the criteria by which he would determine where others fit into God's economy of salvation, that is, who was *in* and who was *out*. And to Fisk this was more than just a spiritual assessment of a person's standing with God. This was the way he assessed their value as human beings, as salvific grace was the power that gave rise to those human qualities that allowed regenerate beings to create a humane society.

With a perceptual grid shaped by these influences Fisk prepared to make the dramatic move from a settled New England existence to an unsettled expatriate existence in a part of the world few Americans had visited and even fewer understood. The dramatic nature of this move is hard to imagine in our global village. Attempting to understand what it entailed in terms of Fisk's perception of the religious other will be the purpose of what follows.

# PART TWO

# The Ottoman Empire

*I am a Pilgrim, a Traveler, a Stranger. I have no home on earth. I see it in the skies.*

THE REV. PLINY FISK 1825

# 6

## Smyrna and Scio

### PREPARING TO LEAVE

A YEAR BEFORE FISK and Parsons slipped out of Boston harbor on a frigate that would take them on the first leg of their journey east, they made a pledge to each other that resembled in tone, if not in substance, a marital contract. Fisk and Parsons were traversing the globe to enter into regions of "deplorable ignorance and degradation"[1] where no other American missionaries had gone. Their success in carrying out the orthodox mission would depend on an intense relationship of mutual affirmation and support.

> As Christians, as ministers and missionaries, we have been separately consecrated to God; we do now, in a united private capacity, not as an unmeaning ceremony, but with sincerity of heart, and with earnest prayer for divine assistance, give ourselves to each other. We enter into a holy covenant, by which we engage, with divine assistance, to keep ourselves from every employment which may impede our progress in the work, to which we are sacredly devoted. We are to live in love; to maintain the most perfect harmony of feeling, of design and of operation; to unite our strength, our talents and our influence, for the conversion of the heathen ... We give ourselves to each other in all our *afflictions, temptations and persecutions,* having our hearts knit

---

1. "Report of the Prudential Committee: Palestine Mission" *The Missionary Herald,* Vol. 15, Dec. 1819,
265.

together as the heart of one man, and performing all the duties of Christians and friends. And while we take this covenant upon ourselves, it is with earnest prayer, that in life we may *long* be united, and in death not far divided.[2]

Even before they took this pledge Fisk and Parsons, who had been friends in piety since their time together at Middlebury, recognized how important it was to proceed as a bonded pair. A month earlier they had set aside several days for fasting and prayer to prepare for what lay ahead. As part of this time of spiritual preparation they asked and answered five questions, the fifth of which was: "What are our peculiar duties to each other?"[3] This is the answer they gave:

Our hearts should be knit together as the heart of one man. Our employments, our duties, our plans must aim incessantly at the same object. We must possess the most implicit *confidence* in each other's pursuits, and seize every opportunity to impart mutual consolation, and to inspire as holy resolution in the work of the Lord.[4]

Armed with this "holy resolution" Fisk and Parsons boarded the frigate, Sally Ann, in Boston Harbor at 10 am on Wednesday, November 3, 1819, to commence their journey first to the Mediterranean island country of Malta and then to the Turkish seaport of Smyrna (Izmir) which the Prudential Committee had designated as their entry point into the Ottoman Empire.[5]

Given the "numerous and deeply interested"[6] crowds who had packed the Park Street and Old South churches the previous Sunday to hear their farewell addresses,[7] it can be assumed that a large crowd was there to see them off. Unfortunately, Fisk's family members weren't

2. Morton, *Memoir of Rev. Levi Parsons*, 159.

3. Ibid., 158.

4. Ibid.

5. "She[the Sally Ann] is expected to touch at Malta; and, after several days, to go thence to Smyrna. This is precisely such a destination that would have been chosen, had the voyage been planned solely for the mission." Report of the Prudential Committee, "Palestine Mission," *Missionary Herald* 15 (1819) 296.

6. Bond, *Memoir*, 96.

7. "Not only the pews, but the aisles, stairs, both galleries, and all the avenues, were thronged, so that it was with great difficulty that the boxes could be circulated for the collection. Many aged persons and many ladies, were obliged to stand during the whole services; and yet, the profoundest attention was observable to the close." Ibid.

among them. Knowing they weren't going to be able to make the trip to Boston, Fisk had traveled to Shelburne the week before for a tearful goodbye. There, says Bond, "he delivered an affectionate and solemn farewell address, and took leave of the people, expecting to see their faces no more."[8] It would be the last time he would see them.

## THE JOURNEY BEGINS

Fisk's solemn and sad farewell underscores how difficult it is for a twenty-first century person to envision what it meant for Fisk and Parsons to make this journey. They were saying goodbye to family members they thought they would never see again with their only means of communication being letters that could take up to a month each way. They were moving to a region of the world they considered to be a place of spiritual darkness, political despotism and moral degradation with few eye-witness accounts to challenge the stereotypes. And they were among the first Americans to attempt such a move.

A.L. Tibawi notes that the first American vessel to reach Constantinople was the frigate *George Washington* in 1800.[9] And while there was a lucrative trade that developed around this time between Boston and Smyrna,[10] only one American merchant family was known to have established a home there—the Perkins family of Boston—who took up residence in Smyrna in 1811.[11] The one short-term exception to this was a man named William Stewart whom Thomas Jefferson appointed as America's first consul at Smyrna in 1803. But he only stayed a year mainly because during that time no American ships came to port.[12] Fisk and Parsons would not be the first Americans to go to the region. But they would be among the first, and they would travel to parts of the Ottoman Empire to which no Americans had traveled before.

## IN QUARANTINE IN MALTA

On December 24 the Sally Ann came within sight of Valletta, the capital of Malta. That sight would have been a relief for Fisk and Parsons, partly

8. Bond, *Memoir*, 95.

9. Tibawi, *American Interests in Syria*, 2.

10. "In the first decade of the nineteenth century, an average of twelve vessels called every year with cargo valued at about one million dollars." Ibid.

11. Ibid.

12. Finnie, *Pioneers East*, 25.

because it had been a long journey, partly because Fisk was seasick for a good deal of the time. Their arrival in Malta also gave them the opportunity to meet a British missionary who had been working in the area for several years along with a Maltese doctor who served as his mission partner.

The British missionary was an agent of the Church Mission Society (CMS) named William Jowett.[13] Jowett, whose articles and letters were frequently published in the *Missionary Herald*,[14] had arrived in Malta in 1815 when the CMS sent him there for "the diffusion of Christian truth among the Jews, Mahometans and pagans," and "the acquisition of information relative to the state of religion and society."[15] By the time Fisk and Parsons arrived he had already made several journeys through the region, including trips to Egypt and the Turkish provinces of the Ottoman Empire.

Jowett's Maltese companion and friend was a chemistry professor named Dr. Cleardo Naudi whom Fisk would later describe as "a zealous friend to Bible Societies and Missions."[16] Fisk and Parsons also learned upon their arrival that another British missionary couple, the Rev. and Mrs. Samuel Wilson, had been working alongside Jowett and Naudi for the past year. All would help Fisk and Parsons gain firsthand knowledge of the region as well as offer the kind of fellowship and encouragement we can assume they would have craved after a long journey in a small ship with men who knew nothing of revivalist Christianity.[17]

Unfortunately, when the ship came to port Fisk and Parsons learned that Maltese customs mandated a fifteen-day quarantine for all passengers and crews of ships entering their harbors as a way of preventing the spread of the plague that was threatening lives in other Mediterranean ports. Given that the Sally Ann's day of departure for Smyrna was earlier than the terminal point of the mandated quarantine, this meant that a

---

13. Ibid.

14. See *the Missionary Herald*, 16 (1820) 221–28, for a letter Jowett wrote after meeting with Fisk and Parsons.

15. Tibawi, *American Interests in Syria*, 12.

16. Ibid.

17. Fisk reported that he didn't find among the ship's crew any "very special indication of the divine presence," despite the fact that they came regularly to prayer meetings and services Fisk and Parsons held on board ship on the journey to Malta. *Letter to the Corresponding Secretary of the ABCFM*, December 23, 1819, Box 6: 3, CLA.

face-to-face visit with Jowett and the others was out of the question.[18] Fisk expressed his disappointment at this.[19] They were, however, able to converse at a distance, first from ship to shore then across a safe divide in the on-shore quarantine station known as the Lazaretto.[20]

Fisk's conversations with the Jowetts, Naudis and Wilsons confirmed their value as sources of useful information and warm Christian fellowship, even at a quarantined distance. They were insiders, which made their information even more valuable than it might have been coming from another source. Jowett was a particularly rich source of information, giving Fisk and Parsons "many useful hints & facts & opinions . . . which I trust will be of use to us in regard to health, studies, traveling & Missionary labor."[21] Naudi helped them to determine where to focus their linguistic studies, telling them they should learn Italian first, then Greek, then Arabic, which is a course Fisk would attempt to follow in the next few years.[22] As for where they should do this, Jowett recommended the island of Scio as the best place to study modern Greek, while their Palestinian destination would be the best place to study Arabic.[23] Perhaps more important in terms of what Fisk gained from these conversations is what it told him about the region in general. It was much less threatening than he had assumed. "Conversations with these men," said Fisk in the diary entry he made for January first, "has endeared me to this place very much. It has made the Mediterranean seem quite like home."[24]

For a short time Fisk and Parsons debated whether they should delay their trip to Smyrna to draw more deeply from the well of information provided by these seasoned missionaries. But financial considerations and their sense that the Prudential Committee would not approve a decision to alter their course so early on in the venture determined that they needed to continue the course the ABCFM had set for them.[25]

Before they left Malta Fisk and Parsons received a gift from the Jowetts that would later inspire Fisk to re-envision his missionary purpose. It

18. Fisk Diary, vol. 1, entry for December 27, 1819, BLA.

19. Ibid.

20. Ibid., entry for December 26, 1819.

21. Ibid., entry for December 30, 1819.

22. Ibid., entry for December 29, 1819.

23. Ibid., entry for December 30, 1819.

24. Ibid., entry for January 1, 1820.

25. Fisk's and Parsons's *Journal*, entry for January 8, 1820, BLA.

was the memoir of the late celebrated British missionary, Henry Martyn[26] who had pioneered Protestant missionary work among Muslims in India and Persia.[27] Fisk would soon add Martyn to his panoply of revered missionary saints.[28] Martyn's memoir would, in fact, become to Fisk as Brainerd's was; a source of inspiration that would, at the same time make Fisk acutely aware of his missionary inadequacies.[29]

## IN SMYRNA

### Initial Impressions

Fisk and Parsons left Malta for Smyrna on November 9, 1820. They arrived a week later. Two days after their arrival Fisk shared his first impressions in a letter he wrote to his father. The next day Parsons did the same in a letter to his sister. A quick comparison of how they framed their first impressions reinforces the impression that these were two very different people.

Fisk's letter is a simple recounting of people they had met and things they had done followed by some basic information about Smyrna itself. It was factual information presented in a detached, analytical style.

> Yesterday we spent the whole day in town. It will comfort you to know, that we have already found a few friends. Capt. Edes went with us first to Messrs. Van Lennep's. There are two brothers of this name who live together. They are merchants, were born in Smyrna of Dutch parents, and are respectable and rich. . . .
>
> We called next on Mr. John Lee's. He is a native of Smyrna by English parents; his wife is a French lady. He is also a rich merchant, and a man of extensive knowledge.
>
> We called next on Mr. Perkins. There are two merchants here by this name, who are brothers, from Boston; one however has lived here about twenty years, and the other a longer time . . .

26. Martyn was born in 1781 and died on October 16, 1812 in Tokat, Turkey after having served as chaplain to the East India Company, which allowed him to travel in the region to engage in the kind of religious conversations with Muslims that Fisk would aspire to. See Sargent's *Memoir of The Rev. Henry Martyn*.

27. Fisk Diary, vol. 1, entry for January 5, 1820.

28. "Martyn's memory will shine with eternal luster," says Fisk after reading the memoir on his way to Smyrna, "theirs [the other more secular authors he is reading] will fade & vanish." Fisk Diary, vol. 1, entry for January 16, 1820.

29. In an entry in his diary dated January 23, 1820, Fisk records this reaction to reading Martyn's Memoir: "The more I read of it, the more I feel ashamed of my ignorance & barrenness and fickleness." BLA.

The men I have mentioned all live near together, in Frank-street, which is inhabited principally by merchants from Europe; English, Scotch, Dutch, Russian, Austrian, Spanish, and Portuguese.

This is a place of extensive trade. There are perhaps 100 vessels now in harbor. Three are American. We expect to hire a room, and live here for the present to study languages. The prospect is, that we shall find our situation pleasant. Surely the goodness of God calls for our gratitude, and our entire devotedness to his cause.[30]

In contrast to Fisk's letter Parson's letter kept the factual information to a minimum. What captured his interest was the historical and spiritual significance of the exotic scenes that had passed before their eyes.

On our passage to Smyrna, what an interesting portion of the world opened to our admiring curiosity! These seas have been honored with the presence of Xerxes, Alexander, Demosthenes, Socrates, and what is more, St. Paul on his heavenly mission of subduing the world to the Prince of Peace. As we passed we could point to the west, and say, "there the great apostle of the gentiles, on Mars-hill, declared to the pagan Athenians the God whom they ignorantly worshipped;" to the east, "there the beloved disciple John was in the isle of Patmos for the testimony of Jesus;" to the north, "there St. Paul and Silas sang praises to God in the prison of Philippi;" to the north-east, "St. Paul kneeled down, and prayed with them all, and they all wept sore."[31]

Fisk was factual, Parsons religiously romantic. Fisk collected information, Parsons found spiritual significance in his surroundings. They went to Smyrna with the pledge of a bonded union. But it wasn't a marriage of like-minded persons. Apart from a common missionary purpose and evangelical fervor they had little in common. But given the fact that they had just traded their insider status in the orthodox fortress in America for outsider status in the Ottoman Empire their pledge of solidarity would be solidified in what would resemble a tribal friendship. The two would become one.

## INTERPRETIVE THEMES IN SMYRNA

In Smyrna Fisk would have his first live encounters with the Ottoman religious other; Christian, Muslim and Jew. An examination of these early

30. Bond, *Memoir,* 108–9.

31. Morton, *Memoir of Rev. Levi Parsons,* 234.

encounters yields interpretive themes that would come to define Fisk's assessment of the religious other throughout his time in the Ottoman Empire. What follows is an elucidation and examination of these themes as they first arose out of the discourse Fisk developed during his time in Smyrna and the island of Scio from January, 1820 to January, 1822.

## Theme #1: Objectifying the Religious Other

One of the tasks Fisk took up almost immediately upon his arrival in Smyrna was something he had already begun on the journey over. He collected what he called useful information for examination and classification with the aim of developing a descriptive narrative for the home audience.

This spirit of inquiry was encouraged by the ABCFM. It was, in fact, built into the instructions they gave to Fisk and Parsons prior to their departure; instructions that were, by necessity, vague and generalized because of "the novelty and uncertainty of the ventures they were undertaking."[32] Included in these instructions was the mandate to obtain "such information, of various kinds, as will be of importance in their subsequent course."[33]

The ill-defined nature of these instructions gave Fisk free reign to indulge his analytical proclivities. Like a tourist with a camera in an ex-localemeticulously descriptive account of his surroundings even when there was no clear missional purpose in doing so. This included what he saw from the ship during the time he was in quarantine in Valetta harbor.

> The harbor in which we lie is a narrow body of water extending from the sea to the shore with Valetta on one side and the Lazaretto or Hospital on the other. Where we lie it is about 80 or 100 rods wide. The town lies S.E. of us. We cannot see the walls for an extent of 1 mile or 1 ½ in nearly a straight line. The walls are irregular and I should judge from 50 to 200 feet high. The domes of several churches & convents—the wheels & upper part of two windmills, one for grinding grain, the other for grinding tobacco into snuff, unnumbered houses of various sizes and forms & the irregular walls & rocks on the shore present an interesting view.[34]

32. Khalaf, *Protestant Missionaries*, 164.

33. Ibid., 266.

34. Fisk Diary, vol. 1, entry for December 27, 1819.

It is hard to know exactly what Fisk had in mind when he made these kinds of observational entries in his diary (which he did often) nor is knowing this critical to the purpose of this book. What *is* worth exploring is his tendency to do the same for people he met.

In his seminal missiological work, *Transforming Mission: Paradigm Shifts in Theology of Mission,* the late South African missiologist David Bosch noted that one of the ways the Enlightenment impacted Christian thinking was through its emphasis on a "strict separation between *subject* and *object*."[35] The world in this case became a specimen to be examined and utilized. What would become apparent already during Fisk's time in Smyrna is that he would apply this kind of objectification not only to the places he visited, but also to the people he met. He examined them at a distance, even when he was meeting them up close. They were objects to be observed and classified as much as people to be loved, specimens for evangelical examination and experimentation. It wasn't difficult in this case to maintain his orientalist/orthodox memes as they became to him what scientific formulas are to chemists: the interpretive keys he used to unlock the otherwise exotic, mysterious Orient.

An example of this can be found in a diary entry Fisk made for April 7, 1820, where he described what he saw at the first Armenian church he visited.

> When we entered the gate the yard was filled with people and a procession was passing round the church. We crowded forward & followed the procession into the church. It resembled very much the one we saw last in the Catholic church of St. Mary. But there was a much greater display of wealth & ornaments. The clergy & a number of men & boys who accompanied them were richly dressed in silk [indistinguishable word] yellow or blue gaily ornamented & embroidered with gold—with sparkling sashes suspended from the shoulders.[36]

This detailed description went on for another page as Fisk recorded everything he observed of the liturgical practices of a church and people he knew nothing about. Yet despite his ignorance he had no qualms about interpreting what it meant.

> Beside the altar stood 2 candles each about 8 feet long & as large as I could clasp with both hands. These I was told are to be

35. Bosch, *Transforming Mission,* 270.

36. Fisk Diary, vol. 1, entry for April 12, 1820.

> kept burning 40 days, beginning tomorrow or next day.—These
> people have lights enough in their churches but alas! they still
> walk in darkness.[37]

Fisk didn't always end his observational entries with a critique. Sometimes he made his observations with no commentary, at other times he expressed appreciation for what he saw, particularly when he observed something that resonated with his evangelical/orthodox sensibilities. But no matter what response he made, the effect was to keep him at a relational distance from the objects of his curiosity.

This was a constant factor in the way Fisk perceived the religious other during his time in the Ottoman Empire as can be seen when comparing what he wrote about the service at the Armenian church to similar observations he made during a visit to the humble home of a Palestinian Christian named Antoon Malem during a trip he took from Jerusalem to Nazareth in November of 1823. Instead of simply enjoying the hospitality of this family, which was welcoming and warm, Fisk used the opportunity to make observations about their home and dress. This included counting the number of silver beads Antoon's wife and daughter had in their necklaces, an act that one can assume to have been disturbing to his Arab host and hostess.

> The dress of the family was very plain & indeed ragged, but the
> women wore the usual ornament of the fair sex in the place,
> i.e. strings of small pieces of silver over the forehead & hanging
> down on both cheeks. The mother had in her string 200 pieces
> worth I supposed about 30 or 40 dolls. The elder daughter had
> about 100 each but of less value in proportion; say 6 or 8 dolls.[38]

By this time Fisk's Arabic was of such fluency that he would have been able to carry on an intelligent conversation with this family. But the impression given is that what was said was far less important to him than the minutiae of this family's simple existence. They were specimens to be studied rather than neighbors to be loved. Fisk's initial response to the religious other would be to objectify them in the same way he objectified his surroundings.

---

37. Ibid.
38. Fisk Diary, vol. 3, entry for November 17, 1823, DFL.

## Theme #2: Struggling with the Occidental Religious Other

Marshall Hodgson speaks of the nineteenth century being a time of "the great western transmutation" when the technological achievements of the Industrial Revolution and the intellectual impact of the French Revolution had shifted the global power equation decisively towards the West.

> [T]he Europeans (including, of course, their overseas descendents) had by 1800 reached a decisively higher level of *social power* than was to be found elsewhere . . . Individual Europeans might still be less intelligent, less courageous, less loyal than individuals elsewhere; but, when educated and organized in society, the Europeans were able to think and to act far more effectively, as members of a group, than could members of any other societies.[39]

The impact this had on the Ottoman Empire was to make the Porte and local pashas in the increasingly decentralized empire more cognizant of their need to draw on western expertise and trade for their own political survival which, in turn, increased European influence and presence in their territory. Sultan Selim III opened this door in the late eighteenth century with reforms aimed at modernizing his military. This happened at the same time Hodgson identifies as the decisive turning point for the "great western transmutation." The sultan who held court in the empire during Fisk and Parsons' time, Mahmud II, both inherited and expanded these reforms.[40]

Standford Shaw gives some indication of the difference this made for the growing ranks of European diplomats, military experts and businessmen who took up residency in the empire during Selim III and Mahmud II's reigns.

> The time of the French Revolution saw a tremendous relaxation in the social barriers which isolated the Europeans in the Ottoman Empire from the Ottomans among whom they lived. In previous centuries the few foreigners who did reside in the Sultan's dominions isolated themselves almost entirely in their own compounds. Mutual distrust and even hostility and scorn,

39. Hodgson, *The Venture of Islam*, 177–78.

40. Lewis notes that the reforms initiated by Selim were due at least in part to his "growing interest in European affairs" through a correspondence he carried on with the king of France before his ascension to the throne. Selim began his reforms with the modernization of the army, but also opened up diplomatic channels in a way that hadn't been done previously. See Lewis, *Emergence of Modern Turkey*, 39 and 60–61.

combined with a more practical and justified European fear of contracting the plague then widespread in the empire, limited contact to purely formal occasions.

But new developments during Selim's reign made it impossible for this kind of isolation to continue. The very fact that foreign diplomats, merchants, and soldiers were living in Istanbul in far greater numbers than in earlier times made it inevitable that opportunities for contact would greatly increase.[41]

This was the setting into which Fisk and Parsons entered when they arrived in Smyrna. It would make it relatively easy for them to have access to people at all levels of Ottoman society, including the growing European community of diplomats and merchants who lived in the expatriate enclave along "Frank Street" in Smyrna.

As noted earlier there was one American family living in Smyrna, a Bostonian merchant family named Perkins. Before they left Boston Perkins' relatives gave Fisk and Parsons parcels and letters to deliver to their family members in Smyrna. Fisk and Parsons made this delivery soon after their arrival. To show their gratitude the Perkins invited them for dinner. Soon Fisk and Parsons were getting invitations to the homes of other rich expatriate merchant families. Among these were the merchants mentioned in Fisk's letter to his father: the Dutch Van Lenneps and the British-French Lees, all of whom lived at a level of comfort and luxury with which Fisk and Parsons were both unfamiliar and uneasy. They certainly were not used to seeing the kind of food Lee put on his table.

> "We saw on the table various kinds of meat, as Wild Boar, Buffaloe [sic] Tongues, Lamb, etc. Pudding, pies, jelly and again many kinds of fruit."[42]

The conversation and socializing Fisk and Parsons' experienced at Lee's table were outside the parameters of their experience. There were, said Fisk, "many ceremonies, some instructive discourse, some vanity & trifling."[43] This is not what Fisk had envisioned when he signed up to become a missionary. Brainerd's self-sacrificing and physically exacting experience with first nation peoples was his model. What he and Parsons were experiencing in the company of these rich merchants, by contrast,

41. Shaw, *Between Old and New*, 194.

42. Fisk Diary, vol. 1, entry for January 17, 1821.

43. Ibid.

represented a seductive enticement to remove the element of self-sacrifice from the missionary enterprise.

One night after dinner and drinks at the Van Lennep's home followed by musical entertainment from the wives and children, Fisk confided in his diary:

> I have no doubt that Satan had a hand in this. He intends by using the friendly politeness of these merchants to put our principles and our purposes to the test, to make us by familiarity, become less opposed to these amusements & give a sort of sanction to them. But my hope and prayer and determination is that Satan shall be disappointed that by and large we may have religious conversation and prayers & instruct the children on such occasions. Perhaps God has given these families a disposition friendly toward us that we may be an influence with them & be of use to their souls.[44]

Despite the reservations Fisk expressed here and elsewhere about keeping company with European expatriates, at no time is there any indication that he made an attempt to break ties with them. This was particularly true of the Van Lennep family who would give Fisk shelter during violent days in Smyrna at the onset of the Greek rebellion. The best explanation for this is that there was a cultural bond between the missionaries and the merchants and diplomats and ship captains whose company they sought and cultivated which allowed Fisk to maintain social intercourse with them despite their nominal Christianity and materialism. But it remained a tenuous relationship, nothing resembling the friendship Fisk had with Parsons or others of his evangelical/orthodox clan. The Europeans remained outsiders to him, not because they were European, but because they weren't adequately Christian. "I am heartily disgusted with so much ceremony, trifling, compliments & waste of time," he said after another evening at the Perkins. "O that we could find one family where we could go and sing & pray and talk freely about experimental religion."[45]

What is beginning to emerge here is a picture of isolation, first because of Fisk's objectification of his Ottoman neighbors, second because the "insider-outsider" paradigm he adopted essentially left everyone except him and Parsons outside his circle of relational significance. Despite being surrounded by people who reached out to befriend them and

44. Ibid., entry for January 19, 1821.
45. Ibid., entry for January 25. 1821.

support them and offer them gracious hospitality, Fisk and Parsons would be socially isolated during much of their time in the Ottoman Empire.

## Theme #3: The Distancing Effect of a Text-based Mission

During their initial time in Smyrna Fisk and Parsons visited sites both in the city and in its outlying districts to gather useful information, distribute Christian literature and seek out religious conversations. One of the first trips they took outside the city was in the company of the chaplain at the British consulate, a man Fisk identified as Rev. Williamson, who took them to the nearby village of Bournabat. This gave Fisk his first opportunity to visit a mosque.

When the trio went to look at the mosque in Bournabat they found a Turk there who graciously invited them in. When he asked them to take off their boots as is the practice at all mosques, they refused. It was too difficult to take them off, they said. Apparently their gracious host did not challenge their lack of sensitivity. He allowed them in. Later Fisk would frame his visit to the mosque, as he would often do, in the context of his evangelical vision.

> This was the first time I ever examined a mosque. O that these mosques might become places of Christian worship. [46]

Williamson also took Fisk and Parsons to a Greek Orthodox Church. There they met three hospitable Orthodox priests who gave them a tour of the facilities.[47] After their tour the head priest invited the missionary trio to his room where he offered them a glass of wine. We can assume that they had some kind of conversation, despite the language barriers. But Fisk wrote nothing about this. He simply said that they gave the monks three modern Greek Bibles then left.[48]

Two things are worth noting here. The first is the graciousness of Fisk's hosts, which made little impression on him. He made note of it, but showed little evidence of appreciating the humanity of the gesture. The second was Fisk's practice of handing out Christian literature with the assumption that this in and of itself was a redemptive exercise, as though the words of scripture needed no relational reinforcement. The mission he and Parsons pursued was, in this case, text-based, which had the effect

46. Ibid.
47. Ibid.
48. Ibid.

of reinforcing Fisk's tendency to maintain a relational distance from his neighbors.

### Theme #4: Conflicting Expectations: a Perceptual Gap

Cultural historian Hilton Obenzinger believes that the text-based approach to mission taken by Fisk and Parsons had a powerfully transformative effect on Ottoman society over time even though the transformation effected was not one they either sought or anticipated.

> The missionaries' task was "the universal diffusion of the word of life." (Parsons, 20), and they sold or gave away thousands of Bibles and tracts in Arabic, Greek, Turkish, Hebrew, and other languages to pilgrims, merchants, and clerics who had never before seen any book treated as a commodity or given away free as propaganda, much less religious texts in the vernacular. The two missionaries set out for spiritual combat against entire civilizations in a complex textual and linguistic field completely unfamiliar to them: in the Ottoman Empire, religious affiliation was entirely communal and firmly bound by authoritative—and authoritarian—clerical interpretation of sacred text, whether Koran, Torah, or Bible. The strange disbursements of the Protestant "Biblemen" along with their ambitions for religious and social mobility, individual conversion and direct communication with the deity, for example—threatened more than religious sensibilities. These missionaries were diffusing market relations, introducing both the machinery and the mentality of print-capitalism, a decisive component in the development of nationalist consciousness. The seed planted by Parsons and Fisk played a significant role in generating, particularly among the Christian minority in Lebanon, a nascent Arab nationalism.[49]

Obenzinger's thesis underscores a gap that existed between what Fisk and Parsons intended to achieve and what they actually achieved, which, as noted in the introduction, is also the underlying premise of the work of Ussama Makdisi and Samir Khalaf. Khalaf is unequivocal about this.

> [T]he establishment of the "Syrian Mission" and all the compelling socio-cultural transformations it initiated and sustained were consequences of fortuitous and unintended consequences …The ardent emissaries carried over with them a set of basic

---

49. Obenzinger, "Holy Land Narrative," 245.

premises, values, and expectations which served to sustain their evangelistic precepts. Yet, in virtually all respects, what they ended up doing was antithetical to their original and avowed intentions.[50]

Fisk, of course, could not have understood nor appreciated these long term "unintended" consequences, but he did understand that there was a gap that existed between the transmission and reception of the message he wished to convey. And the fault, as he saw it, was almost entirely the inability or unwillingness of his hearers to grasp the simple unadorned Truth of the Gospel.

This is apparent already in one of the first conversations Fisk recorded in Smyrna. This was a conversation with a young Greek Christian named John Issaverdous. Issaverdous apparently enjoyed Fisk's company. He frequently visited and appeared to become as close as anyone to becoming a genuine friend to Fisk.

On this occasion Fisk and Issaverdous read scripture together. Their texts were John 1 and Matthew 24, which led Fisk to offer what he considered to be a perfectly reasonable explanation about how God could be human and divine, seen and unseen. But Issaverdous didn't get it.

> He stated the difficulty in the declaration no man hath seen God & the account given of Moses in the Mount.—I find no difficulty in my own mind, yet I find it extremely difficult to make it plain.[51]

In this case Fisk's response could be read as a critique of his own inability to communicate as well as he would have liked in Italian. But on other occasions Fisk would express a similar frustration over what he perceived to be the inability of his conversation partners to grasp a truth to which he believed any reasonable person would readily assent.

This would be the case with a Maltese Catholic priest named Father Grassi who became Fisk's first Arabic instructor during a time of spiritual refreshment in Malta in the spring of 1822. The date is telling, as it suggests that this was a consistent theme in Fisk's approach to the religious other. Fisk recorded a number of conversations he had with Padre Grassi between June and September of 1822. Most he recorded verbatim, which was a practice he followed on a regular basis with conversations he considered worth preserving. The format was that of a debate, as would be

---

50. Khalaf, *Protestant Missionaries*, xv.

51. Fisk Diary, vol. 1, entry for February 11, 1820.

the case with many of the verbatim conversations Fisk recorded. It was a format that resonated well with his training in apologetics. And he usually took care to ensure that he was the one to determine the shape of the discourse as it was important to him to keep the conversation focused on what he perceived to be the unique errors of the particular religious community his conversation partner represented.

The topics Fisk chose to discuss with Grassi were matters such as prayers to Mary and the saints, confession, the authority of scripture versus church councils, the pope and purgatory. This was the verbal counterpart to Fisk's text-based mission as it relied almost exclusively on the power of words to effect change.

On one occasion, Fisk directed the conversation to the subject of the Sabbath, complaining about what he considered the frivolous disregard of the Maltese for the sanctity of the day. This is how Fisk recorded the exchange:

> I described the manner in which the Maltese devote the Sabbath to amusement & enquired what he thought. "It is not right," said he. "It is a profanation of the day," said I. He seemed to think that too hard a term, & then assigned the hackneyed excuse that men who are at work all the week must have some time for diversion & if they attend Mass on Sunday morning, God will not be angry with them for devoting the rest of the day to recreation.
>
> If such are the views of the Priests what must the people think? I could not help thinking of Jer. 23. 11, 13, 13–21. 25–32 etc.[52]

To this Fisk would later add a postscript as a final comment on all the conversations he had with Grassi:"He manifests nothing like a serious regard for the truth."[53]

What is striking in Fisk's response to these conversations is not only his frustration with Grassi's line of argumentation, but also the fact that Grassi was to him a representative figure. "If such are the views of the Priests, what must the people think?" wrote Fisk, underlining "priests" and "think" to emphasize his frustration at what he perceived to be the unreasonable nature of Catholics in general.

Fisk expected that people would be readily convinced by the reasonable nature of his explanations and arguments. When they weren't the

---

52. Fisk Diary, vol. 2, entry for August 5, 1822, DFL.

53. Ibid., entry for September 19, 1822.

only conclusion he could draw is that they were inherently unreasonable, a trait which he attributed to a flaw not only in their own character, but also in the community they represented. When Fisk accused Padre Grassi of not having anything like "a serious regard for the truth" it was both Grassi and Catholics in general he had in mind.

At issue here was the fact that the evangelical/orthodox paradigm Fisk used to make his arguments was not the same paradigm used by his Ottoman hosts. It was a rational model built on the ideological framework of American revivalism. Fisk's failure to understand this, choosing instead to dismiss his conversation partners as unreasonable and irrational, would serve both as a continual source of frustration for him and another means by which the religious other would be kept at a relational distance.

## IN SCIO

Among the information Fisk and Parsons picked up from table talk in the expatriate dinner circuit was that the nearby island of Scio was a good place to spend the summer. They had also heard from missionaries in Malta that they would get good Greek instruction there. One night they mentioned their desire to make this trip to a couple of Greek brothers they met over dinner at the Van Lenneps' home. The brothers, who were wealthy merchants from Scio, offered to give them free passage on their return voyage. That night the missionary duo decided to spend the summer in Scio.[54]

### Theme #5: Otherness as Threat

Fisk's time in Scio was a mixed blessing. It began with a bout of homesickness that quickly developed into full blown culture shock. The evidence is found in the way Fisk began to exhibit a nostalgia he hadn't shown before, nor would again, as he contrasted his life in the Ottoman Empire with what had become in his mind an idyllic life in America.

On one occasion Fisk wrote in his diary about a group of women he had seen in the marketplace "walking & looking about with many a coquettish air" whom he immediately compared to good Christian women back home.

---

54. Fisk Diary, vol. 1, entry for April 29, 1820.

[A]s if not content with being found the beautiful part of creation they vainly attempt to increase their charms with painted cheeks.—I often contrast their appearance with that of intelligent, modest, pious young ladies in America.[55]

A visit Fisk made to a Catholic service during a religious holiday in this same time frame would evoke from him a sarcastic disparagement of Christianity in Scio, almost certainly based on a comparison in his mind between the Eastern Church and New England revivalist Christianity. "If the holiness of this country can be estimated by the number of holidays—canonized Saints—Priests—prayers—churches, etc, etc, etc, it would seem little inferior to Paradise itself."[56]

What bothered Fisk most, however, was what he would later express to Padre Grassi: peoples' cavalier disregard of the Sabbath, treating it as if it were "merely a day of festivity, visiting or idleness."[57] This we can assume was in contrast to what Fisk perceived to be the quiet, sanctified Sabbaths he had enjoyed in Massachusetts.

This was one of the few times Fisk showed this level of comparative frustration with his surroundings. I would suggest that the reason is that Fisk was suffering from culture shock, the symptoms of which intercommunication specialist James W. Neuliep describes as "disorientation, misunderstandings, conflict, stress, and anxiety."[58] In this Fisk was no different than travelers today whose psyches and bodies resist the disorienting onslaught of cultural and religious otherness with the one caveat that unlike today's travelers, Fisk would not have been able to identify the nature of his malady. Culture shock was not a part of early 19th century conceptualizations.

Although at this point this was a temporary condition for Fisk it would be descriptive of ways he would attempt to cope with otherness at other stressful moments in his missionary journey, particularly the time immediately following Parsons' death. That would be grief, as opposed to culture shock. But many of the symptoms would be the same. It would cause him to experience otherness both as a source of frustration and threat.

---

55. Fisk Diary, vol. 1, entry for May 29, 1820.

56. Ibid., entry for June 2, 1820.

57. Ibid., entry for June 7, 1821.

58. Neuliep, *Intercultural Communication*, 385.

## RETURN TO SMYRNA

Fisk and Parsons returned to Smyrna in October of 1820. Almost immediately after they arrived they made plans to do something they had been hoping to do for some time; visit the sites of the seven churches of Revelation. This would be Fisk's first opportunity to visit places with biblical significance. His analytical curiosity combined with his passion for the Bible would make this a trip particularly interesting for him. It would be the same for those who eagerly followed the accounts of his journeys in the *Missionary Herald*.[59] This is what gave the Palestine mission such great appeal. Fisk and Parsons were living in Bible Lands.[60]

## *Theme #6: Reading Ottoman otherness through a biblical lens*

For the most part Fisk played the role of empirical observer on this trip, simply reporting what he saw.

> Went up to the old castle, north of the town. Vast walls are still standing composed principally of granite, with some fine pillars of marble. The castle includes five or six acres of ground, and about half way down the hill is a wall which includes several times as much. Within the castle are large subterranean reservoirs which used to serve for water and provisions. Most of the walls are evidently not very ancient, and are said to be the work of the Genoese.[61]

But when his party reached the site of the ancient city of Sardis, Fisk adopted a posture that he would assume on other occasions when visiting sites with biblical significance. He described not what he saw, but what he didn't see; the former glory of Sardis becoming the interpretive lens through which he judged its present squalor.

> Our eye has affected our hearts while we saw around us the ruins of this once splendid city with nothing now among it of value, its inhabitants but ignorant, stupid, filthy Turks & the only men who bear the Christian name at work all day at their mill. Everything seems as if God cursed the place & left it to the dominion of Satan.[62]

59. The successor to the *Panoplist*.

60. Bird would use this in the title for the book he wrote on the history of the mission in which he would play a major role himself: *Bible Work in Bible Lands*.

61. Bond, *Memoir*, 127.

62. Fisk Diary, vol. 1, entry for November 12, 1820.

Hilton Obenzinger describes the kind of attitude on display here as reading biblically significant landscapes through a "textual lens."[63] It would become typical of Fisk's perspective on biblically significant sites.[64] At times Fisk would go so far as to ignore the present reality altogether in favor of a retelling of the biblical narrative as though what happened at that site two thousand years ago was its definitive reality.

This was not unique to Fisk. Robert L. Wilken attributes it to Christian Holy Land pilgrims of most any era. It's one of the conclusions he reaches in his thorough examination of the early history of Christian perceptions of the Holy Land. This is how he characterizes those perceptions:

> For Christians the Holy Land is not simply an illustrious chapter in the Christian past. As Jerome wrote to his friend Paula in Rome urging her to come and live in the Holy Land, "The whole mystery of our faith is native to this country and city" . . . No matter how many centuries have passed, no matter where the Christian religion has set down roots, Christians are wedded to the land that gave birth to Christ and the Christian religion.[65]

## Parsons' Departure and Separation Anxiety

When Fisk and Parsons returned from their seven churches tour, they revived a discussion they had been having about the opportune time to extend their mission to Jerusalem. Soon after they started this discussion they received a letter from a British missionary named John Connor who advised them against making it a place of permanent residence. "It is the nurse of the most violent party spirit and the prolific hot-bed of religious contentions," he wrote. And that wasn't all.

> It is an isolated spot & carries on no commerce. It rarely sees a stranger except during the Easter ceremonies. The Turks are haughty and fanatic and detest the Franks, while the Arab robbers will prevent you from moving freely and fearlessly in their neighborhood. The Christian population of Jerusalem is not great and a considerable portion of it consists of Catholics, with

---

63. Obenzinger, "Holy Land Narrative and American Covenant," 247.

64. Here it should be noted that Fisk was constantly skeptical about the location of holy sites, prefacing his comments with "they say that" or "it is claimed that." It was yet more evidence of his low opinion of his Christian hosts, one other thing in which they couldn't be trusted.

65. Wilken, *The Land Called Holy*, 254.

whom you would be able to do nothing, as the Latin Convent there is decidedly hostile to the circulation of the scriptures.[66]

Fisk and Parsons saved this letter, but apparently paid little heed to its advice. The ABCFM had conceived their mission with the goal of establishing a permanent mission station in Jerusalem or Bethlehem. Even if there were obstacles to fulfilling that purpose, their commitment never wavered.

The only two questions Fisk and Parsons felt the need to answer as they pondered this purpose were when and how. They answered the "when" by determining that they shouldn't delay the trip any longer. They answered the "how" by deciding to have one of them stay in Smyrna and the other proceed to Jerusalem to scout out the territory for a future long-term residence. The distribution work was going well in Smyrna with Greek schools in the area readily accepting their material. Fisk had also been preaching on a regular basis at the British chapel while the consulate searched for a permanent replacement for Williamson who had finished his term of service and returned to Britain. It was not a good time to abandon the work in Smyrna.

Because Fisk had committed himself to preaching at the chapel the decision was made to have Parsons make the initial foray into the Holy Land. While logical, this was a difficult decision to make, particularly for Fisk who struggled with the idea of being on his own. He took comfort in the fact that it would only be a temporary separation.

> On the whole it seems so far as we can judge that the interests of our mission are likely to be most effectively promoted by a temporary separation. We contemplate it with reluctance, but our rising murmurs are hushed by contrasting our case with the separation to which our brethren were called who went first to India. We hope to be again united after a short time, to prosecute the original plan of our mission.[67]

## Theme #7: Rethinking the Orthodox Paradigm

Parsons left Smyrna on December fifth, a departure Fisk marked with a melancholy entry in his diary: "To be separated from my only Christian

---

66. *Letter from Rev. J. Connor, from Constantinople*, November 17, 1820, box 9:5, CLA.

67. Fisk Diary, vol. 1, entry for November 29, 1820.

brother is a trial indeed. But duty calls and we must obey."[68] This entry and others that followed suggest a time of despondency for Fisk. "Preach to 60 or 70 from Isa. 55: 5" was his only entry for December 10. "Studied the English prayer book in Greek" was his entry on December 11. He also showed signs of allowing his thoughts to drift in directions they hadn't gone before. It is reasonable to assume that Parsons' departure was the reason.

Of most interest is an entry Fisk made in his diary related to a visit he had made to a Greek school less than a week after Parsons' left. As he was leaving the school one of the teachers told him that he would pray to the Virgin Mary on his behalf. "This is not uncommon with the Greeks," wrote Fisk when he recorded the incident in his diary, "especially when they have received a favor."[69] Then Fisk asked an uncharacteristic question:

> A great part of their [Greek Orthodox] prayers are addressed to Mary or other saints or to Angels. Query. Is this idolatry?[70]

This is not the response one would have assumed Fisk to make to such an offer. The expectation would be for him to reject it out of hand, or at least explain in his diary why the person who suggested it was wrong to do so. It was wrong because it was idolatry. But here he shows some hesitation and uncertainty even appearing to contemplate the possibility that it might be a legitimate spiritual practice. Shortly after this he would put the same question to a ministerial friend in America.

> When we said Christ was the only Mediator; he replied, that Christ was Mediator when on earth, that he is not Mediator now, but Judge. "For this reason," he says, "we pray to angels and saints, and especially to the Mother of God, as our Mediator." *Is this idolatry, or is it not?* They say to us; "You ask saints on earth to pray for you; why not then ask saints in heaven to pray for you?" When you write again, tell me what you think of this [emphasis added.].[71]

It is a surprising shift in Fisk's perception of the Orthodox other, unexpected from a man who up to this point had shown no indication

68. Ibid., entry for December 5, 1820.
69. Ibid., entry for December 14, 1820.
70. Ibid.
71. Bond, *Memoir*, 145.

of deviation from the evangelical/orthodox worldview. The question is: why?

I believe the reason can be found in Parsons' absence, as one of the roles he played in Fisk's life was to keep him grounded in the evangelical/orthodox vision. Fisk's analytical mind determined truth on the basis of evidence. Given this proclivity it is perhaps possible to see in this query an example of his mind taking him where the evidence led; the Orthodox argument for saint veneration making sense to him. Without Parsons there to remind him that such a conclusion would put him outside the accepted orthodox boundaries Fisk felt free to probe the issue beyond where he would normally go.

There is no evidence that Fisk followed this line of inquiry any further. Soon, in fact, he would return to his accusations of Catholic and Orthodox idolatry. But the fact that he asked the question at all does indicate a possibility that his analytical nature might have led him in the long run (if he had lived longer than he did) to question other elements of the evangelical/orthodox paradigm, including essentialist memes of the religious other.

## WARS AND RUMORS OF WAR: THE GREEK REBELLION

Several of the themes listed above would give definition to Fisk's response to the greatest crisis of his ministry, the Greek war for independence, whose effects began to be felt in Smyrna by the spring of 1821. How Fisk dealt with the turmoil caused by the war reveals much about his perspectives of the religious other at this time.

The first entry Fisk made in his diary about the uprising was on April 12, 1821, the day he was returning from a three-day visit to the site of the ancient city of Ephesus in the company of George Perkins and several of Perkins' friends who were visiting from Boston.[72] Rumors about a Greek revolt in Moldavia and Wallachia had been swirling around Smyrna even before they left. As they rode into the city after their visit to Ephesus they discovered that the rumors were true.

> We had left town with some apprehensions that a disturbance might take place as there were accounts of a rebellion in Molda-via . . . We therefore approached Sm. with some apprehensions . . . We had hardly entered Turk town (the Turkish quarter of the city) when on a sudden we saw the people around us in motion

72. Fisk Diary, vol. 1, entry for April 9, 1821.

& in a very few minutes the street was filled with armed Turks. It was impossible to learn the cause of this sudden movement. In answer to our enquires one Turk told us that the Greeks had rebelled & all were under arms. Another said the Franks (i.e. the Europeans) had taken arms against the Turks. A third said the Turks were going to attack the French ship of war which lay in the harbor. We could not learn the truth & were not a little alarmed. We were entirely in the hands of the Turks and if there had been in fact any rebellion or disturbance it is impossible to say what might have befallen us.[73]

The Greek rebellion had been in the planning stages since at least 1814 when a secretive Freemasons' society known as the *Philiki Eteria* (Friendly Organization) was organized by Greek expatriates in Odessa to "bring about, in time, the liberation of the fatherland."[74] By 1820 this organization had identified a leader for the rebellion, a charismatic Greek soldier named Alexander Ipsilantis, several of whose family members had served as Ottoman-appointed governors of Moldavia and Wallachia.[75] In the spring of 1820 Ipsilantis resigned his post in the Russian army and for the next year worked with the members of the *Philiki Eteria* to put in motion what was needed to initiate what they hoped would lead to an independent Greek state.

The campaign in Moldavia and Wallachia was a diversionary tactic.[76] And it was not successful. "Ipsilantis' expedition achieved nothing," says historian David Brewer.[77] But it was the spark that would energize Greeks to rise up against the Ottoman Turks throughout the Greek-speaking provinces in the spring and summer of 1821 in what would quickly become a vicious and bloody affair as the Turks responded swiftly and violently to the provocations. For the rest of Fisk's time in the Ottoman Empire the war would rage off and on with particular fury in the Greek-speaking provinces. It would serve as the backdrop for a difficult season of ministry that would reinforce the negative attributions Fisk gave not only to Turks but to Ottoman peoples in general.

73. Ibid., entry for April 12, 1821.

74. Brewer, *Greece & the Hidden Centuries,* 238.

75. Ibid.

76. "One of the reasons for starting the revolt there was, says Xanthos, 'in order to attract all the attention and forces of the enemy to the Danubian regions, so that the Greek lands should remain with only small enemy forces.'" Ibid., 244.

77. Ibid.

## Fisk's Response

Fisk's initial response to the conflict was to treat it as a disruptive annoyance, as he was more concerned with what it would mean for his ministry than he was about what it meant for the people who were suffering its effects. "While this state of things continues," he wrote in his diary, "it will prevent me from travelling and from engaging very largely in the distribution of books."[78] He wrote something similar to Parsons two days later without expressing much sympathy for the war's victims.

> I do not apprehend any immediate personal danger. But these movements will, of course, prevent my labors among the Greeks at least for a time.[79]

It wasn't long before Fisk found his fears realized as the violence made its way to Smyrna making his visits to schools and monasteries and other religious institutions next to impossible. Fisk had little else to do at this point than to record what he was able to learn about the violence that was now all around him. Over the next few months he would devote the bulk of his diary entries to descriptions (sometimes eyewitness descriptions) of horrific scenes of carnage, misery and death.

This started immediately after Fisk returned from his trip to Ephesus, when he recorded information about "assassinations" and "house plunderings."[80] In one case he recorded an incident where Turks broke into a house, killed the father and kidnapped the daughters. The day before Fisk himself had met a man with an angry wound on his head who had been attacked by Turks simply because he was Greek.[81] The fact that Fisk entered this into his diary on a Sunday without making his usual comments about the service he had attended or the scripture he had read, indicates how deeply disturbed he was by these events.[82] And this was just the beginning of a conflict that would get much more brutal and bloody, with Fisk reporting dozens of people killed every day.

Fisk took no side in the conflict. He wrote about Turkish atrocities. He also wrote about Greek atrocities. The same day he wrote about the assassinations and house plunderings, he also included this: "Greek ships

---

78. Fisk Diary, vol. 1, entry for April 1, 1821.

79. Letter from Fisk to Parsons, April 14, 1821, Box 6: 17, CLA.

80. Fisk Diary, vol. 1, entry for May 14, 1821.

81. Ibid., entry for May 13, 1821.

82. Fisk Diary, vol. 1, entry for May 13 and 14, 1821.

in the Archipelago have taken a Turkish man of war at Milo & a merchant vessel from Egypt & put all the people on board of both of them to death."[83] And when he reported about the war in general it wasn't to lay blame on one side or the other. It was to make a generic statement about the war itself. "[T]he war seems thus far to be of a most horrid character."[84]

Two observations can be made here. One is that Fisk was doing what he had done from the beginning of his time in the Ottoman Empire. He was collecting information. The war was the dominant event of that time. It was coloring all that happened in Smyrna. Like a good investigative journalist, Fisk was gathering information to make sure that the "intelligence" he passed on to the home front was accurate.

The second observation is to note where this investigative approach positioned Fisk in Ottoman society. It had the effect of reinforcing his outsiders' status.

It is important to point out that this is definitive of expatriate status during most any civil war. But Fisk's outsider status was accompanied by an apparent lack of empathy for any of the parties involved, which is not what one would expect from a person engaged in Christian ministry. What concerned Fisk appears to have been less the devastating effects of the violence on the lives of his neighbors than the disruption it was causing to his missionary work. Numerous examples from Fisk's diary could be shown to illustrate this. Typical is what Fisk wrote to a pastor friend in Vermont just when the violence was reaching its peak:

> Last year our prospects were very encouraging, and we hoped that our labors might be soon attended with spiritual blessings to our fellow men. This year we are surrounded with more than Egyptian darkness. This country is now subject to all the horrors of rebellion, civil war, massacres, and assassinations. Murders and assassinations have taken place almost daily in this town for three or four months. That dreadful disorder, the plague, has also existed among us for a month past, though it has now abated, and our fears, as to that, have subsided. These disturbances have prevented me from travelling, and almost entirely from distributing the Scriptures and Tracts.
>
> We already know enough of this country, to expect our plans to be often interrupted by one adverse event or another. Yet this

---

83. Ibid., entry for May 14.
84. Ibid., entry for May 25.

does not at all diminish our conviction that missionary labors
here will produce at some future day very important results.[85]

One does not have to read too carefully between the lines to recognize a lack of empathy. Fisk "already" knew "enough of this country"
to assume that the Ottomans would naturally and normally act this way.
In Fisk's mind it was part of the Ottoman nature to be less humane than
Christians in America. He wasn't entirely without sympathy, but his
disdain for the people and culture kept him from having a heightened
concern for their plight. More critical to his thinking was the negative
impact on his work. He wanted the conflict to end so he could get on with
the business of bringing "spiritual blessings to our fellow men."

## CONTEMPLATING AN EXIT FROM SMYRNA

On August 4, just as the conflict was beginning to wear him down,[86] Fisk
met a British "traveler"[87] while he was making his rounds of the European consulates. This was a man Fisk identified as Captain Hamilton,
noting that Hamilton had spent the past year in Egypt and Syria. Fisk was
clearly interested in what Hamilton had to say as he devoted several diary
entries to it. What particularly piqued his interest was what Hamilton
told him about travel in Syria. It was perfectly safe, said the Captain, as
. . . "[t]he Turks in Syria are very civil. There is not the least danger."

Soon after this meeting, Fisk met another British traveler whom
he identified as the Honorable Mr. Bradish. Fisk was so taken by what
Bradish had to say that he went to visit him every day during the two
weeks he spent in Smyrna. He was particularly taken by what Bradish
said about the semi-autonomous ruler of Egypt, Muhammad 'Ali Pasha,
whom he described as "a man of talents . . . who has made such improve-
ments in the government & state of the country that the productions
have increased 10 fold." Bradish also praised the Pasha for sending young
men to European universities and hiring European technocrats to help

85. Cited in Bond, *Memoir*, 154–55.

86. "In reflecting today on my situation & that of Br.P.—on the events which are
now taking place in the country & the prospects of our missions I have felt a degree of
despondency such as I have seldom experienced. Yet I know that God reigns & I desire
to trust in his mercy." Fisk Diary, vol 2, entry for July 28, 1821, DFL.

87. A term used to describe Europeans who traveled through the region doing
what Fisk may have wished to do himself —collecting information about interesting
sites and people to satisfy their own curiosity or to write books to satisfy the curiosity
of European and American readers.

modernize his country. To Fisk it would have represented the kind of openness he had hoped to find in the Ottoman Empire. If the Pasha welcomed western technology and expertise, perhaps he might also embrace the civilizing religion that made them possible.[88]

The news from Hamilton and Bradish allowed Fisk to think more seriously about his and Parsons' plans to move on from Smyrna. Smyrna had never been their final destination. Jerusalem was. The intent was for them to establish a residency there together based on the "intelligence" Parsons would gather during his initial visit. And now, after hearing what the two travelers said, Fisk had come to realize that Egypt might also be a good place to visit. Given the current violence in Smyrna and the disruption it had brought to Fisk's work, leaving Smyrna sooner rather than later suddenly became an attractive prospect. This is almost certainly what lies behind the way Fisk chose to characterize the conflict caused by the Greek revolt to the corresponding secretary of the ABCFM.

> Egypt seems the one part of the Turkish Empire which remains quiet, and Egypt, is in fact rather a tributary kingdom than a Turkish province. I ought also to except Mount Lebanon whose inhabitants are governed by their own Prince & where the Turks have neither access nor influence. Whether Armenia is affected at all I do not know. Probably not. But the greater part of Turkey is in a state of the greatest agitation. Human blood flows freely. All the selfish, revengeful, cruel and licentious passions of which human nature is capable are indulged without restraint. When & how these dreadful events are to be made subservient to the cause of Christ and the diffusion of truth is for him to decree ... It is our part to submit to his will; while we weep over the miseries and depravity of our fellow men and to improve what few opportunities we have of doing good while we wait to see obstacles removed & a wider field opened up before us.[89]

88. This sentiment is based on an intriguing comment Fisk wrote in his diary after meeting one of the Egyptians to whom Bradish referred during the short time Fisk was in Cairo. When this educated Turk told Fisk that he was committed to the modernization program promoted by the Pasha, Fisk's response was this: "To hear a learned Turk speak deliberately of attempting to civilize his countrymen, produced a peculiar effect on my mind." It is not much of a stretch to assume that the peculiar effect this had on Fisk's mind was related to his belief that Christianity and the ameliorating effects of Western education and technology were inextricably linked together. Cited in Bond, *Memoir*, 208.

89. Letter to the Corresponding Secretary of the ABCFM, October, 1821, box 6:29, CLA.

The stage was now set for Fisk and Parsons' next move, this time as a team to Jerusalem by way of Egypt. It would give them the opportunity to meet new varieties of Eastern Christians, as well as allow for more opportunities to distribute literature and engage the religious other in spiritual conversations. What it was that prompted them to make this move, however, was not something that Fisk either anticipated or welcomed. It would lead to the most devastating moment of his young life and end the dream of a joint mission in Jerusalem.

# 7

# Egypt, Syria, Palestine, and Lebanon

## PARSONS' ILLNESS AND TRIP TO ALEXANDRIA

PARSONS RETURN TO SMYRNA in December of 1821 would signal a new phase of Fisk's ministry, both in terms of geographical focus and opportunities for learning about and developing conversational relationships with Jews and Muslims. The geographical shift happened earlier than Fisk assumed it would, the result of a serious illness Parsons had contracted in Syria. It was so serious that a doctor recommended that he and Fisk travel to Egypt in the belief that Parsons' health "would be greatly improved by the voyage & the mild winter of Egypt."[1] This gave Fisk the justification he was looking for to move into the next phase of his and Parsons' plan to establish a permanent mission station in Jerusalem. Egypt would be their first stop on their way to the Holy Land. Or so they hoped.

## IN AND AROUND ALEXANDRIA

### A Time for Recuperation

When they arrived in Alexandria Fisk fully expected Parsons to recover from his illness. The doctor in Smyrna had assumed this would happen. A physician Fisk contracted to look after Parsons after they were settled in Alexandria believed the same, even though he was less certain that Parsons would fully recover. "He will get better," he told Fisk, "but will never be well in this climate. There will always be a tendency to a swelling

---

1. Fisk Diary, vol. 1, entry for December 24, 1821.

of the liver & an irregular state of the bowels."[2] Based on this diagnosis Fisk used the time in Alexandria to continue what he had begun in Smyrna and Scio. He became fully engaged in mission activity.

## Discovering Diversity among Jews and Muslims

Fisk had had a limited number of contacts with Jews and Muslims in Smyrna, nothing significant enough to challenge his orthodox preconceptions. This would change in Alexandria where he was able to engage in significant religious conversations with two Jews whose contrasting personalities and perspectives would make generalizations more difficult.

The first Jew with whom Fisk would develop a conversational relationship was a customs agent named Giuseppe. Giuseppe showed an interest in Fisk's Hebrew books when he was going through Fisk's bags in the customs house, which led Fisk to invite him to his room for further discussions. Giuseppe accepted the invitation and would over the course of the next few months make regular visits to Fisk's and Parsons' temporary residence to converse about religious matters.

Fisk recorded several of the conversations he had with Giuseppe during this time. What is striking about these conversations, particularly the conversations Fisk had with Giuseppe before Parsons' death, is their conciliatory tone. This is in contrast to what can be noted of the conversations Fisk recorded in his diaries with Eastern Christians as Fisk's conversations with Giuseppe were less debates laced with frustration than opportunities to exchange information. This is seen already in the first conversation Fisk recorded.

> I enquired "What do you Jews believe & expect concerning the Messiah?" "That he is to come, we know not when, but some say after 200 years, that he will be a great Prophet, etc." I then stated to him what we believe concerning Jesus, his divinity & atonement, the apostasy & depravity of man & the way of salvation; to all which he listened with apparent attention but made no reply.[3]

What is notable here is the fact that Fisk made no attempt to correct Giuseppe's beliefs about the Messiah, which is what he usually did with Christians when they said something he believed to be in error. There appears in this case to be a genuine interest on Fisk's part to learn what it is Jews believe. He also used the occasion to explain to Giuseppe what he

2. Ibid., entry for January 31, 1822.

3. Ibid.

believed about Jesus, but in a less contentious tone than previous conversations. It was more dialogue than proselytism.

The other Jewish conversation partner Fisk had during his short time in Alexandria was Parsons' physician, a German doctor named Marpurgo. Both Fisk and Parsons saw the doctor's visits as an opportunity for religious conversations. "We had hoped," said Fisk, "that after becoming a little acquainted we might be able to introduce some religious discussions."[4] That was not difficult to do in this case, as Dr. Marpurgo was a gregarious companion who enjoyed speaking about religious matters.

Fisk took great interest in what Marpurgo had to say, recording his words both in the context of dialogical exchanges and, almost uniquely, as direct quotations on various subjects outside the context of dialogue, suggesting that Fisk valued the doctor's opinions.

In his conversations with Dr. Marpurgo Fisk came to realize that he was a different sort of Jew than Giuseppe, as the doctor was much more critical of his community and traditions. The Jews of Alexandria, said Marpurgo, are "ignorant, superstitious & barbarous,"[5] not to mention avaricious. "For $100 they would consent that there should never be a Messiah."[6] When Fisk asked Marpurgo what he thought about the Talmud Marpurgo told him that "it is a perfect Babel, a confusion of language, a confusion of logic, of theology & everything else. In a volume you will scarcely find 12 verses that are good."[7] Hearing this, Fisk determined that Marpurgo was a "free thinker."[8] The contrast with the more devout, spiritually-inclined Giuseppe couldn't have been greater.

What Fisk learned from these initial encounters with Jews in Alexandria was something that at least had the potential to whittle away at the hard edges of one set of his orientalist/orthodox memes, as he now became aware in a way he hadn't been before, of a diversity in the Jewish community that belied easy categorizations.

Fisk would gain a similar awareness of diversity in the Muslim community when he met a western educated Muslim in Cairo after Parsons' death. This was a man Fisk identified as a Turk named Osman Effendi,

4. Ibid., entry for January 23, 1822.

5. Ibid.

6. Ibid.

7. Ibid.

8. Ibid.

who was one of the bright young men the Pasha had sent to Europe as part of his modernization program.[9] Fisk was clearly captivated by him.

> The most interesting thing I saw at Cairo was the pasha's Literary Institution. Some years ago the pasha sent several young men, some Mussulmans, some Christians, to Europe to receive an education. After several years residence in Italy and France, a part of them have returned to Egypt. One, Osman Effendi, a Turk, is now at the head of the Institution. I visited him twice. When I expressed to him the satisfaction, with which I contemplated the commencement of the Institution and its prospects, he replied: "We have done something; but we find many difficulties in the way, which must always be the case in the first efforts towards civilizing the people of a country." *To hear a learned Turk speak deliberately of attempting to civilize his countrymen produced a peculiar effect on my mind* [emphasis added].[10]

The "peculiar effect" this had on Fisk's mind was almost certainly related to the challenge this encounter provided to Fisk's generalized categorizations of Turks and Muslims (two identifiers that Fisk would often employ as synonyms). Like many of his cultural and orthodox peers, Fisk linked civilization to Christianization. To have a Muslim interested in pursuing what was essentially in Fisk's mind a Christian project would have made it difficult to hold onto at least one set of pejorative classifications. The educated Turk might have been an exception to the rule, but the fact that there may have been other exceptions would mean that the rule itself would be harder to uphold over time.

### Parsons' Final Letter to Fisk

As indicated above Fisk fully expected Parsons to recover. Parsons, in contrast, was fully aware of his fragile state and didn't expect to recover. He said so in a letter he wrote to Fisk two weeks before he died, even though the two of them were living in the same boarding house at the

---

9. The Egyptian Pasha, Muhammad 'Ali, sent hundreds of young Egyptians and Turks to Europe to acquire the education needed to help him run his ambitious modernization program, the need for which was given added significance after the French invasion and occupation of 1798. It became necessary particularly after the pasha came to realize that the European managers he had originally hired were too expensive for him to turn a profit from the modern industries they served. See Daly, ed., *The Cambridge History of Egypt*, 162.

10. Cited in Bond, *Memoir*, 208.

time. This letter represented what Parsons considered to be his final words of advice to his missionary partner.

> In view of my present weakness we are both bound to think of a separation by death. Having my mind on such an event, I commence this letter for the purpose of noticing, from time to time, as I may have a little strength, hints of usefulness with regard to our important mission.[11]

What follows in this letter is a list of fourteen "hints of usefulness" marked with Roman numerals. On the top of the list was Parsons' expression of confidence in the ultimate success of their mission. "Never did the glorious harvest seem so nigh," he wrote. He also hoped that other missionaries would soon join Fisk and gave him recommendations for the best way forward. Seek out "easy, meek, & spiritual conversations" with the religious other, he urged, as he believed this was one of the most important ways Fisk could accomplish his mission. He also urged Fisk to pay special attention to the pilgrims who visited Jerusalem, a place Parsons identified as "the most promising station in the known world." There were more specific directions, as well, as Parsons urged Fisk to examine the books at the library of the Monastery of the Holy Cross in Jerusalem, along with developing a catalogue of what was available there to send to the church in America. Mostly he wanted Fisk to know that he needed to be patient, as "these operations may be gradual, & often weary you, but the day will burst upon your waiting eyes like the visions of heaven!" This was Parsons as Fisk would come to venerate him in his death, calmly facing his end with a Brainerd-like spirit of self-sacrifice.

## Parsons' Death and Fisk's Response

Just over two weeks later, on February 10, 1822, Parsons was gone. Fisk was with him when he died. With great anguish he recorded what transpired.

> At half past 3 Antonio[12] called me. O how heart rending was the moment. He was gasping for breath, unable to speak & apparently insensible to all around. I stood by his bedside, spoke to him, attempted to revive him, but in vain. We sent with all

11. Letter from Parsons to Fisk, January 23, 1822, Box 6:13, CLA. All quotes in this paragraph are taken from this letter.

12. Antonio was a servant Fisk hired to be Parsons's caretaker in what he had hoped to be a time of recuperation.

haste for the Physician. I stood by his side. I wept. I called him, but he made no reply, nor even gave me a parting look. I wept. I attempted to pray & commend his soul to the Blessed Redeemer, whom he had so faithfully served. At a quarter past four the muscles of his face were knit together as if in pain. It was the dying struggle. His features become placid again. His pulse ceased to beat. His breath stopped. His Spirit took its immortal flight.

After the first pang of separation I stood pensive by his side, thinking of the scenes which were opening to his view "what glories, O what glories!"—then my thoughts turned to my own lonely situation. He will pray, sing & converse with me no more. He will counsel, comfort, guide, reprove, direct & strengthen me no more. O what a loss, no one can duly appreciate it who knew him less intimately than I. How mild, how humble, how diligent, how affectionate, how devout, how pure he was! But he is gone. He will not give me another word, not another look. Divine Redeemer; prepare me to meet him where we shall be purer & happier than it was possible to be in this world.[13]

Parsons' funeral was held that afternoon, his body interred in a section of the cemetery of a Greek monastery reserved for foreigners.[14] There weren't many there to see him off as he and Fisk knew few people in Alexandria. Maltese who were boarding in the same house as Fisk, a handful of expatriate ship captains, the British Consul and "a few others" made up the party who processed to the grave site. Once there Fisk read scripture, made a brief address and prayed for grace "to improve as we ought the solemn warning" and for Parsons' relatives that they might be "prepared for the heavy & distressing tidings."[15]

The days that immediately followed found Fisk in a state of near paralysis, his only consolation putting pen to paper to record his thoughts and share the sad news with Parsons' relatives and the Prudential Committee. He also made a resolution to carry on the work he and Parsons had begun with new resolve; honoring Parsons' now sainted memory by embracing what he believed to be Parsons' intense fervor for lost souls. Parsons' death, wrote Fisk in his diary the next day, was "a loud call to me, to be more diligent & faithful & more entirely devoted to my master's work."[16]

13. Fisk Diary, vol. 2, entry for February 10, 1822.

14. Ibid.

15. Ibid.

16. Ibid., entry for February 11, 1822.

## A Revived Fervor, a More Confrontational Approach

On the Thursday of that week Giuseppe came to visit, Fisk recorded the conversation. It was in great contrast with the conversation he had had with Giuseppe before Parsons' death.

The conversation began with Fisk reading Genesis 49:10. He then asked Giuseppe what was meant by *Shiloh*, trying to get him to see that it was a reference to Jesus as Messiah. Giuseppe responded by giving an answer Fisk deemed unacceptable. Then Fisk spoke his mind with a forcefulness not evident in his previous conversations.

> I can tell you how it is, said I, the Messiah came 1800 years ago
> & your Fathers rejected him & you persist in their course &
> though the evidence is abundant from your own Prophets, you
> refuse to believe![17]

Hearing this Giuseppe stammered out a response saying that he was different from other Jews, but also protested that it was difficult for him to let his family know what he believed because when he spoke favorably of Christianity they opposed him. Fisk was unsympathetic. He closed the conversation by urging Giuseppe to embrace the truth no matter what the consequences, and then "exhorted him to study the word of God till he should find his Savior."[18]

Beside himself with grief over Parsons' death, Fisk responded, at least initially, by adopting what he believed to be Parsons' more focused approach on corrective evangelism. Now, instead of an exchange of information, he would directly challenge error. Fisk's initial response to Parsons' death was to revert to an earlier polemical spirit.

## Experiencing Otherness as Threat

Another response grief evoked in Fisk was a revival of the critical spirit evidenced during the time he was experiencing culture shock in Scio. At that time he contrasted an idealized past with a despoiled present. This time it took the form of verbally lashing out at an environment that felt less hospitable than it had before. Ottoman otherness was now perceived as a threat to his orthodox values.

Several encounters Fisk had with his neighbors over the next few weeks illustrate the extent to which this critical spirit had captured his

17. Ibid.
18. Ibid.

mind. On one occasion he told his fellow boarder —a Maltese Catholic —that transubstantiation was biblically wrong and rationally untenable, and did so with an abrasiveness that he had rarely shown previous to this.[19] He told a Greek merchant that the kind of Christianity with which he was familiar could hardly be called Christianity at all. "I endeavored to show him that there is an important difference between that bigotry & superstition which are sometimes called Christianity & Christianity itself."[20] And instead of expressing happiness when a Jew named Joseph told him that he had read the entire New Testament and found it to be very good, Fisk greeted the news with a dismissive critique of western Asians in general. "I perceived by conversing with him that he had read it in that hasty & unprofitable manner *which is common in the East* for he knew very little about it [emphasis added]."[21]

There are two things we can perceive in this alteration in Fisk's attitude. The first was a natural response to grief that carried similar symptoms to culture shock. The second is related to Fisk's new relationship with his now departed friend. The saintliness Fisk observed in Parsons leading up to his death was now magnified by his death leaving Fisk to devote himself to a more intense form of piety and evangelical fervor that translated into a more confrontational approach.

One can't help but recognize a certain irony in this transformation, as one of the things about which Fisk was most critical was the Orthodox and Catholic veneration of saints, or as Fisk put it, their saint *worship*. It was one of his most consistent critiques of what he determined to be the derelict Eastern Churches. The irony is found in the fact that Fisk's desire to honor his friend's memory by emulating his piety could be seen as a form of veneration approaching that which Catholics offered to canonized saints. It was the same kind of veneration Fisk gave to his other missionary heroes, David Brainerd and Henry Martyn. And it was more than just hero worship. It approached the spiritual dimension of saint veneration. This can be seen in an astonishing claim Fisk made in a letter he wrote to the corresponding secretary of the ABCFM on the day of Parsons' death. What Fisk said in this letter about Brainerd and Martyn he would now be able to say about Parsons, as well.

19.  Ibid., entry for February 21, 1822.

20.  Letter from Fisk to Evarts, February 28, 1822, box 6:30, CLA.

21.  Fisk Diary, vol. 1, entry for February 27, 1822.

Now that God in his righteous Providence has seen fit suddenly to remove from me my dear brother Parsons, I recollect with melancholy satisfaction the many conversations I have had with him. In our intercourse last evening he said; "I hope God will spare your life to labor in this mission, till your head blossoms for the grave." We spoke of the employments of departed saints, as engaged with angels in praising God, and rejoicing perhaps with them in the conversion of sinners. We conversed of being *conducted to glory* by some ministering spirit, and for aught we know, by Abraham, or Moses, or *Brainerd, or Martyn.* "But be this as it may," he said, "if Christ receives us to himself, that will be enough [emphasis added]."[22]

## A BRIEF STAY IN CAIRO

### Continued Grief, Continuing Criticism

At the end of February Fisk was ready to move on. And since he and Parsons had determined that they should visit Egypt then proceed to Jerusalem, Fisk made the decision to travel on to Cairo which he saw as the next step towards an eventual trip to Jerusalem. He wrote very little in his diary during this time so it is difficult to discern exactly what was on his mind. But the very sparseness of the entries indicates that his grief lingered, as did his bitter spirit. Two examples of entries Fisk made in his diary during the time he traveled to Cairo and lived in Cairo will suffice to illustrate this.

The first is an entry Fisk made on the river cruise to Cairo from Alexandra. As the vessel made its way up the Nile river valley Fisk found himself doing what he had done at the Sardis site. He contrasted idealized biblical scenes of Egyptian glory with the poverty and misery he saw in villages on the river banks. This time Fisk put the blame on Islam.

> Here, too, that union of ignorance & fanaticism, & intolerance & barbarity, which are combined in Islamism[23] which "destroys everything & repairs nothing" has spread wide its desolations.[24]

A month later, after having been in Egypt only three months where he met very few Egyptians and was unable to communicate adequately

22. Bond, *Memoir,* 178.

23. Evidence that the term "Islamism" was coined long before journalists started using it post 9/11, albeit with an entirely different connotation from its current use.

24. Fisk Diary, vol. 2, entry for March 4, 1822.

with those he did meet, Fisk, nonetheless, felt justified in pronouncing an anathema on Egyptian society in general in a letter he wrote to a friend. It was the fullest expression of his grief-fueled bitterness.

> Alas! How fallen is Egypt! The great body of the population in respect to food, clothing, houses, labor, and education are just about on a level with the slaves in America.
>
> As to the moral state of the country, I will not attempt a description; for you would never forgive me, if I should barely name the vices that are general and fashionable. The common proofs of human depravity appears feeble indeed, when compared with notorious facts, and the general state of things in this country. The Gospel only can purify this polluted land.[25]

## *A Decision to Seek Recuperation in Malta*

Despite his grief and bitterness, Fisk managed to draw a few moments of pleasure out of his trip to Cairo. The first was his visit with the educated Turk, Osman Effendi mentioned above. The second was a therapeutic trip to the pyramids which allowed him to re-focus his thoughts and energy on the kind of information-gathering task he enjoyed. But this did nothing to re-energize him for mission. He himself came to realize that he couldn't continue as he had as he was not only grief-stricken, but spiritually, mentally and emotionally exhausted. This realization also made him cognizant of his need for a retreat in the company of the only people with whom he felt: his fellow missionaries, most of whom were in Malta at this time. The fact that a new ABCFM missionary couple had just arrived in Malta, the Rev. and Mrs. Daniel Temple, made it even easier for Fisk to make the decision to delay his trip to Jerusalem. This is how he explained the decision to the Prudential Committee:

> I will not deny that, after the journeys and voyages, the studies and anxieties, the scenes of massacre and plague, the various disappointments of the last two years, and the seclusion from Christian society, especially after the death of my fellow-laborer, I did feel the need of being for a short time quietly with a few Christian friends, where I might collect my scattered thoughts, review the way in which the Lord has led me, and, as I hope, be

---

25. Cited in Bond, *Memoir*, 206.

prepared to engage in my work with renovated vigor of body and mind.[26]

## RESPITE IN MALTA

### *Pondering Missionary Methodology*

The quarantine restrictions were still in force when Fisk arrived in Malta. This allowed him time to reflect on an issue with which he had been struggling for some time. It was an issue he shared in a letter he wrote to his theological mentor from Andover Seminary, Dr. Leonard Woods. The issue was trying to determine the proper approach a missionary should take to the religious other.

The dilemma for Fisk was related to methodology: should he be firm or gentle in his approach; confrontational or respectful? The way Fisk framed the issue in the letter suggests that he was leaning towards a more confrontational approach. But he wasn't sure if this was justified by the biblical account.

> I have considered with some care the gradual and gentle methods by which our Saviour made known his Gospel, and corrected the erroneous opinions of his apostles. Still when it becomes as a practical question, I often find it difficult to decide, how far fidelity to my Saviour requires boldness and unyielding perseverance; and how far it requires quiet and patient waiting, till 'he who now letteth be taken out of the way.[27]

The reason why this methodology was a dilemma for Fisk was because he feared that the "gradual and gentle methods" of Jesus would leave people mired in their sins. His was a corrective mission. How could he correct errors if he didn't confront them?

> [W]e have sometimes seen men sin without reproving them, and have heard errors advanced without contradicting them; lest we should raise a war, or provoke opposition, which would defeat our plans. Human wisdom, the maxims of the world, love of ease and safety, all conspire to recommend to the missionary in Turkey a timid, flexible, time-serving policy; with perhaps some Jesuitical maxims occasionally. I am not insensible of the danger to which I am exposed. Though it be difficult for you to

---

26. Ibid., 201.

27. Ibid., 203.

decide as to particular cases, yet I shall be very glad to know distinctly and fully, what have been your thoughts and impressions on this subject; particularly when you have looked at our journals, and thought about the peculiar state of this country.[28]

It is not known what response Woods made to this query. What is certain is that this issue would continue to confound Fisk for some time as he alternated between the two approaches.

## Keeping the Outsider Out

Fisk's time in Malta accomplished the purpose for which it was intended. By the middle of May there is evidence that he had begun to recover his sense of spiritual and psychological equilibrium. He began to write more frequently and voluminously in his diary. He also resumed his religious conversations, the first being one that would reveal much about his attitude towards those who sought to cross over from their spiritual world into his, a movement that defined the very essence of Fisk's missionary purpose. This was a conversation Fisk had with an elderly Jew he identified as Mr. Cohen.[29]

Cohen came to Fisk requesting baptism. This should have been welcome news to Fisk as it was evidence that the evangelical witness was bearing fruit. But Fisk did not see in this man what he wanted to see. He didn't find in him evidence of the kind of piety his revivalist faith demanded. "He wishes to be baptized," writes Fisk, "he seems serious, modest & humble, but is ignorant & does not give satisfactory evidence of piety."[30]

In the introduction to the previous chapter I noted how Fisk's evangelical/orthodox worldview required a stark differentiation between insiders and outsiders. That differentiation is on display here. While Fisk didn't reveal exactly what criterion he used to reject Mr. Cohen's request we can assume that it was drawn from the Edwardsian morphology of conversion mentioned in chapter one.[31] Put simply, Mr. Cohen's experience did not match his own. He didn't have what it took to step inside the revivalist paradigm.

28. Ibid., 204.

29. Fisk Diary, vol. 1, entry for May 17, 1822.

30. Ibid.

31. See chapter 2, n35.

Fisk would never meet anyone who fulfilled his revivalist standards during his time in the Ottoman Empire, nor would he see evidence of spiritual revival among Oriental Christians. While there may have been a number of reasons for this, certainly one is the criteria he used, which were so narrowly specific to the ethos of revivalist culture that there were few Ottoman citizens who could have met it.

The anthropological insights of Clifford Geertz are instructive as a guide to understanding the attitude this represented, particularly what he says in his book *The Interpretation of Cultures* about religion as a cultural system.

> In religious belief and practice a group's ethos is rendered intellectually reasonable by being shown to represent a way of life ideally adapted to the actual state of affairs the world view describes, while the world view is rendered emotionally convincing by being presented as an image of an actual state of affairs peculiarly well-arranged to accommodate such a way of life. This confrontation and mutual confirmation has two fundamental effects. On the one hand, it objectivizes moral and aesthetic preferences by depicting them as the imposed conditions of life implicit in a world with a particular structure, as mere common sense given the unalterable shape of reality. On the other, it supports these received beliefs about the world's body by invoking deeply felt moral and aesthetic sentiments as experiential evidence for their truth. Religious symbols formulate a basic congruence between a particular style of life and a specific (if, most often, implicit) metaphysic, and in so doing sustain each with the borrowed authority of the other.[32]

Fisk (and Parsons when he was alive) carried with him an "image of an actual state of affairs peculiarly well-arranged to accommodate" a way of life that "objectiviz[ed] moral and aesthetic preferences" unique to western culture as filtered through a revivalist sub-culture. This "image" was largely unavailable to the thought perceptions and experiences of the Ottoman other, even those who may have sought, as Mr. Cohen sought, to cross over into Fisk's spiritual world. This explains not only Fisk's rejection of Mr. Cohen's request, but also his continual frustration at the inability of his conversation partners to grasp his logic.[33] In terms

---

32. Geertz, *The Interpretation of Cultures*, 89–90.

33. As was the case with Padre Grassi's inability to understand Fisk's strict Sabbatarianism.

of his missionary calling, what this meant is that Fisk was rarely able to cross the relational bridge that would have allowed him to engage his neighbors in an incarnational witness. In terms of his personal life, it meant that he would constantly struggle with feelings of isolation and loneliness. And the tighter he clung to his insider's status the lonelier he became.

## FISK'S NEW MISSIONARY PARTNER: JONAS KING

Soon after Parsons' death Fisk had come to realize his need to find another traveling companion as the ministry tasks he and Parsons had envisioned for themselves, particularly the distribution work, were too much for one man alone. It was in Malta that Fisk identified the person he believed to be the perfect candidate for Parsons' position. This was a former Andover classmate named Jonas King, who was at that time studying Arabic in Paris in the hope of becoming a missionary in the Muslim-majority world.

King was a highly competent scholar who would become the first of the ABCFM missionaries to master Arabic. Makdisi, who is otherwise critical of King, describes him as the only one of the early missionaries who was able to "immerse himself in an Arabic environment."[34] Like Fisk, King grew up on a Massachusetts' farm, had a valid experimental conversion narrative and received a proper orthodox education, in his case at Williams College and Andover Seminary.[35]

## PREPARING A TRAVELING TEAM

Fisk's invitation to King was in response to a letter King had earlier written to Fisk offering his services when word got out in Andover circles that Parsons was seriously ill. In this letter King told Fisk that he would be willing to join him for at least three years "should Mr. Parsons be called from his labors."[36] Given that Parsons had not yet died it was an audacious offer. This audacity was, in fact, a hint of things to come, as the unabashed self promotion it represented would mark the ministry of this controversial figure almost from the moment he arrived in the Ottoman

---

34. Makdisi, *Artillery of Heaven*, 91.

35. King's story is found in a book that was published by the American Tract Society in 1879: Haines, *Jonas King: Missionary to Syria and Greece.*

36. Letter from King to the ABCFM, Paris, 12th August, 1822, Box 13: 4, CLA.

Empire.[37] But Fisk didn't know this at the time. He only knew that King's passions, education and commitment were well suited to the task. He would not replace Parsons in Fisk's affections, but he would be a suitable missionary partner.

After a time of fund-raising, King traveled to Malta to meet Fisk with the purpose of going on with him to Egypt, Syria and Palestine. Fisk was ready to make this move. "On his arrival," he wrote in a letter to the Prudential Committee after the arrangements had been made for King to come, "I expect to go with him into Egypt to spend the winter & the spring or if Providence permit, in Syria."[38]

Fisk was also anticipating the arrival of Joseph Wolff, who had requested the opportunity to accompany him and King to Jerusalem. Wolff was the son of a Bavarian rabbi who had converted to Christianity in Europe and was now traveling through the region under the auspices of the London Jews Society.[39] He was a zealous missionary whom Obenzinger describes as "boldly disputatious . . . a flamboyant missionary to the Jews who would incessantly upset the American Board's sense of evangelical decorum."[40] What Fisk appreciated was Wolff's commitment to an evangelical witness among Jews, particularly given the importance of that witness to the ABCFM's purposes for the Palestine mission. The appreciation was reciprocal as Wolff indicated in a journal entry he made soon before traveling to Malta to meet Fisk and King.

> As Messrs. Fisk and King are going back to mount Sinai and Jerusalem, I hesitated not to determine myself to go with them. God be praised that thou hast finally heard my prayers, and hast given me two fellow-labourers, two Gentile fellow-laborers, with whom I go back to Jerusalem, to speak once more on the Saviour's mercy, on the Saviour's love towards poor Israel![41]

King arrived in Malta on the twelfth of November, an occasion Fisk marked with an appreciative but not overly enthusiastic entry in his diary. "For this event," he writes, "I bless & praise God & pray that it may

---

37. King became the subject of national interest when he was arrested in Athens in 1846 on charges of attempting to subvert the Greek Orthodox faith. As will become apparent, there may have been some justification for the ire his ministry raised. See Haines, *Jonas King: Missionary to Syria and Greece*, 304–17.

38. Ibid.

39. Obenzinger, "Holy Land Narrative and American Convenant," 256.

40. Ibid.

41. Wolff, *Missionary Journal and Memoir of the Rev. Joseph Wolf*, 320.

be the means of mutual comfort to us & of good to others & of glory to our Savior."[42] Wolff arrived soon after. Wolff marked the occasion with a prayer indicating a temperament and outlook that stood in stark contrast to Fisk's analytical stoicism.

> If it is thy will, send me back to Jerusalem with these two good Gentile preachers, such zealous preachers of thy Gospel. Ought I not to be ashamed for myself, to observe so much love in two Gentiles towards my brethren, when I am often so lukewarm! O Lord, send me out with them, and keep us all three under thy holy protection, and give us thy Holy Spirit, and an abundance of the river of that love which thou hast displayed towards sinners on the cross! There thou didst plead the sinner's cause—let us likewise plead the sinner's cause; and let us not only preach the Gospel to Jews, but likewise to the children, the descendants of Ishmael. Lord, let us shew by our life and example, that we are thy children, sent forth to seek the lost sheep wherever thou dost send us.[43]

Fisk, King and Wolff would spend another six weeks together in Malta preparing for their journey by worshiping and praying together, discussing strategy and gathering materials for distribution. Jowett also spent time with them sharing out of his wealth of experience and knowledge of the region. Jowett's advice was that they spend a "considerable time (five years, or perhaps on the spot three years) in learning the language, customs, and prejudices of the people, before attempting publicly to combat their errors; after which time it is a positive duty to gird ourselves with primitive courage and zeal, and openly combat Mohammedanism."[44] Fisk also counseled a gradual approach, noting that direct evangelism among Muslims was not appropriate at this time.

> Preach . . . among the Christians, and revive Christianity, and let Turks see what it is. Ask them about their religion, and tell them about ours; give them the Bible, but not with the avowed object of converting them.[45]

Fisk recognized in Wolff and King volatile spirits that needed to be checked, particularly when it came to the sensitive area of Christian

---

42. Fisk Diary, vol. 2, entry for November 12, 1822.

43. Ibid., 322.

44. Haines, *Jonas King: Missionary to Syria and Greece*, 90.

45. Ibid.

evangelism among Muslims. What he should have been equally concerned about was what King would do among Eastern Christians. Already before they left Malta King showed evidence of a problematically contentious nature during a visit the trio made to a Catholic church and convent outside Valetta. This is how King's biographer records the incident.

> In the church of St. John, also in a convent of Franciscan monks, Dr. King spoke boldly against the worship of images. One priest admitted that it was forbidden in the Old Testament, but not in the New. He was reminded of the text, "Little children, keep yourself from idols." Entering the outer door of another convent, and seeing several nuns who quietly retired, except one, who turned her face to the wall, Dr. King, with something of the humor of Mark Twain, asked a bystander, "What have these women done, what crimes have they committed, that they have to be shut up here?"[46]

It was a foretaste of things to come.

## OPPOSITION IN ALEXANDRIA

The missionary trio traveled to Alexandria for the first leg of their journey through the region in January of 1823. Here they would encounter something Fisk had never encountered before: strong opposition. It happened in a Catholic "convent."[47]

King had met the superior of this monastery before, perhaps in France. But the superior wasn't there when they visited. So they took the occasion to engage two monks in the kind of guided evangelical conversation Fisk sought with Eastern Christians. The topic was praying to Mary and the saints. The response was not unexpected. "They zealously defended the practice," said Fisk, "on the authority of Popes, Fathers & Councils."[48] It was similar to many conversations Fisk and Parsons had had with Catholics in Smyrna and Scio. But when they went to visit the curate, whom Fisk described simply as a "man with a long white beard,"[49] the conversation turned to confrontation.

46. Ibid., 91.

47. Fisk uses the term "convent" to describe both nunneries and monasteries. It appears to be a generic word for such establishments. This was a Catholic monastery of undetermined provenance.

48. Fisk Diary, vol. 2, entry for January 19, 1823.

49. Ibid.

The curate asked them if they had come to his monastery to dispute. They said, no, they had come to meet the Superior, and were disappointed to find that he wasn't there. They also, according to Fisk, said that they had come as seekers desiring to know the truth and "stood at the door & conversed some time about the means of learning the truth, prayer, a humbler, docile, impartial mind, the spirit of the Gospel, praying to the Virgin, etc."[50]

Then for no apparent reason the curate flew into a rage, and "spoke in a most violent & angry manner against the Bible Society & the English & their Missionaries, said they are all out of the Church, without a priesthood, & going to hell, etc."[51] He also said that he would "preach against them with all his might," collecting whatever books they distributed to destroy them. "I think I never saw a man manifest a more infernal spirit," added Fisk as a postscript to the visit.[52]

This was Fisk's account of the visit. King's was different. In King's account Fisk was a minor character, almost as if he hadn't been there at all. And, unlike Fisk, King made it clear that he *had* come to dispute. This is how King's biographer records the incident based on King's journal. It starts with King telling his story:

> Two of the monks met us at the door and said that he (the superior of the convent) had gone out. I made some little conversation, and they invited us into their room. "Do you devote yourselves," said I, "continually to prayer and fasting?" "Yes, we pray to God the Father, Son, and Holy Ghost, and the Virgin and the saints." "Ah," said I, "to the Virgin and the saints? This is a thing that I have never seen in the Bible. We are commanded to pray to God and to Christ, but I have nowhere seen that we are commanded to pray to the saints." Quite a discussion followed, in the course of which the curate talked very loudly against the English, who, he said, were all excommunicated, were without a priesthood, were all going to the house of the devil, and would be damned . . . The monks who stood by seemed a little ashamed.

King continued:

> It may be thought rash and imprudent by some to address the Roman-catholics with so much plainness as I did the curate,

50. Ibid.
51. Ibid.
52. Ibid.

but I know not what else to do. They have perverted the Word
of God and taken away the key of knowledge from the people,
and introduced into the church as real idolatry as the worship of
Venus or of Jupiter Ammon.[53]

Numerous examples could be given from King's journals to show
that this disputatious attitude and approach would characterize many of
his encounters with the religious other, particularly Catholics to whom
he seemed to have a particular aversion. An additional example from the
time he would spend in Jerusalem indicates how consistently he maintained this approach. This happened in November of 1823.

Two Catholics came to my room & read in my Arabic New Testament, & conversed on the subject of religion. I endeavored to
show them, that they & their priests were covered with gross
darkness, & that with all their prayers & confessions, & Ave Ma-
rias, they were in danger of going down to everlasting perdition,
& that because they know not the sinfulness of their hearts &
had never exercised any true faith in Jesus Christ.[54]

The reaction of the curate suggests that King's account was the more
accurate of the two. And while Fisk himself didn't record it this way,
there is no evidence that he was critical of King for taking this aggressive
stance. It may, in fact, have confirmed Fisk's own inclination to take a
more confrontational approach.

This incident initiated a time of opposition that would dog Fisk,
King and Wolff wherever they went during their time in Alexandria, especially after the superior of the convent rallied other priests to his cause.
It would prove to be a foretaste of a greater confrontation that would
occur between the missionaries and the Maronite establishment in Lebanon just after Fisk's death.

Makdisi devotes a good deal of time characterizing the nature of
this conflict in his book *Artillery of Heaven: American Missionaries and
the Failed Conversion of the Middle East*. He believes it was inevitable.

[T]he first American missionary encounter with the Arab world
very much represented the contradiction and struggle between
two different and fundamentally antithetical readings of the
world. One reflected a determination to refashion that world

---

53. Haines, *Jonas King: Missionary to Syria and Greece*, 95–96.

54. Jonas King Journal, to the Paris Missionary Society, October 29, 1823, box
13:2a, CLA.

on evangelical terms at a time of ascendant Anglo-American power, the other, a violent refusal to accept these terms.[55]

The response of the curate, who would later be joined by the entire Catholic hierarchy in Alexandria, gives credence to Makdisi's thesis. The violence of the response suggests a belief on their part that the missionary message represented a threat to a way of life that had been constructed over the centuries around the protective shield of confessional communalism. The American missionary message threatened that communalism with its appeal to the individual conscience and its links to the growing power and presence of Europeans in Ottoman society. It was, as Makdisi rightly points out, a clash of "two powerful currents of history."

> The former was represented by an expansive American missionary movement for which unconstrained individual freedom of conscience had to lead inevitably to an evangelical Protestantism, and no accommodation with other religions could be tolerated. The later emerged out of an Ottoman Arab orthodoxy that regarded the mutual recognition of different religious communities as a guarantee of order and harmony in a profoundly unequal multi-religious Islamic society.[56]

Makdisi's point about the inevitability of this conflict is well taken. But it is worth asking whether the violence of the Catholic response, both here and in Lebanon, might have been tempered by a less aggressive evangelism, certainly less aggressive than what King represented. The fact that this opposition only started after King's arrival does suggest that this might have been the case. In this sense we could say that the Catholic response might have had as much to do with the *way* the missionaries presented their message as the message itself. Would it have been different if Parsons' advice to Fisk to engage the religious other through "easy, meek, & spiritual conversations" had become their guiding principle? Unfortunately that will never be known because that was neither the approach taken by King nor indeed by Fisk in the wake of Parsons' death.[57]

55. Makdisi, *Artillery of Heaven*, 5.

56. Ibid.

57. Makdisi focuses on what this battle meant for the most celebrated convert of these first missionaries, As'ad Shidyaq, who was drawn to King's forceful challenge of Catholic teaching. "The very bluntness of King's style won him admirers," writes Madisi, "among whom was As'ad Shidyaq, who intensively taught him Syriac in Dayr al-Qamar in the summer of 1825." Makdisi, *Artillery of Heaven*, 93. What should be noted here is that Fisk died before the controversy surrounding Shidyaq's conversion

## CAIRO AND A TRIP TO UPPER EGYPT

### *Warm Receptions*

The missionary trio didn't stay long in Alexandria, which may have had something to do with the opposition they encountered there. By the end of January they made preparations to move on to Cairo.

On their way to Cairo they stopped at Rosetta where they found a welcome reception in the court of a local Ottoman official Fisk identified as the "Musselim" (the Turkish governor)."[58] They went there to seek his approval for their visit, which was both an act of courtesy and custom. What they found when they arrived was an "affable" man whose welcome was much warmer than what they had received at the Catholic convent.

> He received us very agreeably. We left our shoes at the door & entered his room. He directed us to sit on the sofa near him. Coffee was served first & then long elegant pipes. The Musselim appeared to be 35 or 40 years old with a long black beard; 5 or 6 men, I suppose uleman or Moollahs were sitting with him & 8 or 10 soldiers armed with pistols & long swords were standing before him. Mr. Wolf conversed with him in Arabic. He was quite affable.—A Moollah sat on his right whom he recommended to us as a very learned man, who knows medicine, astronomy, everything else. Before we came away Mr. Wolf proposed sending him some Arabic books. He said tieeb (very well). We accordingly sent him a Test. a Psalter, & a copy of Genesis but he sent them back after looking at them saying "These books are not for us."[59]

Fisk was discouraged by the governor's response to their gift,[60] but clearly delighted at the reception he gave them. Subsequent encounters with Turkish officials would reinforce the impression he got from this visit; that in general they were hospitable, agreeable and respectful in their conversations on religious matters, more so than some of the Christians Fisk encountered. It would encourage Fisk to approach Muslims with less apprehension than he had previously exhibited which would lead to extended conversations later on.

---

exploded.

58. Fisk Diary, vol 2, entry for January 23, 1823. The term "musselim" is a mysterious one appearing in other transliterated forms in the literature of the era as "mutasallim" yielding the meaning of "deputy governor."

59. Ibid.

60. "This repulse was rather mortifying & discouraging to us." Ibid.

The trio arrived in Cairo on the twenty-ninth of January and almost immediately began making plans for a trip to Upper Egypt. This trip would occupy the bulk of their time in Egypt and be a source of great encouragement to Fisk as the Coptic Orthodox Christians they met on their journey down the Nile were for the most part hospitable and eager to receive what they had to offer. On one occasion Fisk was so encouraged by the response that he broke his strict Sabbatarian observations. This was in the town of Akhmim where a large number of Copts came to their boat to purchase Bibles on the Sabbath. There were, wrote Fisk,

> a multitude literally clamorous for Bibles. It is lawful to do good on the Sabbath days. The Sabbath was made for man & not man for the Sabbath. God will have mercy rather than sacrifice. We cannot spend the Sabbath preaching to these people, but we can sell them the word of God itself. We on the whole thought it our duty to not send the multitude away & accordingly offered our books.[61]

The trip to Upper Egypt also gave Fisk the opportunity to engage in his favorite pastime as he filled his diary with observations about the celebrated ruins he visited in Luxor and various sites along the Nile. It was an exercise that both evoked his admiration for the civilization that produced these magnificent monuments and drew his pious derision.

> Afterwards we spent a season together in social worship, on which occasion we read the account of Brainerd's conversion & some extracts from his journal. This led us to contrast this monument of Brainerd, & his character with the character of Busiris, Osymandia, Cheops, & Cephrenes & the monuments which they raised to perpetuate their glory. All their cities, mausoleums, temples & pyramids seemed like children's toys compared with the crown of glory which Brainerd wore. They shall perish, most of them indeed have perished already, but this shall remain forever.[62]

## Contemplating Religious Conversations with Muslims

The trip to and through Upper Egypt was a satisfying one for Fisk on several different levels. But there was a cloud hanging over it occasioned by information the missionary trio received from the British Vice-Consul

61. Ibid., entry for February 23, 1823.

62. Ibid., entry for March 2, 1823.

just before and after their trip. The issue was a great disturbance that had arisen among Muslims in Rosetta in the wake of their visit. This is how Fisk summarized the contents of the first letter they received from the Vice-Consul about this matter:

> A high degree of fanaticism had been excited among the Mussulmans at Rosetta by our conversation, preaching & distributions of books & that immediately after our departure the Musselim gave orders to collect all the books that we had distributed, put them in a case & sent them to the Pasha.[63]

A second letter the Vice-Consul shared with them upon their return to Cairo was from the Pasha himself requesting that the Vice-Consul ask the missionaries to stop distributing Christian literature among Muslims (which apparently King and Wolff had done during their time in Rosetta). This was disturbing news to Fisk as it meant that the man who had absolute authority in Egypt was now aware of their activities.

While Fisk responded with caution to this news he, at the same time, gave an indication that there had been a shift in his thinking regarding evangelism among Muslims. It was a shift almost certainly caused by his new-found appreciation for diversity in the Muslim community.

Fisk began his response with a dairy entry he made about the need to stay focused on missionary activity among indigenous Christians.

> This serves to confirm me in the opinion I have for some time entertained that it is our duty made plain by the dispensations of Providence, to labor principally & almost exclusively for the present among Xns & Jews. Here is a wide & promising door open before us & it seems improper to cause it to be shut against us by attempting to force open a door which Providence seems to have shut against us.[64]

The caveat came in what he wrote next, which, despite the warning contained in the Pasha's letter, left the door open to evangelism among Muslims.

> Now & then we meet a Mussulman who has traveled in Europe—or who reads European books, or who is liberal & tolerant in his ideas. To such persons & to our teachers & to persons with whom we become acquainted we may speak of Christ & give the Gospel. Mussulmans also come sometimes to purchase

63. Ibid., entry for February 6, 1823.
64. Ibid.

ss. of their own accord—By enlightening & reforming the Xns of Turkey we are removing the stumbling blocks & preparing the way—& raising up Agents to bear a part, when the way shall be prepared, in convincing the followers of the false Prophet of their errors & of the truth.[65]

What can be ascertained from this is that Fisk was thinking of his own missionary role, one that would involve more intentionality in the development of conversational relations with Muslims. He was now aware that there were some who would be more open than others to a Gospel witness, countering an earlier impression of fanaticism among Turks and Muslims in general. It was a shift in his missiological perspective that was at the same time indicative of his ability to think about Muslims less collectively than individually.

## JOURNEY TO JERUSALEM

### Encounters with the Muslim Other

Soon after their return to Cairo Fisk, King and Wolff made preparations for a journey by caravan to Jerusalem. It was the ultimate goal of Fisk's mission now made bittersweet by the fact that he wasn't making it with Parsons. Among Fisk's traveling companions for this challenging desert journey were Muslim camel drivers and guides and guards representing a variety of different cultures and religious expressions, including at least one Kurd and two Sufis. The fact that Fisk devoted the bulk of his diary entries on this trip to conversations he had with Muslims along with observations he made about their behavior gives credence to what was indicated above about a shift in his thinking. He was now intentionally seeking out encounters with the Muslim other.

The encounters Fisk had with Muslims on this trip were simple and brief, at least partly because Fisk's broken Arabic didn't allow for anything more than this when King or Wolff weren't around to translate for him. They were simple encounters, but significant enough to record in his diary. The first entry he made was about a conversation he had with the caravan guide, Hagdi[66] Mustapha. Mustapha was a Dervish and while Fisk would have known about Sufi Dervishes from his studies at Andover, he was curious to see how Mustapha would describe himself.

---

65. Ibid.

66. Fisk's transliteration of the Muslim honorific *hajji*.

I asked Hadgi Mustapha what a Dervish is. He said one that eats what he has today & trusts God for the future. I asked if the Dervishes are priests. He said they were among Turks what priests are among Greeks.[67]

Fisk made no comment either critical or otherwise about this conversation, which would be the case with all of the entries he made about such encounters on this journey. He was collecting information about Islam and Muslims whom he now envisioned as conversational partners for an evangelical witness. No commentary was needed in this case. On one occasion, however, he took a more actively evangelistic role. This was an encounter he had with his other Dervish traveling companion, a Russian Muslim named Hagdi Mohammed.

The encounter happened one evening after the caravan had stopped to make camp. After they had pitched their tents Mohammed invited Fisk, King and Wolff to sit with him on a blanket he spread out on the sand. He asked to see their books. The missionaries showed him what they had in Arabic and Turkish, mainly scripture portions and Bibles. Mohammed, in turn, showed them his Arabic and Persian manuscripts.[68]

As they sat together Mohammed read the first chapter of Genesis. After he finished he declared that "it was very good."[69] This prompted another Muslim to take the book from Mohammed to read the same passage. He, however, took exception to the verse that said: "God rested on the seventh day" almost certainly due to its explicit anthropomorphism. An angry exchange ensued between this man and Wolff who did his best to explain it in a way that would fit Islamic sensibilities. Mohammed remained silent through this exchange, which may have led Fisk to think that he was convinced by Wolff's explanations. As they were headed back to their tents for a night's rest, Fisk gave Mohammed his copy of Genesis.

In just a few days into their journey Fisk had already had more religious conversations with Muslims than he had had during the entirety of his two years in the Ottoman Empire. And despite the cautions he had issued after learning of the Pashas' disapproval of missionary activities among Muslims, he showed no sign that he was going to follow his own advice, as he distributed scriptures to a Muslim who was not among the educated elite who fit Fisk's exception to his rule. It was evidence that Fisk

67. Ibid.

68. Ibid, entry for April 11, 1823.

69. Ibid.

was re-envisioning his missionary purpose to include a more intentional evangelical witness to Muslims.

## IN AND AROUND JERUSALEM

On the twenty-fifth of April, after a journey of just over a month, Fisk's caravan approached the city that inspired Fisk the way it had inspired thousands of other Christian pilgrims. It brought to mind scenes of biblical glory, leading Fisk to do what he had done in Sardis: read present reality through the lens of an idealized biblical past. It would also, perhaps even more powerfully, bring to mind the memory of his dear departed friend.

> As we drew near the city I recollected how my dear Br Parsons, when wars & rumors of wars obliged him to leave the city, turned back his eyes as he ascended the hill W. of Jerusalem & wept & said "If I shall find favour in the eyes of the Lord, he will bring me again & shew me both it & his habitation." II Sam 15.25. Alas, for me, these words were fulfilled in a much higher sense than he then anticipated. I cannot for a moment doubt that he did find favor in the eyes of the Lord & though he was not permitted to return to the earthly Jerusalem yet his Divine Savior has given him an infinitely higher felicity, that of seeing & enjoying the bliss of that eternal habitation in which the Divine glory dwells. We had prayed hundreds of times together that we might be permitted to weep & rejoice & sing & pray & praise together at these holy places & live & labor together in the city where David dwelt & where David's son & Lord expiated the sins of a world. Infinite wisdom has seen fit to order it otherwise. I bow submissively & pray for grace to adore my Redeemer in every disappointment & in every duty.[70]

### Depression and Despondency in the Holy City

Almost certainly it was this memory that colored Fisk's perceptions of Jerusalem the first night he spent there, as it was not a happy occasion for him.

> In the evening I found myself depressed & desponding.—My fancy painted the prospect before me in this city in dark colours.[71]

70. Fisk Diary, vol. 3, entry for April 25, 1823.
71. Ibid.

Another factor may have determined this response to his first night in Jerusalem: a strained relationship with his new missionary partner. Fisk had not bonded with King as he had with Parsons, which could perhaps best be explained by noting the contrast between Parsons' and King's personalities. Where Parsons was pietistically evangelical, King was contentiously polemical. Where Parsons stressed a gentle evangelism, King was confrontational. The contrast this represented would almost certainly have reminded Fisk how much he missed his friend, deepening his sense of isolation even in the company of missionary companions.

There are several indications that Fisk's relationship with King was a disappointment to him. The first is the fact that the diary entries Fisk made for the long trip from Cairo to Jerusalem rarely mentioned King at all. "I" in this case is far more prevalent than "we." Another indication is what Fisk did the day after they arrived in Jerusalem. He went to the Church of the Holy Sepulcher on his own.[72] That would not have been the case if Parsons had been with him. They would have gone together. Fisk and Parsons had been a team. Fisk and King weren't.

Fisk's visit to the Church of the Holy Sepulcher was an emotional moment that briefly lifted his spirits. "Today," he wrote in his diary, "I have felt encouraged. Jerusalem seems much more like home now than it did last evening.[73] But this sentiment was short-lived as most of the diary entries he made and letters he wrote during this first trip to Jerusalem give evidence of a bitter spirit reminiscent of his time of cultural shock in Scio and grief after Parsons' death.

Hints of the emergence of this bitter spirit are recognizable already in a letter Fisk sent to Daniel Temple just over a week after his arrival in Jerusalem.

> I know not how to describe my feelings since I have been here. I have experienced sudden alternations of fear and hope, despondency and confidence, timidity and courage. I cannot move my eye without seeing awful evidence that the curse of God rests on Jerusalem. Turkish avarice and despotism, Jewish unbelief and hardness of heart, and the superstition and idolatry of nominal Christians—for these things I weep. The associations connected with these places affect me more deeply, than I had anticipated.[74]

72. "I made my first visit to the sepulcher of my Lord." Ibid., entry for April 26, 1823.

73. Ibid.

74. Cited in Bond, *Memoir*, 295.

Fisk went even further in his denunciation of the people of Jerusalem in a second letter he wrote to Temple a month later. "The people here," he wrote, "are the worst set of beings I ever saw."[75]

What this indicates when read in light of earlier observations suggest that there was a direct corollary between the intensity of his feelings of estrangement and isolation and the bitterness of his orientalist/orthodox denunciations. That this was the case during his time in Jerusalem is perhaps most evident in a letter he sent to one of his "missionary brethren" just days before he left Jerusalem for Beirut.

> O what amazing events have taken place on this ground. But now the daughter of Zion sits solitary—the wrath of God burns hot against Jerusalem. It seems to me that if there is a city on earth, that is peculiarly abandoned, and devoted to sin, it is this very city, where the blood of redemption flowed. True there is no Juggernaut here, but there is idolatry as gross as that of India. Why does not the earth again quake, and the rocks again rend, and Mount Calvary open to swallow up those who dare thus profane this sacred spot?[76]

Michael B. Oren in his book, *Power, Faith and Fantasy: America in the Middle East 1776 to the Present* makes the claim that Fisk was, near the end of his life, "exhausted, ill stricken, and demoralized" due to constant harassment at the hands of Muslims and Maronites.[77] This is not correct. Fisk received very little harassment from Muslims and Maronites who, for the most part, treated him with gracious hospitality. What demoralized him were feelings of estrangement from a society with which he never made peace at least partly because he made few attempts to do so. He was, in his own words, "a pilgrim, a traveler, a stranger" with "no home on earth,"[78] even though he was surrounded by people who offered him gracious hospitality and kindness. It was a largely self-imposed isolation that sapped his spirits and kept him from finding reasons to either respect or appreciate his neighbors.

75. Letter from Fisk to Temple, June 11, 1823, box 6:35, CLA.

76. Cited in Bond, *Memoir*, 312.

77. Oren, *Power, Faith, and Fantasy*, 96.

78. Fisk Diary, vol. 3, entry for June 2, 1823, DFL.

## AN INTERLUDE IN BEIRUT

The next move Fisk made was to Beirut where he sought out the company of the British and American missionaries who were gathered there, who by this time included two new ABCFM missionary families, Mr. and Mrs. Isaac Bird and Mr. and Mrs. William Goodell. Fisk used this time as he had used his previous time in Malta, to re-energize his fatigued spirits.

The time Fisk spent in Lebanon is one of the reasons why Ussama Makdisi and Samir Khalaf included him in their books, as the focus of their scholarship is on the impact made by the early ABCFM missionaries on Lebanese society. Khalaf, oddly,[79] writes about Fisk *and* Parsons' time in Lebanon in order to ask and answer the questions: "What was Mount Lebanon like at the time? What impressions did those early encounters leave on them? How were they perceived?"[80] even though they were never in Lebanon together. Makdisi in his book, *The Artillery of Heaven,* devotes much of his attention to working out the long-term implications of the conflict between the missionaries and Maronites that arose over the conversion of As'ad Shidyaq to Protestantism in 1825.[81] But Fisk's role in this conflict was negligible as Shidyaq's conversion happened after Fisk's death. In point of fact, Lebanon was for Fisk more of an interlude than a place to engage in significant missionary service. He and Parsons were the initiators of a mission that would impact Lebanese society in the ways Makdisi and Khalaf claim, but others, most notably King, Bird and Goodell, were the key actors in that drama.

## BACK TO JERUSALEM

### *Henry Martyn and an Orientalist Fantasy in Acre*

After this interlude in Beirut, Fisk would make two more trips to Jerusalem as well as a journey to Aleppo and northern Syria. Most critical to assessing his developing attitude to the religious other is what he recorded in his diary after visiting a mosque in Acre on his first return trip to Jerusalem, as it gives evidence of the previously mentioned re-imagining of his mission to be more inclusive of a missional engagement with Muslims.

79. As far as we know Parsons visited neither Beirut nor the Lebanese mountains.

80. Khalaf, *Protestant Missionaries*, 165.

81. "What follows is the story of a foundational encounter between Americans and Arabs. It traces the arrival of the first American Protestant missionaries to the Arab provinces of the Ottoman Empire, and the ensuing persecution and death of one of their earliest converts." Makdisi, *Artillery of Heaven*, 1.

What we learn from the entry Fisk made after visiting the mosque is that this re-imagining was inspired by Henry Martyn's memoir.

Earlier I indicated that Fisk and Parsons canonized Martyn as one of their missionary saints. They did so for a different reason than what had prompted them to do the same for David Brainerd. They revered Brainerd for his self-sacrificing lifestyle. Martyn's ministry didn't have that same self-sacrificial quality. He was a chaplain to the British East India Company for most of his career. He would have made a comfortable living from that occupation. It was not his sacrificial lifestyle that Fisk and Parsons admired. It was his pioneering work among Muslims. He was, as his biographer, George Smith, put it: "Saint and Scholar: First Modern Missionary to the Mohammedans."[82]

Unlike Brainerd, Martyn was Fisk's contemporary. He died in 1812 and his memoir (the one Fisk received as a gift from the Van Lennep's) had just been published the year when Fisk and Parsons made their journey to the Ottoman Empire.[83] As such Martyn's story reflected contemporary realities in a setting similar to the one in which Fisk was living. This would have made Martyn's missionary model a feasible option for Fisk.

While it is difficult to determine exactly when Fisk began to ponder the possibility of a more intentional conversational relationship with Muslims, a reasonable assumption can be made that the idea began to germinate in his mind as he read and re-read Martyn's memoir in light of his visit with the educated Turk at the Pasha's institute in Cairo. Almost certainly this is what was on his mind when he visited a mosque in Acre in November of 1823 when he recorded in his diary what can best be described as a Martyn-inspired orientalist/missionary fantasy.

Fisk made this visit in the company of the British vice consul in Acre, a man named Mr. Michael. The occasion was the need for Fisk to obtain the necessary travel papers for his on-going journey to Jerusalem. The man they visited was a successor to the infamous Bosnian Mamluk, Ahmad al-Jazzar (the "butcher") who at the height of his power ruled as a semi-autonomous governor of large parts of Lebanon and Palestine from his palace in Acre.[84] His rule ended with his death in 1804 immediately followed by Sulaiman Pasha al-Adil whose nickname (the "just")

---

82. Smith, *Henry Martyn: Saint and Scholar.* This quote is taken from the title to the book.

83. Sargent, *A Memoir of Rev. Henry Martyn.*

84. Kramer, *A History of Palestine,* 61.

suggests a radical shift from his predecessor's policies.[85] He, in turn, was succeeded in 1819 by Abdulla Pasha who committed himself to advancing and enforcing the Sultan's modernization program.[86] It was Abdulla whom Fisk met.

Fisk recorded the details of this visit in his diary, including what he saw in the mosque that was connected to the sitting room where the Pasha met with them. Outside the mosque was an idyllically serene courtyard, the kind of setting that French artists might have romanticized for their orientalist paintings. It was a setting that would lead Fisk to engage in what might best be described as a flight of orientalist/missionary fantasy:

> This court with its fountains & shade is quite in oriental taste & certainly for a hot country it is a most delightful spot. My imagination was filled with the idea of the learned Mussulmans in the times of the Caliphs of Bagdad & Cairo passing their time in such places. I was dressed in my Turban Rhumbaz & Jembbee with a beard already of a tolerable length, & I almost fancied that I could soon become master of Arabic in such a place surrounded by Mussulman doctors. Had I the faith, the wisdom & the learning of Martyn I might perhaps find access to such places & tell the doctors that Jesus is the Son of God.[87]

It is possible that this fantasy took its inspiration from a scene in Martyn's memoir when Martyn was in Persia meeting with Shi'a scholars in a public forum to have what his biographer called his "first public controversy with the Mohammedans" in Shiraz.[88] The fact that it was held in a setting not unlike the courtyard of the mosque in Acre means that the following words from Martyn's memoir might have been on Fisk's mind that day:

> After some hesitation and demur, the Moojtuhid, or Professor of Mohammedan Law, consented to a discussion upon religious topics. He was a man of great consequence in Shiraz, being the last authority in the decision of all matters connected with his profession; so that a contest with him, as it respected rank, prejudice, popularity, and reputation for learning, was manifestly

---

85. Ibid.
86. Ibid.
87. Ibid., entry for November 3, 1823.
88. Sargent, *Memoir*, 334.

an unequal one. Mr. Martyn, however, fearlessly engaged in it, knowing in whom he had believed.[89]

From this point on we find evidence in Fisk's letters and diaries that he was determined to translate this fantasy into reality. He was aware that it wouldn't happen exactly as he envisioned it (in a sensuous setting surrounded by learned Muslim scholars), but the basic thrust of the fantasy—Fisk being to Ottoman Muslims as Martyn was to Persians—would now lead him to seek out opportunities to engage in religious conversations with Muslims, or at least be open to the possibility when opportunities arose.

## Meeting Muslims in Jerusalem

There is evidence that Fisk intentionally sought out conversational relationships with Muslims on his second trip to Jerusalem. The evidence is found in the person he hired to teach him Arabic. Before he had hired Christian language instructors; this time he chose to hire a Palestinian Muslim named Jar Allah.

### JAR ALLAH

There is an interesting possibility that Jar Allah was a member of an illustrious Palestinian family with purported blood ties to the Prophet Muhammad. According to the:

> The Jarallahs belonged to Jerusalem's old Muslim elite, and were counted among the city's *ashraf* or descendants of the prophet Muhammad. Family members held religious posts in Jerusalem for hundreds of years and emerged at the end of the nineteenth century among the local Ottoman bureaucratic-landowning class, although less influential than the Husaynis and Nashashibis.[90]

This gave added significance to the relationship Fisk developed with his instructor even though he probably wasn't aware of any of this at the time. Most important to him was the fact that he was taking the necessary steps to initiate an intentional evangelical witness to Muslims.

---

89. Ibid.

90. Online reference from the *Gale Encyclopedia of the Middle East and North Africa*, http://www.encyclopedia.com/doc/1G2-3424601417.html (accessed July 12, 2016).

What we find in examining the diary entries Fisk made to record the conversations he had with Jar Allah was that he had reverted to his earlier non-confrontational approach, something approaching dialogue, albeit in an evangelical key. He used explanation more than argumentation to get his point across. And he showed a genuine interest in learning from Jar Allah what it is Muslims believe. He assumed in this case the dual role of teacher and student.

We see this in a conversation Fisk recorded in his diary on March 9, 1824. It is worth quoting at length.

> Read Heb. 1 in Arabic with my Master Jar Allah. He immediately noticed the manner in which Christ is mentioned as the son of God & said that in their view it was infidelity to call him so. I stated it as a doctrine in which all Christians agree. But I told him we do not believe Jesus is the son of God in the same sense in which I am the son of my Father, for this was impossible. I then showed him in Luke 1. 35 the reason assigned by the Angel why Jesus should be called the Son of God.
>
> He raised his hands & exclaimed, as if almost overcome on hearing this explanation, "God preserve you." It would be wrong however to infer from this exclamation that he fully understood what I said or that he was satisfied with it. It only shows at most that my explanation served to render the doctrine in some measure less offensive to him than it was before.
>
> He says Mussulmans believe that the Angel blowed [*sic*] into the side of Mary in consequence of which she conceived Jesus. He was born also from the side not as other children are.— When the Jews perceived that she was pregnant, they came to her & demanded "How is this? You are a virgin. How then came this in your womb?" She replied "Ask it, & it will answer you." They did so & the embryo replied "I am Abd Allah (the slave of God) & God has sent me with his gospel."
>
> Jar Allah says he goes to the place of Christ's birth at Bethlehem & kisses the stones & covers his face, & does the same at the tomb of the Virgin Mary in the valley of Cedron. He speaks of Christ & so do the other Turks, under the name of our Lord Jesus (Issa). Mary they call our Lady Miriam. They speak also of our Lord Abraham, our Lord Isaac, our Lord Moses, etc. He says our Lord Jesus is the greatest of the Prophets except Mohammed, & if one should speak against Jesus the Turks would put him to death.
>
> I asked him whether Musssulmans ever pray to Mohammed. He at first said "Yes." I asked in what manner & he replied they

pray that peace may be upon him. "But, said I, this is praying for him not to him. Do you ever say in your prayers, O Mohammed do this & do that?" "Never, never," he said, but he told me afterwards that they beseech God to do things for the sake of Mohammed, & they consider him as a Mediator between God & man.[91]

Two things are worth noting here. The first is that Fisk is less intrusive in his questioning with Jar Allah than he had been in previous conversations with Christians. He lets Jar Allah set the conversational agenda. The result is a more free-flowing dialogue than what was evident in the debates Fisk set up with Christian priests and monks. It was the kind of conversation that a Christian might envision having with a Muslim today.

The second thing worth noting is the fact that Fisk recorded the conversation without comment. There is much in what Jar Allah said that Fisk would not have agreed with. But he allowed it to stand on its own. It could be that this is because Fisk felt that what Jar Allah said was so self-evidently wrong that it didn't need refutation. But more possible is that he recorded it this way because he was less interested in giving a proper orthodox response to Muslim error than gathering information that would help him understand Muslims better. And he did it with the respect that a good student gives to his or her professor.

### Shekh Khaleel

This same pattern is found in a conversational relationship Fisk developed with a second Arabic instructor he engaged during his third and final visit to Jerusalem in the spring of 1825. By this time there is no doubt that Fisk had made the development of conversational relationships with Muslims the *sine qua non* of his missional purpose. This is apparent in the fact that Fisk devoted nearly the entirety of his final diary to a verbatim account of an ongoing religious conversation he had with this instructor, a Palestinian Muslim named Shekh Khaleel.[92]

What we learn about Shekh Khaleel from these long conversations is that his understanding of his own faith was on the level of a populist

---

91. Fisk Diary, vol. 3, entry for March 9, 1824.

92. Almost certainly "Shekh" is Fisk's transliteration of the Arabic honorific "shaikh."

form of Islam, what some missiologists today designate "folk Islam."[93] It is evident in his matter-of-fact treatment of miraculous events combined with a literalist reading of the more mythic elements of the Qur'anic account such as sensuous descriptions of paradise and reference to spiritual beings such as the two angels, Harut and Marut (mentioned in Surah 2:102) following a long-standing tradition of associating them with sorcery.[94] What isn't certain is whether or not Fisk was able to contrast this form of Islam with other forms he had encountered in previous conversations. It isn't possible to ascertain this because Fisk recorded these conversations verbatim with no accompanying commentary.

It is possible that this extended conversation took place in Arabic, as Fisk was studying Arabic with Shekh Khaleel six hours a day with a break only for tSunday Sabbath observance. What we could be looking at in this case is Fisk's translation of Arabic lessons that he chose to frame in the form of a religious discussion. It isn't certain. What is certain is that these conversations were critically important to Fisk as he not only recorded them verbatim in dozens of pages of his diary, he also included Qur'anic references and material he had drawn from whatever texts he was able to find on Muslim belief and practice. So once again Fisk was taking on the role of student and teacher. What follows is an excerpt from the first conversation Fisk recorded to give an idea of the shape these conversations took. I will set off Fisk's Qur'anic references and notes in italics.

> "Conversations with Shekh"
>
> F: "When you say the Coran descended from Heaven, do you mean that it came down already written?"
>
> S: "No. Gabriel brought down the words & gave them to Mohammed & scribes who wrote them."
>
> F: "Is the promise of women to believers in Paradise to be understood literally or figuratively?"

---

93. See Parshall's book *Bridges to Islam* for a missionary's definition of this kind of populist Islam.

94. Joseph A. Islam speaks of a "popular" Islamic belief that associates dark magic with Harut and Marut then refutes it with a *tafsir* (interpretation) of Surah 2:102 indicating that what these two beings brought with them from heaven was not knowledge of sorcery, but divine wisdom to guide the umma. Shekh Khaleel's version represents the "popular" Islamic belief. See Islam, "Did Harut and Marut Teach Dark Magic?," *The Qur'an and it Message*, March 19, 2012, http://quransmessage.com/pdfs/Harut%20and%20Marut.pdf (accessed July 12, 2016).

S: "Literally"

F: "There are some in our country who insist that Mussulmans understand this figuratively but others say literally."

S: "The latter are right."

F: "A Christian who had turned Mussulman (J.B. English) told me that the best commentators understand it figuratively."

S: "Then he is not yet a Mussulman. Why Paradise if there are no women there?"

F: "The excellence of Paradise consists in being with Saints & Angels, & in being like them, in the presence of God, free from trouble & above all free from sin."

*Ch. 2 p. 13 "We gave Jesus the son of Mary revelations—(manifestations) & strengthened him by the Holy Spirit"*

F: "What is the Holy Spirit?"

S: "It is the word of God; -Jesus is also called the Holy Spirit."

F: "Is not this name given also to Gabriel?"

S: "Yes. He is also called the Holy Spirit."

*Chap. 1. p. 15—Enchantment—taught by Devils & sent down by two Angels, Haroot & Maroot at Babel. No possibility of Salvation to those who learn this art.*

Shekh says "I was once with a man who knew and I told him I wished to know what it was. He then raised his long robe a little from his feet & immediately thousands of mice issued from his feet & filled the room. He raised his robe a second time & a multitude of weasels came out who immediately devoured all the mice. I saw it with my own eyes."

F: "What became of the Weasels?"

S: "The man raised his robe a third time & they all returned immediately whence they came."

F: "Where are Haroot & Maroot now?"

S: "I have never seen them, but it is said they are in Babylon still, hung up with their heads downwards. Some say they are not Angels but two Kings."

F: "How do men learn this art?"

S: "They go to these Angels in Babylon—become infidels, & then at the command of the angels, take water & cast it into a hot oven that is there & thus understand the art at once without study. They can then teach the art to others."[95]

Later conversations were wide-ranging, covering aspects of Islamic practice ("Do you ever beat your wife?"),[96] Islamic cosmology ("Our earth is the upper one of 7"),[97] and the existence of spiritual beings. For the most part Fisk set the conversational agenda, but he also allowed Khaleel to take the lead, making this more of a dialogue than anything we have seen in Fisk's conversations up to this point. Sometimes the results led to bizarre exchanges such as this one:

> S: "Do you worship the Son of Mary?"
>
> F: "Not the human nature, but the Divine nature that was united with it. We hold it a first principle in religion that prayer & worship are to be offered to no being but him that created the Heavens & the Earth, nor we allow at all the use of pictures or images in our worship."
>
> S: "Did Mohammed ever go to England?"
>
> F: "No."
>
> S. "Then, the English if they live according to their faith as you describe it, will go to Paradise (the Garden)."[98]

This would not have been the kind of conversation Fisk envisioned when he formulated his fantasy in the Acre mosque. Shekh Khaleel was not a scholar. But the effort Fisk invested in these conversations shows that his dream of one day having more substantial conversations with learned Muslims was on his mind. He was doing whatever he felt was necessary to become the next Henry Martyn.

## A PRELUDE TO THE END: A VIOLENT ENCOUNTER WITH A BEDOUIN

Fisk would never leave the Levant, making two more trips to Beirut and one to northern Syria between and after his two visits to Jerusalem. It was on his last visit to Beirut that he would die, possibly from complications

---

95. Fisk Diary, vol. 4, entry for February 9, 1825.
96. Ibid., entry for March 5, 1825.
97. Ibid., entry for March 20, 1825.
98. Ibid., entry for February 24, 1825.

related to injuries he received in a violent encounter with Bedouin near Jerusalem.

The incident in question happened on May 12, 1825. Fisk was traveling with King in an entourage that included armed guards through territory known for Bedouin banditry. That morning two young Bedouin who had been in the employ of the Arab serving as their caravan leader were seized and bound on the suspicion of stealing trunks. "There seemed indeed good grounds for suspicion,"[99] wrote Fisk in the entry he made in his diary reporting the incident. He wondered, however, whether it had been wise for his caravan leader to tie them up as the Bedouin were known to protect their own. That was the case here. Fisk described what happened next as a group of angry Bedouin attacked their caravan to set the prisoners free:

> The attack was furious and wild as the whirlwind of the desert. Had it been their design to take our lives or our property, we were completely in their power. One man in our train received a slight sabre-wound in the arm. Many received heavy blows over the head and back. A heavy blow of a bludgeon grazed my head and spent its force on my arm, which was in consequence lame for several days.[100]

Samir Khalaf believes that the injury Fisk sustained in this attack was a greater blow to his health than Fisk himself realized. "He never fully recovered." says Khalaf. "The assault must have aggravated his already enfeebled physical condition."[101] There is no way to know for certain if Khalaf is correct. What is certain is that within five months Fisk would die in Beirut from an undetermined cause.

## FINAL DAYS IN BEIRUT

### Privileging the Muslim Other

Fisk maintained a strange silence during his last trip to Beirut. There are very few diary entries between the time of his arrival in late May and the time of his death in October. This is probably due to the injuries he sustained in the Bedouin attack. But there is enough in the entries he made, just before and after his return to Beirut, to underscore an interesting

99. Ibid., entry for May 12, 1825.

100. Ibid.

101. Khalaf, *Protestant Missionaries*, 190.

development in his perception of the religious other. His intentional engagement with his Muslim neighbors had led him to be less critical of them than he was of Christians with whom relationships had become strained and contentious. That this was the case can be seen in two contrasting entries he made in his diary during this time.

During a visit to Jaffa on May 2 Fisk attended his first Greek Orthodox baptism which he described as a ceremony which "presented a disgusting & painful compound of frivolous superstitions & unbecoming levity."[102] A week later after passing through territory that many had warned him about crossing due to political troubles in the area, he recorded words of praise for the Muslims he met along the way. "So all our fears concerning this part of our Journey have vanished & instead of insult or detention we meet with nothing but civility."[103]

The question that needs to be left open is whether Fisk's less critical assessment of the Muslim other might have led to a more appreciative attribution in a way that would resonate with Edward Said's conceptualization of a contingent "narrative." It needs to be left open because Fisk would die before such a possibility came to fruition.

## Fisk's Death

Fisk returned to Beirut in May of 1825. He would die in October. This would happen in the company of missionary friends who recorded his parting with even more attention to detail than Fisk gave to Parsons' death, at least partly because he lingered on the verge of death for several days.[104] Bird and Goodell recorded every word he said in those last days, many of which were the expression of a fevered mind. What we learn from the words he spoke while still lucid is that the sense of inadequacy that had haunted him throughout his time in the Ottoman Empire would haunt him till his dying breath.

> It is now about seventeen years that I have professed to be a servant of Christ. But O how have I served him—with how many halting and stumbling and sins. Were it not for the infinite

102. Fisk Diary, vol. 3, entry for May 2, 1825.

103. Ibid., entry for May 9, 1825.

104. Following the pattern of memoirs of the era, Bond devotes a good deal of time to recounting the details passed on to the Prudential Committee from Bird and Goodell recounting the last few days of Fisk's life. This is found in Bond, *Memoir*, 415–24.

merits of Christ, I should have no hope—not one among a thousand of my words has been right—not one among a thousand of my thoughts has been right.[105]

As he lay on his death bed what most impressed itself on Fisk's consciousness was how negligible his contribution had been to the mission he and Parsons had begun with such promise. What he clung to in this case was his Calvinist belief in the perseverance of the saints, knowing that God's acceptance was not dependant on his achievements. "Thanks be to God for so much mercy, and let his name be trusted in for that which is future"[106] were the final words Fisk would say before he was lost to delirium and then to life. Another hand wrote the simple words that would conclude his diary and close the last chapter of his life.

Thus ended the Journals of our good Brother Fisk. On the 11th of October he was too ill at Mr. G's to come out & attend our prayer meeting. He died on the morning of the Sabbath Oct 23rd aged 32 yrs. He was born June 24, 1792.[107]

105. Cited in ibid., 419–20.
106. Ibid., 422.
107. Fisk Diary, vol. 4, entered after Fisk's last entry for May 26, 1825.

# 8

## The Tragedy of Pliny Fisk

### TRANSFORMATION?

MY EXPERIENCE AND EARLIER research on the topic of the transformational nature of missionary encounters with the religious other led me to assume that what I would find in Pliny Fisk's discourse and narrative would be evidence of an alteration in his perceptual paradigm when he crossed from theoretical construct to existential encounter. What I found, instead, was little evidence to suggest that such a transformation occurred.

I say this based on Edward Said's categories of *narrative* and *vision*. As previously noted, Said defined *vision* as a "synchronic essentialism" using "the device of a set of reductive categories (the Semites, the Muslim mind, the Orient, and so forth)" by which to define Middle Eastern peoples.[1] He defined *narrative* as the force that counters vision with the introduction of "diachrony into the system,"[2] thus giving lie to the essentialist memes upon which the orientalist vision is constructed. Diachrony suggests change over time, which means seeing in the other the same contingent possibilities one recognizes in oneself. Fisk himself believed that it was important to approach the religious other with the empathy Said's "narrative" suggests, as one of his expressed motivations for mission was the recognition that all people are his *"fellow* beings."

My expectation in this case was that Fisk would, in the discourse he developed out of his encounters with the Ottoman religious other,

1. Said, *Orientalism*, 240.
2. Ibid.

show evidence of a growing awareness of the kind of humanizing narrative Said commends, if for no other reason than to live out his professed belief in the essential unity of humankind. But there is little to suggest that this transformation occurred in any perceptibly significant way. The classification system he developed during his formative years became more nuanced as he encountered what could be seen as exceptions to his reductive categories among the Jews and Muslims he met in the Ottoman Empire. Positive encounters with individual Ottoman Catholic and Orthodox Christians also pushed the boundaries of his classification system. But he never stopped classifying them, at least not in ways that allowed him to develop anything beyond utilitarian relationships, that is, relationships determined less by friendship than their missiological purpose. Theoretically Fisk determined that all human beings were his "fellow" beings. Practically he lived and died with an "intimate estrangement"[3] from the people he came to serve based at least in part on his consistent use of reductive categories by which to judge them.

While there are numerous examples given in this book to provide evidence for this observation, two entries that Fisk made in his diary just a little more than a year before he died illustrate how consistently he maintained this stance. The first is a comment Fisk made about an Orthodox Archimandrite he met in Damascus in July of 1824 whose intelligence set him apart from other Orthodox leaders he had met. The Archimandrite was, in this case, an exception to a rule Fisk used to classify the Orthodox in general. But the impression given in the entry Fisk made about this encounter suggests that the rule remained the determining description.

> Met a deacon from Cyprus, a pleasant, sociable young man. While we were with him the Archimandrite came in. He is an Arab named Macarios, a man of a very intelligent countenance & dogmatical in his manner of speaking, but not such a *stupid blockhead* as most of the Ecclesiastics in this country [emphasis added].[4]

The other entry may be more telling particularly given what was noted in the previous chapter about Fisk's growing awareness of and appreciation for diversity in the Muslim community. Two weeks previous to his encounter with the Archimandrite Fisk encountered a Muslim shaikh in Damascus renowned for his learning. The reputation of this man led

---

3. See introductory chapter, n. 17.

4. Fisk Diary, vol. 3, entry for July 24, 1824, DFL.

Fisk to assume that he might be like the Turk who so impressed him at the Pasha's institute in Cairo. But it turned out he was less an exception to the rule than its definition. He, like Muslims in general (in Fisk's estimation), exhibited an irrational nature, a pejorative appellation that Fisk attached to Muslims like a second skin. The issue in this case was the shaikh's belief in *jinn*.

> This Shekh is said by the Xns to be the most learned man in Damascus. He is certainly a man of strong mind & well acquainted with Mussulman learning. But he appears to believe all *this nonsense* as firmly as anything whatever [emphasis added].[5]

## Reasons

There are, I believe, several reasons why Fisk was unable, or perhaps unwilling, to transcend "synchronic essentialism" in his estimation of the Ottoman religious other. The first has to do with the fact that his time on the field was too short to allow for the kind of life-transformative experience that has often occurred in others who have immersed themselves in cross-cultural missionary service. One wonders in this case if the amount of time Fisk was pouring into his Arabic studies and extensive religious conversations with Muslims in the later part of his ministry might not have led him to develop a discourse that would have been more in line with Said's contingent narrative than what actually transpired. One wonders particularly because of a trait of Fisk's character that might have allowed this possibility to emerge.

The trait in question is something to which I have been referring throughout this book, which is Fisk's analytical nature. Fisk had a curious mind that led him to observe his surroundings with the eye of an empiricist, always probing to discover as much as possible the factual truth about the people he encountered and places he visited. This could be seen as the basis for the judgments he made about the Archimandrite and the learned Muslim in Damascus. In both cases what drew his admiration and condemnation was their adherence or lack thereof to what he considered to be rational beliefs and behavior. One could assume in this case that the longer Fisk had spent engaging the diverse population of the various places he visited and lived, the more possibility there would have been for him to begin to recognize that the exceptions he was discovering

5. Ibid., entry for July 10, 1824.

to his reductive categories were as definitive of Ottoman reality as the categories themselves.

This would be a reasonable assumption. And it might still have happened that way if he had lived longer. But given the way Fisk chose to exercise his calculating nature it is doubtful, as his approach served to create a relational distance from the people he came to serve.

One of the instructions given to Fisk and Parsons when they were preparing to take up the task given them by the ABCFM was to obtain "such information, of various kinds, as will be of importance in their subsequent course."[6] What has been apparent throughout my examination of Fisk's Ottoman discourse is that Fisk made this a primary ministry task, not only in his exploration of the places he visited, but also of the people he met. They became subjects, or perhaps better, objects, of his analytical research, specimens to be categorized and analyzed for their missiological interest.

Perhaps the most telling illustration of this came in Fisk's visit to the humble home of one of his Palestinian travel guides during the later part of his ministry, a visit to which I alluded in the previous chapter. Here it is worth examining the entry he made in his diary about this incident in a more detailed fashion.

The incident in question happened on November 17, 1823, when Fisk was on a trip visiting Nazareth and its environs. His guide for the trip, a Palestinian Christian he identified as Mallem[7] Antoon Basilos, invited him and his traveling companions to visit his home. When Fisk entered the home to experience what one would assume to have been an opportunity for bonding with a hospitable Arab host, he used the occasion instead to engage in an analytical examination of Antoon's home and family. Here is an excerpt from the lengthy entry Fisk made to mark this occasion:

> I found his house consisted only of a single room. One corner is a kitchen, another a bedroom, a third the nursery & the fourth the divan, that is to say, in one corner was a jug of water, an earthen vessel which served for a fire place, a tin pot for boiling food & a coffee pot, this consisted the furniture of the kitchen. In another corner, the beds of the whole family are piled up together. They consist of thick blankets, which are spread out on the floor at night & Parents, sons & daughters sleep on them in

6. See chapter 6, n34.

7. A possible attempt on Fisk's part to reproduce the Arabic *mu'allam*, "teacher."

their wearing apparel. In the third corner was a cradle, a basket of clothes & a chest, & in the fourth a mat was spread on the floor, & a carpet on a window seat with two cushions. There the Father & I sat, while the rest of the family sat on the floor or prepared coffee, pipes & supper for us.[8]

After recording the names of the family members, and the activity in which they were engaged as Antoon's wife prepared the meal, Fisk continued with observations of the family members themselves:

The dress of the family was very plain & indeed ragged, but the women wore the usual ornament of the fair sex in the place, i.e. strings of small pieces of silver over the forehead & hanging down on both cheeks. The mother had in her string 200 pieces worth I suppose about 30 or 40 dolls [sic]. The elder daughters had about 100 each but of less value in proportion, say 6 or 8 dolls a string & Ghoory wore a string of [?][9] worth perhaps a doll.

Fisk ended his observations with a detailed description of the meal he ate with the family followed by his estimation of their status. Despite their humble circumstances, he observed, "they probably live better by far than the greater part of the inhabitants," which, given other observations Fisk made over the course of his time in the area, was his way of pointing out one of the many flaws he found in Arab society.

What is clear here, as it is in many other entries Fisk made about the people he met during his time in the Ottoman Empire, is that the role he claimed for himself was more akin to that of an investigative journalist than a missionary intent on building incarnational relationships. This had the effect of keeping his Ottoman neighbors at a relational distance, which made it difficult for him to meet them as fellow human beings. The isolation he felt, particularly after the death of Levi Parsons, was in this case largely self-imposed, as there is no evidence that he ever made any significant friendships outside the small circle of missionaries with whom he traveled.

There was another element of Fisk's analytical approach that made it difficult for him to move beyond an orientalist vision. This was the apologetic framework within which he made his analytical judgments, which, as noted earlier, was a critical element of his education at Andover

8. Fisk Diary, vol. 3, DFL, entry for November 17, 1823.

9. Fisk's handwriting is indecipherable here.

Theological Seminary. The effect this had on Fisk and others who pursued an Andover education was to teach him to perceive the religious other as an ideological sparring partner. The fact that Fisk's religious conversations most often took the form of debates indicates how foundational this apologetic emphasis was to his mental universe.

Yet another reason why Fisk's analytical nature did not lead him to a greater appreciation for a Saidean narrative has to do with the criteria he used to make his rational judgments. Reference has been made to the foundational role that Scottish Common Sense Realism played in Fisk's educational experience, both at Middlebury and Andover. This had the effect of giving him an elevated confidence in his ability and right to judge his Ottoman neighbors for beliefs and practices that did not conform to an ortho-praxy that, in his mind, was determinant of the very structure of the universe. His criticism of the learned shaikh in Damascus for his belief in *jinn* can be understood in this context. To believe in *jinn* was, in Fisk's estimation, "nonsense," which is a term suggesting an unacceptable irrationality. Fisk would not have said the same about angels even though Boston rationalists would have challenged that belief on the same basis. Fisk wouldn't have done this because the existence of angels is confirmed by the biblical account. What was rational to Fisk was not only what was verifiable by empirical evidence; it was what was verifiable by biblical evidence, or more to the point, biblical evidence as defined by an evangelical/Calvinist hermeneutic. As long as this remained the determinant framework for Fisk's critical assessment of the beliefs and practices of his Ottoman neighbors (and there is no evidence that it ever stopped being such), he would find it difficult to develop any kind of empathetic appreciation for the narrative that defined his neighbors' existence. Their "otherness" would remain their most compelling descriptor.

The themes developed in the sixth chapter underscore how deeply embedded this analytically-shaped framework was in Fisk's world view. We see it particularly in the first theme ("Objectifying the Religious Other"), which was illustrated by the incident related above when Fisk visited the home of his Palestinian guide. We see it to a lesser, yet no less telling way, in the second theme ("Struggling with the Occidental Religious Other"), which highlights the struggles Fisk had fitting into an expatriate community whose members shared few of his revivalist sentiments. We see it in the third ("The Distancing Effect of a Text-based Mission") and sixth ("Reading Ottoman Otherness Through a Biblical Lens") themes, both of which illustrate his belief that the Bible was both the only valid source for redemptively objective truth and the means by which Fisk could assign value judgments to the contemporary settings of biblically-significant sites. We see it in the fourth theme ("Conflicting Expectations: a Perceptual Gap"), which expresses his frustration over the lack of comprehension he found in his conversation partners when he offered what he believed to be perfectly reasonable explanations of spiritual truth. The fact that they didn't understand was, in his estimation, less a problem with his logic or communication skills than their "stupid blockheadedness." Finally, it is apparent in Fisk's experience of otherness as a threat during times of stress and grief as the distance it created between him and his neighbors made it easy to assign blame for his despondency on a cultural environment that he never learned to call home. The final theme ("Rethinking the Orthodox Paradigm") gave some promise of a more appreciative grasp of narrative with the challenge it posed to a reductive category the evangelical/orthodox used to critique the beliefs of their Eastern Christian neighbors. But there is no evidence that it was anything other than a momentary anomaly in Fisk's more predominant tendency to define the religious other though a set of reductive categories.

## MISSIONARY HEROES

One other element that might have hindered Fisk's ability to see beyond his orthodox/orientalist categorizations was his veneration of missionary heroes, particularly David Brainerd and Henry Martyn, but also his dear friend, Levi Parsons after his untimely death. This is a more difficult factor to assess, as it isn't entirely certain how it impacted his perception of the religious other. There is no doubt that these missionary heroes became his models for ministry, or at least their iconic narratives became his model for ministry. This is almost certainly the source of his constant feelings of missionary inadequacy, feelings that he took to his grave. What isn't as certain is whether this hero worship caused him to solidify his less salutary characterizations of the religious other, believing that there was only one valid way to approach the subjects of missionary service. There is reason to believe that this may have been the case, but it is mentioned here less as a certainty than a plausible conjecture.

## ISOLATION

There is a tragic element to Pliny Fisk's story both in terms of his own life and the goals of the ministry to which he was committed. One of the reasons he devoted so much of his time and analytical inclinations to collecting and analyzing "useful information" about people and places is because he believed it would benefit those missionaries who would follow in his wake. The objectifying nature of his ministry in this case might be said to have led to a more positive result than what is apparent on the surface. But there is little evidence that this was the case. Little of the material he collected was ever published in any form beyond occasional excerpts for the *Missionary Herald* and Bonds' hastily and often poorly constructed hagiography. And it was largely forgotten after the publication of the highly influential and thoroughly researched *Missionary Researches in Armenia: including a journey through Asia Minor, and into Georgia and Persia, with a visit to the Nestorian and Chaldean Christians of Cormiah and Salmas,* by ABCFM missionaries, Eli Smith and H. G. O. Dwight in 1833.[10] The tragedy in this case is apparent.

The other tragedy was the sense of isolation Fisk developed through the distancing effect of his analytical objectification of his Ottoman neighbors. This made it difficult for him to carry out his evangelistic purpose, as the incarnational message of the gospel was negated by his lack of a relational witness. But it took a toll on him, as well, as his isolation produced a spirit of bitterness that had the effect of driving him more deeply into an estrangement from the people he believed God had called him to serve. This was, perhaps, the greatest tragedy as Fisk was surrounded by people who were eager to befriend him with the offer of a gracious Middle Eastern hospitality that makes most missionaries who have had the privilege of living and working in the region reluctant to leave. That was my experience. I had hoped that it would have been Fisk's experience, as well.

The Ottoman Empire was an alien and alienating place to Pliny Fisk when he arrived. It remained that to him till the day he died. His tragedy in this sense was not the failure of his evangelical mission. It was his failure to find the "fellow" in his Ottoman "fellow being." In this case the most fitting epitaph on his life may be the one he wrote for himself.
"I am a Pilgrim, a Traveler, a stranger. I have no home on earth. I see it in the skies."[11]

---

10. Dwight and Smith, *Missionary Researches in Armenia.*

11. Fisk Diary, vol. 3, entry for June 2, 1823.

# Bibliography

Ahlstrom, Sidney. "The Scottish Philosophy and American Theology." *Church History* 24, no. 3 (1955) 257–72.

Allmendinger, David F. *Paupers and Scholars: The Transformation of Student Life in Nineteenth-Century New England.* New York: St. Martin's, 1975.

American Board of Commissioners for Foreign Missions (ABCFM). *First Ten Annual Reports of the American Board of Commissioners for Foreign Missions with Other Documents of the Board.* Boston: Crocker and Brewster, 1834.

———. *Instructions from the Prudential Committee of the American Board of Commissioners for Foreign Missions to the Rev. Levi Parsons and the Rev. Pliny Fisk: missionaries designated for Palestine : delivered in the Old South Church, Boston, Sabbath evening, Oct. 31, 1819.* Boston: Prudential Committee, 1819.

———. "Report of the Prudential Committee: Palestine Mission." *Missionary Herald* 15 (1819) 265–67, 295–96.

Anderson, Rufus. *Memorial Volume of the First Fifty Years of the American Board of Commissioners for Foreign Missions.* Boston: ABCFM, 1862.

———. "Student lecture notes." ABC, box number 30.4. Houghton Library Archives, Harvard University.

Andover Theological Seminary. *Catalogue of the Library Belonging to the Theological Institution in Andover.* Andover, MA: Flagg and Gould, 1819

———. *The Constitution and Associate Statutes of the Theological Seminary in Andover with a Sketch of its Rise and Progress.* Boston: Farrand, Mallory, 1808.

———. *General Catalogue of the Theological Seminary, Andover, Massachusetts, 1808–1908.* Boston: Todd, 1908.

———. *Letter from Professors to ABCFM Commending Andover Students for Missionary Work.* ABC: 6.1—"Testimonials of Missionaries and Assistant Missionaries, including letters from them and papers respecting them till their departure for their respective missions." Houghton Library Archives. Harvard University, Cambridge, MA.

———. *Outline of the Course of Study in the Department of Christian Theology, with References to the Principle Books in the Library, Pertaining to that Department, for the use of the Students in the Theological Seminary, Andover.* Andover, MA: Flagg and Gould, 1822.

Andover Theological Seminary Trustees. *Constitution and Associate Statutes of the Theological Seminary in Andover; with a sketch of its Rise and Progress.* Boston: Farrand, Mallory, 1808.

Andrew, John A. III. *Rebuilding the Christian Commonwealth: New England Congregationalists & Foreign Missions, 1800–1830*. Lexington: University of Kentucky, 1976.

Andrew, John A. III. *Rebuilding the Christian Commonwealth: New England Congregationalists & Foreign Missions, 1800–1830*. Lexington: University Press of Kentucky, 1976.

Anonymous. *Abstract of an Account of the Manner in which the united Brethren preach the Gospel and carry on their Missions among the heathen* (no date given). Unpublished manuscript. Volume7: Dissertations. Franklin Trace Library Special collections, Andover Newton Theological School, Newton Center, MA.

*Asiatick Researches*. Vol. 1. Unpublished Manuscript. Volume7/Dissertations. 1811. Franklin Trace Library Special collections, Andover Newton Theological School, Newton Center, MA.

Bailey, Sarah Loring. *Historical Sketches of Andover (Comprising the present towns of North Andover and Andover)*. Boston: Houghton, Mifflin, 1880.

Banner, Lois Wendland. "The Protestant Crusade: Religious Missions, Benevolence, and Reform in the United States, 1790–1840." PhD diss., Columbia University, New York, 1970.

Barber, John Warner. *Historical Collections Relating to the History and Antiquities of Every Town in Mass with Geographical Descriptions*. Worcester, MA: Lazell, 1848.

Baxter, Richard. *The Saints Everlasting Rest*. New York: American Tract Society, 1845.

Beaver, R. Pierce. "The Concert of Prayer for Missions." *Ecumenical Review* 10, no. 4 (1958) 420–27.

Beaver, R. Pierce, ed. *Pioneers in Mission: The Early Missionary Ordination Sermons, Charges, and Instructions: A Source Book on the Rise of American Missions to the Heathen*. Grand Rapids: Eerdmans, 1966.

Bird, Isaac. *Bible Work in Bible Lands; or, Events in the History of the Syria Mission*. Philadelphia: Presbyterian Board of Publication, 1872.

Birdsall, Richard. "The Second Great Awakening and the New England Social Order." *Church History* 39 (1970) 360–62.

Bond, Alvan. *Memoir of the Rev. Pliny Fisk, A.M. Late Missionary to Palestine*. Boston: Crocker and Brewster, 1828.

————. *The present state of Mohamedanism* (Dec 17, 1816). Unpublished manuscript, Volume7/Dissertations. Franklin Trace Library Special collections, Andover Newton Theological School, Newton Center, MA.

Bosch, David J. *Transforming Mission: Paradigm Shifts in Theology of Mission*. Maryknoll, NY: Orbis, 1992.

Brauer, Jerald, C. "Conversion: From Puritanism to Revivalisim." *Journal of Religion* 58, no. 2 (1978) 227–43.

Breitenbach, William. "Piety and Moralism: Edwards and the New Divinity." In *Jonathan Edwards and the American Experience*, edited by Nathan O. Hatch and Harry S. Stout, 177–204. New York: Oxford University, 1988.

Brewer, David. *Greece & the Hidden Centuries: Turkish Rule from the Fall of Constantinople to Greek Independence*. London: Taurus, 2010.

Brown, Ralph H. "The American Geographies of Jedidiah Morse." *Annals of the Association of American Geographers* 31, no. 3 (1941) 125–217.

Brown, William. *The History of the Propagation of Christianity among the Heathen since the Reformation, in Two Volumes*. New York: Low, 1816.

Brown, William Adams. "A Century of Theological Education and after." *Journal of Religion.* 6, no. 4 (1926) 363–83.

Buchanan, Claudius. *Christian Researches in Asia: With Notices on the Translation of the Scriptures Into the Oriental Languages.* Boston: Armstrong, 1811.

Burgess, Ebenezar. *Address to the Society of Inquiry* (Sept 26, 1815). Unpublished manuscript, Volume7/Dissertations. Franklin Trace Library Special collections, Andover Newton Theological School, Newton Center, MA.

Burnham, A.W. *Some Account of the Denomination of Christianity Called Quakers or Friends* (July 8, 1817). Unpublished manuscript, Volume7/Dissertations. Franklin Trace Library Special collections, Andover Newton Theological School, Newton Center, MA.

Byington, Cyrus *What considerations will justify a student at this Eminary in declining to engage in a mission to the heathen?* (Jan, 1818). Unpublished manuscript, Volume7/Dissertations. Franklin Trace Library Special collections, Andover Newton Theological School, Newton Center, MA.

Calhoun, George A. *What are the reasons which should induce the members of this Seminary to give special attention to the subject of missions?* (March, 1816). Unpublished manuscript, Volume 7. Dissertations. Franklin Trace Library Special collections, Andover Newton Theological School, Newton Center, MA.

Chaney, Charles L. *The Birth of Missions in America.* Pasadena, CA: William Carey Library, 1976.

Clark, Joseph S. *Historical Sketches of the Congregational Churches in Massachusetts with an Appendix.* Boston: Congregational Board, 1858.

Conforti, Joseph A. *Jonathan Edwards, Religious Tradition & American Culture.* Chapel Hill: University of North Carolina, 1995.

———. *Samuel Hopkins and the New Divinity Movement.* Grand Rapids: Eerdmans, 1981.

Cracknell, Kenneth. *Justice, Courtesy and Love: Theologians and Missionaries Encountering World Religions, 1846–1914.* London: Epworth, 1995.

Daly, M. W., ed. *The Cambridge History of Egypt.* Vol. 2, *Modern Egypt, from 1517 to the End of the Twentieth Century.* Cambridge: Cambridge University, 1998.

DeJong, James A. *As the Waters Cover the Sea: Millennial Expectations in the Rise of Anglo-American Missions, 1640–1810.* Laurel, MS: Audubon, 2006.

Dogan, Mehmet Ali, and Heather Starkey, eds. *American Missionaries and the Middle East: Foundational Encounters.* Salt Lake City: University of Utah, 2011.

Dwight, Timothy. *Discourse on Some Events of the Last Century Delivered at the Brick Church of New Haven on Wed., Jan. 7, 1801.* New Haven: Ezra Read, 1801.

———. *The Duty of Americans, at the Present Crisis, Illustrated in a Discourse, Preached on the Fourth of July, 1798 by the Reverend Timothy Dwight. D.D. President of Yale College; at the Request of the Citizens of New Haven.* New Haven: T. and S. Green, 1798.

———. *A Sermon Preached at the Opening of the Theological Institution in Andover; And at the Ordination of Rev. Eliphalet Pearson, LL.D, September 28th, 1808.* Boston: Farrand, Mallory, 1808.

———. *Travels in New England and New York.* Vol. 2. Edited by Barbara Miller Solomon with the assistance of Patricia M. King. Cambridge, MA: Belknap, 1969.

Edwards, Jonathan. *An Account of the Life of the late Reverend Mr. David Brainerd, Minister of the Gospel, Missionary to the Indians, from the honourable Society in*

Scotland, for the Propagation of Christian Knowledge, and Pastor of a Church of Christian Indians in New Jersey.* Boston: Henchman, 1749.

———. *A Faithful Narrative of the Surprising Work of God in the Conversion of Many Hundreds of Souls in Northampton, Massachusetts, A.D. 1735.* New York: Dunmig and Spalding, 1832.

———. *An inquiry into the modern prevailing notions respecting that freedom of will which is supposed to be essential to moral agency, virtue and vice, rewards and punishment, praise and blame.* 1735. Reprint, New York: Mariner, 1970.

———. *The Life of David Brainerd.* Edited by Norman Pettit. New Haven: Yale University, 1985.

Elsbree, Oliver Wendell. *The Rise of the Missionary Spirit in America, 1790–1815.* Williamsport, PA: Williamsport Printing & Binding, 1928.

———. "The Rise of the Missionary Spirit in New England, 1790–1815." *New England Quarterly* 1, no. 3 (1928) 295–322.

Emmons, Nathanael. *Sermons to Young People: Preached AD 1803, 1804.* New Haven: Sidney's, 1806.

Fehler, Brian. *Calvinist Rhetoric in Nineteenth-Century America: The Bartlet Professors of Sacred Rhetoric of Andover Seminary.* Lewiston, NY: Mellen, 2007.

Ferm, Robert L. "Seth Storrs, Congregationalism, and the Founding of Middlebury College." *Vermont History: The Proceedings of the Vermont Historical Society* 69, supplement (2001) 253–66.

Finkel, Caroline. *Osman's Dream: The Story of the Ottoman Empire, 1300–1923.* London: Murray, 2005.

Finnie, David H. *Pioneers East: the Early American Experience in the Middle East.* Cambridge, MA: Harvard University, 1967.

Fisk, Pliny. *A comparative view of the claims of the eastern and western missions upon the American churches (Feb 25, 1817).* Unpublished manuscript, Dissertations. Volume7/Dissertations Franklin Trace Library Special collections, Andover Newton Theological School, Newton Center, MA.

———. *Address to the Society* (Sept 22, 1818). Unpublished manuscript, Volume7/ Dissertations. Franklin Trace Library Special collections, Andover Newton Theological School, Newton Center, MA

———. *Brethren Journal translated from the original code* (1818) . Franklin Trace Library Special collections, Andover Newton Theological School, Newton Center, MA.

———. *Chh. Covenant* (1808). . Franklin Trace Library Special collections, Andover Newton Theological School, Newton Center, MA

———. *Confidential Letter from Fisk to Jeremiah Evarts. June 21, 1825.* Slot 4. Unit 5 (ABC 16.5), Reel 502, Congregational Library and Archives, Boston.

———. *Constitution of the Society of Brethren* (no date given). . Franklin Trace Library Special collections, Andover Newton Theological School, Newton Center, MA.

———. *Copy of a Report of Labors in Salem Performed in the spring Vacation, 1818.* Unpublished manuscript, Dissertations. Volume7/Dissertations Franklin Trace Library Special collections, Andover Newton Theological School, Newton Center, MA

———. Extracts of Letter from Fisk to Mr. Vande Lennep from Beyrout. June 17, 1824 Slot 14. Unit 5 (ABC 16.6). Reel 514. Congregational Library and Archives, Boston..

————. *Fisk Journal entry from Malta. Feb. 22, 1823.* Slots 6–8.Unit 5 (ABC 16.6). Reel 513. Congregational Library and Archives, Boston.

————. *Fisk Journal from Dec. 6, 1820 to Feb. 14, 1821.* Slots 6–8.Unit 5 (ABC 16.6). Reel 513. Congregational Library and Archives, Boston.

————. *Fisk Journal from Feb 17, 1821 to May 10, 1821.* Slots 6–8.Unit 5 (ABC 16.6). Reel 513. Congregational Library and Archives, Boston.

————. *Fisk Journal from May 27, 1821 to Oct 2, 1821.* Slots 6–8.Unit 5 (ABC 16.6). Reel 513. Congregational Library and Archives, Boston.

————. *Fisk Journal sent to Evarts. July 14–Oct 26, 1823.* Slot 12.Unit 5 (ABC 16.6). Reel 513. Congregational Library and Archives, Boston.

————. *Fisk Journal sent to Evarts. Oct 28–Nov. 23, 1823.* Slot 12.Unit 5 (ABC 16.6). Reel 513. Congregational Library and Archives, Boston.

————. Fisk letter from Alexandria Feb 28, 1822 [unknown addressee] Slots 6–8.Unit 5 (ABC 16.6). Reel 513. Congregational Library and Archives, Boston.

————. Fisk letter to Jeremiah Evarts from Smyrna. May 30, 1821. Slot 9.Unit 5 (ABC 16.6). Reel 513. Congregational Library and Archives, Boston.

————. Fisk to Goodell and Temple. Nov 4, 1823 Slot 4. Unit 5 (ABC 16.5), Reel 502, Congregational Library and Archives, Boston.

————. Fisk to Temple, Jan 12, 1823 from Alexandria Slot 4. Unit 5 (ABC 16.5), Reel 502, Congregational Library and Archives, Boston.

————. Fisk to Temple from Jerusalem. June 11, 1823 Slot 4. Unit 5 (ABC 16.5), Reel 502, Congregational Library and Archives, Boston.

————. Fisk to Temples, Birds & Goodells from Syria. Oct. 2, 1823 Slot 4. Unit 5 (ABC 16.5), Reel 502, Congregational Library and Archives, Boston.

————. Fisk to Temple, March 29, 1823 from Cairo to Malta. Slot 4. Unit 5 (ABC 16.5), Reel 502, Congregational Library and Archives, Boston.

————. Fisk to Temple, Jan. 20, 1823 from Alexandria to Malta Slot 4. Unit 5 (ABC 16.5), Reel 502, Congregational Library and Archives, Boston.

————. Fisk to Temple from ? Sept 13, 1823 Slot 4. Unit 5 (ABC 16.5), Reel 502, Congregational Library and Archives, Boston.

————. Fisk to Temple from Aleppo. Sept 11, 1824 Slot 4. Unit 5 (ABC 16.5), Reel 502, Congregational Library and Archives, Boston.

————. Fisk to Temple from Beyroot. July 12, 1823 Slot 4. Unit 5 (ABC 16.5), Reel 502, Congregational Library and Archives, Boston.

————. Fisk to Temple from Beyroot. July 5, 1825 Slot 4. Unit 5 (ABC 16.5), Reel 502, Congregational Library and Archives, Boston.

————. Fisk to Temple from Beyroot. Oct 25, 1823 Slot 4. Unit 5 (ABC 16.5), Reel 502, Congregational Library and Archives, Boston.

————. Fisk to Temple from Beyroot. Sept 19, 1825 Slot 4. Unit 5 (ABC 16.5), Reel 502, Congregational Library and Archives, Boston.

————. Fisk to Temple from Cairo. April 1, 1823. Slot 4. Unit 5 (ABC 16.5), Reel 502, Congregational Library and Archives, Boston.

————. Fisk to Temple from Jaffa. March 16, 1825 Slot 4. Unit 5 (ABC 16.5), Reel 502, Congregational Library and Archives, Boston.

————. Fisk to Temple from Jerusalem. April 1, 1824 Slot 4. Unit 5 (ABC 16.5), Reel 502, Congregational Library and Archives, Boston.

————. Fisk to Temple from Jerusalem. Dec, 12, 1823 Slot 4. Unit 5 (ABC 16.5), Reel 502, Congregational Library and Archives, Boston.

————. Fisk to Temple from Jerusalem. Feb 9, 1824 Slot 4. Unit 5 (ABC 16.5), Reel 502, Congregational Library and Archives, Boston.

————. Fisk to Temple from Jerusalem. Feb. 29, 1824 Slot 4. Unit 5 (ABC 16.5), Reel 502, Congregational Library and Archives, Boston.

————. Fisk to Temple from Jerusalem. Feb. 3, 1824 Slot 4. Unit 5 (ABC 16.5), Reel 502, Congregational Library and Archives, Boston.

————. Fisk to Temple from Jerusalem. May 17, 1823. Slot 4. Unit 5 (ABC 16.5), Reel 502, Congregational Library and Archives, Boston

————. Fisk to Temple from Jerusalem. May 2, 1823. Slot 4. Unit 5 (ABC 16.5), Reel 502, Congregational Library and Archives, Boston.

————. Fisk to Temple from Sidon. Aug 12, 1823 Congregational Library and Archives, Boston.

————. Fisk to Temples and Goodells from ? March 24, 1823. Slot 4. Unit 5 (ABC 16.5), Reel 502, Congregational Library and Archives, Boston.

————. *Historical Sketch of the Society (1818).* Franklin Trace Library Special collections, Andover Newton Theological Seminary, Newton Center, MA.

————. *Journal begun in Beirut, May 25, 1824 ending in Jerusalem, November 24, 1824.* Slot 4. Unit 5 (ABC 16.5), Reel 502, Congregational Library and Archives, Boston.

————. Letter from Fisk and Parsons to Jeremiah Evarts from Alexandria. Jan 16, 1822. Slot 9.Unit 5 (ABC 16.6). Reel 513. Congregational Library and Archives, Boston.

————. Letter from Fisk to ? (while in quarantine in Malta), April 24, 1822 Slot 4. Unit 5 (ABC 16.5), Reel 502, Congregational Library and Archives, Boston.

————. Letter from Fisk to Daniel Temple (while in quarantine in Malta), April 22, 1822 Slot 4. Unit 5 (ABC 16.5), Reel 502, Congregational Library and Archives, Boston.

————. Letter from Fisk to Daniel Temple from "Grand Cairo," March 10, 1822 Slot 4. Unit 5 (ABC 16.5), Reel 502, Congregational Library and Archives, Boston.

————. Letter from Fisk to Daniel Temple in Malta from Cairo, May, 1822 Slot 4. Unit 5 (ABC 16.5), Reel 502, Congregational Library and Archives, Boston.

————. Letter from Fisk to Evarts from Alexandria. Feb 11, 1822. Slot 9.Unit 5 (ABC 16.6). Reel 513. Congregational Library and Archives, Boston.

————. Letter from Fisk to Evarts from Alexandria. Feb. 20, 1822. Slot 9.Unit 5 (ABC 16.6). Reel 513. Congregational Library and Archives, Boston.

————. Letter from Fisk to Evarts from Beyrout. May 27, 1824. Slot 14. Unit 5 (ABC 16.6). Reel 514. Congregational Library and Archives, Boston.

————. Letter from Fisk to Evarts from Cairo. March 18, 1822. Slot 9.Unit 5 (ABC 16.6). Reel 513. Congregational Library and Archives, Boston.

————. Letter from Fisk to Evarts from Jerusalem. Dec 22, 1823. Slot 9.Unit 5 (ABC 16.6). Reel 513. Congregational Library and Archives, Boston.

————. Letter from Fisk to Evarts from Jerusalem. Feb 20, 1824. Slot 9.Unit 5 (ABC 16.6). Reel 513. Congregational Library and Archives, Boston.

————. Letter from Fisk to Evarts from Malta, Dec 25, 1822. Slot 9.Unit 5 (ABC 16.6). Reel 513. Congregational Library and Archives, Boston.

————. Letter from Fisk to Evarts from Malta. April 18, 1822. Slot 9.Unit 5 (ABC 16.6). Reel 513. Congregational Library and Archives, Boston.

————. Letter from Fisk to Evarts from Malta. July 1, 1822. Slot 12.Unit 5 (ABC 16.6). Reel 513. Congregational Library and Archives, Boston.

———. Letter from Fisk to Evarts from Malta. June 15, 1822. Slot 12.Unit 5 (ABC 16.6). Reel 513. Congregational Library and Archives, Boston.

———. Letter from Fisk to Evarts from Malta. May 23, 1822. Slot 12.Unit 5 (ABC 16.6). Reel 513. Congregational Library and Archives, Boston.

———. Letter from Fisk to Evarts from Malta. May 9, 1822. Slot 9.Unit 5 (ABC 16.6). Reel 513. Congregational Library and Archives, Boston.

———. Letter from Fisk to Evarts from Malta. Nov 21, 1822. Slot 9.Unit 5 (ABC 16.6). Reel 513. Congregational Library and Archives, Boston.

———. Letter from Fisk to Evarts from Malta. Oct 8, 1822. Slot 9.Unit 5 (ABC 16.6). Reel 513. Congregational Library and Archives, Boston.

———. Letter from Fisk to Evarts from Mt. Lebanon. Aug 21, 1823. Slot 9.Unit 5 (ABC 16.6). Reel 513. Congregational Library and Archives, Boston.

———. Letter from Fisk to Evarts from Nazareth. Nov 9, 1823. Slot 9.Unit 5 (ABC 16.6). Reel 513. Congregational Library and Archives, Boston.

———. Letter from Fisk to Hannah Adams. July 24, 1822. Slot 9.Unit 5 (ABC 16.6). Reel 513. Congregational Library and Archives, Boston.

———. Letter from Fisk to Jacob Van Lennep from Cairo. April 3, 1823. Slot 9.Unit 5 (ABC 16.6). Reel 513. Congregational Library and Archives, Boston.

———.Letter from Fisk to J. Evarts & H. Hill. September, 1825. Slot 4. Unit 5 (ABC 16.5), Reel 502, Congregational Library and Archives, Boston.

———. Letter from Fisk to Jeremiah Evarts from Alexandria. Feb. 4,1822. Slot 9.Unit 5 (ABC 16.6). Reel 513. Congregational Library and Archives, Boston.

———. Letter from Fisk to Jeremiah Evarts from Alexandria. Feb. 10, 1822. Slot 9.Unit 5 (ABC 16.6). Reel 513. Congregational Library and Archives, Boston.

———. Letter from Fisk to Jeremiah Evarts from Malta Harbor. Jan 7, 1820. Slot 9.Unit 5 (ABC 16.6). Reel 513. Congregational Library and Archives, Boston.

———. Letter from Fisk to Jeremiah Evarts from Smyrna, May 18, 1821. Slot 9.Unit 5 (ABC 16.6). Reel 513. Congregational Library and Archives, Boston.

———. Letter from Fisk to Jeremiah Evarts from Smyrna, May 17, 1821. Slot 9.Unit 5 (ABC 16.6). Reel 513. Congregational Library and Archives, Boston.

———. Letter from Fisk to Jeremiah Evarts from Smyrna July 6, 1821. Slot 9.Unit 5 (ABC 16.6). Reel 513. Congregational Library and Archives, Boston.

———. Letter from Fisk to Jeremiah Evarts from Smyrna. Aug. 27, 1821. Slot 9.Unit 5 (ABC 16.6). Reel 513. Congregational Library and Archives, Boston.

———. Letter from Fisk to Jeremiah Evarts from Smyrna. Feb. 15, 1821. Slot 9.Unit 5 (ABC 16.6). Reel 513. Congregational Library and Archives, Boston.

———. Letter from Fisk to Jeremiah Evarts from Smyrna. Jan 2, 1822. Slot 9.Unit 5 (ABC 16.6). Reel 513. Congregational Library and Archives, Boston.

———. Letter from Fisk to Jeremiah Evarts from Smyrna. March 17, 1820. Slot 9.Unit 5 (ABC 16.6). Reel 513. Congregational Library and Archives, Boston.

———. Letter from Fisk to Jeremiah Evarts from Smyrna. May 8, 1821 Slot 9.Unit 5 (ABC 16.6). Reel 513. Congregational Library and Archives, Boston.

———. Letter from Fisk to Jeremiah Evarts from Smyrna. Nov 22, 1821. Slot 9.Unit 5 (ABC 16.6). Reel 513. Congregational Library and Archives, Boston.

———. Letter from Fisk to Jeremiah Evarts from Smyrna. Oct 4, 1821. Slot 9.Unit 5 (ABC 16.6). Reel 513. Congregational Library and Archives, Boston.

———. Letter from Fisk to Jeremiah Evarts from Smyrna.Oct. 2, 1821. Slot 9.Unit 5 (ABC 16.6). Reel 513. Congregational Library and Archives, Boston.

———. Letter from Fisk to John W. Langdon from Alexandria, Jan. 25, 1822. Slot 9.Unit 5 (ABC 16.6). Reel 513. Congregational Library and Archives, Boston.

———. Letter from Fisk to R. Anderson from Jerusalem. March 27, 1824. Slot 14. Unit 5 (ABC 16.6). Reel 514. Congregational Library and Archives, Boston.

———. .Letter from Fisk to unknown addressee written on board Ship Sally at Sea. Dec. 16, 1819. Slot 9.Unit 5 (ABC 16.6). Reel 513. Congregational Library and Archives, Boston.

———. Letter from Fisk to W.V. Lennep from Mt. Lebanon. Aug 19, 1823. Slot 9.Unit 5 (ABC 16.6). Reel 513. Congregational Library and Archives, Boston.

———. Letter from Pliny Fisk to Ebenezer Fisk sent to Shelburn, MA from Andover, Nov.17, 1815. Hougton Library at Harvard University, Cambridge, MA.

———. Letter from Rev. J. Connor from Constantinople. Nov 17, 1820 Slot 9.Unit 5 (ABC 16.6). Reel 513. Congregational Library and Archives, Boston.

——— Letters and Journal Entries to ABCFM. Feb 29, 1824. Slot 4. Unit 5 (ABC 16.5), Reel 502, Congregational Library and Archives, Boston.

———. Letters from Fisk to Parsons. April 14, 1821. May 14, 1821. June 30, 1821. May, 1822. Slot 3. Unit 5 (ABC 16.5), Reel 502, Congregational Library and Archives, Boston.

———. *Pliny Fisk Diary, Vol. II & III.* C115 Fisk. Davis Family Library, Special Collections. Middlebury College, Middlebury, VT.

———. *Pliny Fisk Diary Vol. I & IV.* Pliny Fisk Papers, Box 1. Missionary Research Library Archives: Section 2: Near/Middle East. The Burke Library Archives. Columbia University at Union Theological Seminary, New York

———. *Regulations for the government of the Society in their proceedings respecting members, who do not go on a Mission to the Heathen* (1821). Franklin Trace Library Special collections, Andover Newton Theological School, Newton Center, MA.

———. *Sermons preached at Shelburne, Mass. and Wilmington, Vt. dated October 1814-June 1815.* Franklin Trace Library Special collections, Andover Newton Theological School, Newton Center, MA.

———. *The key to the code* (1818). Franklin Trace Library Special collections, Andover Newton Theological School, Newton Center, MA.

Fisk, Pliny, and Jonas King. *Journal of Fisk and King. Description of Holy City & Journal Entries [indeterminate date]* Slots 10 & 11.Unit 5 (ABC 16.6). Reel 513. Congregational Library and Archives, Boston

———. *Journal of Fisk and King. January 8, March 24, 1823.* Slots 10 & 11.Unit 5 (ABC 16.6). Reel 513. Congregational Library and Archives, Boston

———. *Journal of Fisk and King. June 2, 1823–July 14, 1823.* Slots 10 & 11.Unit 5 (ABC 16.6). Reel 513. Congregational Library and Archives, Boston

———. *Journal of Fisk and King. March 24–May 5, 1823.* Slots 10 & 11.Unit 5 (ABC 16.6). Reel 513. Congregational Library and Archives, Boston

———. Letter with Journal Entries from Fisk and Jonas King to Evarts from Mt. Lebanon. July 23, 1823. Slots 10 & 11.Unit 5 (ABC 16.6). Reel 513. Congregational Library and Archives, Boston.

Fisk, Pliny, and Levi Parsons. *Fisk and Parsons Journal.* MRL 2: Pliny Fisk Papers, Box 1. Missionary Research Library Archives: Section 2: Near/Middle East. Burke Library Archives (Columbia University Libraries) at Union Theological Seminary, New York.

———. *Journal from Parsons & Fisk from August 1st–Sept. 1, 1820.* Slots 6–8.Unit 5 (ABC 16.6). Reel 513. Congregational Library and Archives, Boston.

———. *Journal from Parsons & Fisk from Oct 31–Dec 5, 1820 from Smyrna.* Slots 6–8. Unit 5 (ABC 16.6). Reel 513. Congregational Library and Archives, Boston.

———*Journal from Parsons & Fisk from Sept 2–Oct 24, 1820 from Scio.* Slots 6–8.Unit 5 (ABC 16.6). Reel 513. Congregational Library and Archives, Boston.

———. Letter from P & F to ABCFM from Smyrna. Mar 10, 1820. Slots 6–8.Unit 5 (ABC 16.6). Reel 513. Congregational Library and Archives, Boston.

———. Letter from P & F to ABCFM. Dec 25, 1821 Slots 6–8.Unit 5 (ABC 16.6). Reel 513. Congregational Library and Archives, Boston.

———. Letter from P & F to ABCFM. Dec. 13, 1821 Slots 6–8.Unit 5 (ABC 16.6). Reel 513. Congregational Library and Archives, Boston. Congregational Library and Archives, Boston.

——— Letter from Parsons & Fisk to ABCFM near Malta. Dec 23, 1819. Slots 6–8.Unit 5 (ABC 16.6). Reel 513. Congregational Library and Archives, Boston.

———. Letter from Parsons & Fisk to Evarts. March 11, 1820 from Smyrna Slots 6–8. Unit 5 (ABC 16.6). Reel 513. Congregational Library and Archives, Boston.

———. Letter from Parsons & Fisk to Jeremiah Evarts from Smyrna. Dec. 31, 1821. Slots 6–8.Unit 5 (ABC 16.6). Reel 513. Congregational Library and Archives, Boston.

———. Letter from Parsons & Fisk to Jeremiah Evarts from Smyrna. Jan. 22, 1822. Slots 6–8.Unit 5 (ABC 16.6). Reel 513. Congregational Library and Archives, Boston.

———. Letter from Parsons & Fisk to Jeremiah Evarts from Smyrna. Jan. 7, 1821. Slots 6–8.Unit 5 (ABC 16.6). Reel 513. Congregational Library and Archives, Boston.

———. Letter from Parsons & Fisk to Samuel Worchester. Dec 4, 1820. Slots 6–8. Unit 5 (ABC 16.6). Reel 513. Congregational Library and Archives, Boston. Congregational Library and Archives, Boston.

———. Letter from Parsons & Fisk to Samuel Worchester. Oct 31, 1820. Slots 6–8.Unit 5 (ABC 16.6). Reel 513. Congregational Library and Archives, Boston.

———. Letter from Parsons & Fisk to ABCFM from on board ship to Greece. Nov 3, 1819. Slots 6–8.Unit 5 (ABC 16.6). Reel 513. Congregational Library and Archives, Boston.

———. Letter from Parsons & Fisk to ABCFM from Smyrna. [unknown date] Slots 6–8.Unit 5 (ABC 16.6). Reel 513 Congregational Library and Archives, Boston..

———. Letter from Parsons & Fisk to ABCFM from Smyrna. Feb. 8, 1820. Slots 6–8. Unit 5 (ABC 16.6). Reel 513. Congregational Library and Archives, Boston.

———. Letter from Parsons & Fisk to ABCFM from Smyrna. Jan 21, 1820. Slots 6–8. Unit 5 (ABC 16.6). Reel 513. Congregational Library and Archives, Boston.

———. Letter from Parsons & Fisk to ABCFM. Sept12, 1820 Slots 6–8.Unit 5 (ABC 16.6). Reel 513. Congregational Library and Archives, Boston.

———. Letter from Parsons & Fisk to Samuel Worchester. Oct 27, 1820. Slots 6–8.Unit 5 (ABC 16.6). Reel 513. Congregational Library and Archives, Boston.

———. Letter from Parsons and Fisk to ABCFM. Sept 10, 1820. Slots 6–8.Unit 5 (ABC 16.6). Reel 513. Congregational Library and Archives, Boston.

———. Letters from Fisk and Parsons to ABCFM. Jan. 21, 1820. Feb 1, 1820. July 7, 1820. Slot 2, Unit 5 (ABC 16.5), Reel 502, Congregational Library and Archives, Boston.

————. *List of Books for a Missionary Library in Smyrna* Slots 6–8.Unit 5 (ABC 16.6). Reel 513. Congregational Library and Archives, Boston.

————. *Parsons & Fisk Journal Entries (excerpts). March 11th–July 31st,1820.* Slots 6–8. Unit 5 (ABC 16.6). Reel 513. Congregational Library and Archives, Boston.

————. *Parsons and Fisk Journal.* MRL 2: Pliny Fisk Papers, Box 1. Missionary Research Library Archives: Section 2: Near/Middle East. The Burke Library Archives. Columbia University at Union Theological Seminary, New York

Forman, Charles W. "A History of Foreign Mission Theory in America." In *American Missions in Bicentennial Perspective*, edited by R. Pierce Beaver, 69–140. Pasadena, CA: Carey, 1977.

Foster, Frank Hugh. *A Genetic History of New England Theology.* Chicago: University of Chicago, 1967.

Geertz, Clifford. *The Interpretation of Cultures.* New York: Basic, 1973.

Goen, C. C. "Jonathan Edwards: A New Departure in Eschatology." In *Critical Essays on Jonathan Edwards*, edited by William J. Sheick, 151–65. Boston: Hall., 1980.

Goodell, William. *Brief History and Present State of Armenia and as a Mission Field* (Dec, 1818). Unpublished manuscript, Volume7/Dissertations. Franklin Trace Library Special collections, Andover Newton Theological School, Newton Center, MA.

Granquist, Mark. "'The Role of 'Common Sense' in the Hermeneutics of Moses Stuart." *Harvard Theological Review* 83, no. 3 (1990) 305–19.

Graves, Allen. *On the establishment of a missionary seminary in the United States* (Jan, 1815). ). Unpublished manuscript, Volume7/Dissertations Franklin Trace Library Special collections, Andover Newton Theological School, Newton Center, MA.

Greven, Philip. *The Protestant Temperament: Patterns of Child-Rearing, Religious Experience, and the Self in Early America.* Chicago: University of Chicago, 1977.

Gribbin, William. A Mirror to New England: The Compendious History of Jedidiah Morse and Elijah Parish. *New England Quarterly* 45, no. 3 (1972) 340–54.

Griffin, Charles J. G. "Sins of the Fathers: The Jeremiad and the Franco-American Crisis in the Fast Day Sermons of 1798." *Southern Speech Communication Journal* 47 (1982) 389–401.

Griffin, Edward D. *The Kingdom of Christ: A Missionary Sermon Preached Before the General Assembly of the Presbyterian Church in Philadelphia, May 23rd, 1805.* Greenfield, MA: Denio, 1808.

Grigg, John A. *The Lives of David Brainerd: The Making of an American Evangelical Icon.* Oxford: Oxford University, 2009.

Haddock, Charles B. *Paganism —origin and progress* (March, 1818). Unpublished manuscript, Volume7/Dissertations Franklin Trace Library Special collections, Andover Newton Theological School, Newton Center, MA.

Hall, Robert. *Modern Infidelity Considered with Respect to its Influence on Society: in a Sermon, Preached at the Baptist Meeting, Cambridge.* Charlestown, MA: Etheridge, 1801.

Hallock, William A. *The Mountain Miller: An Authentic Narrative.* Published along with *The Shepherd of Salisbury Plain* by Hannah More. New York: American Tract Society, 1838.

Hart, D. G. "Jonathan Edwards and the Origins of Experimental Calvinism." In *The Legacy of Jonathan Edwards*, edited by D. G. Hart, Sean Michael Lucus, and Stephen J. Nichols, 161–81. Grand Rapids: Baker, 2003.

Henderson, Roger D. "Connotations of Worldview." *Pro Rege.* 15, no. 4 (2012) 10–21.

Hodgson, Marshall G. S. *The Venture of Islam: Conscience and History in a World Civilization.* Vol. 3, *The Gunpowder Empires and Modern Times.* Chicago: University of Chicago, 1974.

Holifield, E. Brooks. *Theology in America: Christian Thought from the Age of the Puritans to the Civil War.* New Haven: Yale University, 2003.

*Holy Land Missions and Missionaries* (reprints of Fisk and Parsons farewell sermons). New York: Arno, 1977.

Hooker, Edward W. *Historic sketch of the order of Jesuits* (date unknown). Unpublished manuscript, Volume7/Dissertations Franklin Trace Library Special collections, Andover Newton Theological School, Newton Center, MA.

Horne, Melvill. *A Collection of Letters Relative to Foreign Missions; Containing Several of Melvill Horne's "Letters on Missions," and Interesting Communications from Foreign Missionaries.* Andover, MA: Ware, 1810.

Hubers, John. "Samuel Zwemer and the challenge of Islam: from Polemic to a Hint of Dialogue." *International Bulletin of Missionary Research* 28, no. 3 (2004) 117–18.

Hutchinson, William R. *Errand to the World: American Protestant Thought and Foreign Missions.* Chicago: University of Chicago, 1987.

Jackson, Leon. "The Rights of Man and the Rites of Youth: Fraternity and Riot at Eighteenth Century Harvard." In *The American College in the Nineteenth Century*, edited by Roger Geiger, 46–79. Nashville: Vanderbilt University Press, 2000.

Jackson, Susan E. *Reminiscences of Andover.* Andover, MA: Andover, 1914.

Jordan, Frederick W. *Between Heaven and Harvard: Protestant Faith and the American Boarding School Experience, 1778–1940.* Notre Dame: Notre Dame University, 2004.

Jowett, William. "Missionary Correspondence." *Missionary Herald.* 16 (1820) 221–28.

Judson, Adorinam. *Letter to Society of Inquiry & Letter to ABCFM .* Archives of the Franklin Trask Library. Newton Center, MA: Andover Newton Theological Seminary.

Kellogg, Ebenezer. *Remarks on South America* (Feb, 1815). Unpublished manuscript, Volume7/Dissertations Franklin Trace Library Special collections, Andover Newton Theological School, Newton Center, MA.

Kett, Joseph F. *Rites of Passage: Adolescence in America, 1790 to the Present.* New York: Basic, 1977.

Khalaf, Samir. *Protestant Missionaries in the Levant: Ungodly Puritans, 1820–1860.* London: Routledge, 2012.

Kidd, Thomas S. *American Christians and Islam: Evangelical Culture and Muslims from the Colonial Period to the Age of Terrorism.* Princeton: Princeton University, 2009.

Kingsbury, Cyrus. *On the establishment of mission schools among the Indians within the territory of the United States* (Aug 15, 1815). Unpublished manuscript, Volume7/Dissertations. Franklin Trace Library Special collections, Andover Newton Theological School, Newton Center, MA.

Kinross, Lord. *The Ottoman Centuries: The Rise and Fall of the Turkish Empire.* New York: Morrow, 1977.

Kling, David W. *A Field of Divine Wonders: The New Divinity and the Village Revivals in Northwest Connecticut, 1792–1822.* University Park, PA: Penn State University, 1993.

————. "The New Divinity and the Origins of the American Board of Commissioners for Foreign Missions." In *North American Foreign Mission, 1810–1914: Theology, Theory, and Policy*, edited by Wilbert R. Shenk. Grand Rapids: Eerdmans, 2004.

————. "The New Divinity and Williams College, 179–1836." *Religion and American Culture* 6, no. 2 (1996) 195–223.

Kramer, Gudrun. *A History of Palestine: From the Ottoman Conquest to the Founding of the State of Israel*. Princeton: Princeton University, 2002.

Kuklick, Bruce. *Churchmen and Philosophers: From Jonathan Edwards to John Dewey*. New Haven: Yale University, 1985.

Lang, Amy Schrager. "A Flood of Errors: Chauncy and Edwards in the Great Awakening." In *Jonathan Edwards and the American Experience*, edited by Nathan O. Hatch and Harry S. Stout, 160–77. New York: Oxford University, 1988.

Leonard, Bill. "Getting Saved in America: Conversion Event in a Pluralistic America." *Review and Expositor* 82, no. 1 (1985) 112–23.

Letter of Recommendation from Andover Professors. ABC: 6 v. 1. Archives of Hougton Library of Harvard University.

Lewis, Bernard. *Emergence of Modern Turkey*. London: Oxford University, 1961.

Lord, E. *A Compendious History of the Principal Protestant Missions to the Heathen Selected and Compiled from the Best Authorities, In Two Volumes*. Boston: Armstrong, 1813.

Makdisi, Ussama. *Artillery of Heaven: American Missionaries and the Failed Conversion of the Middle East*. Ithaca, NY: Cornell University, 2008.

————. *Faith Misplaced: American Missionaries and the Failed Conversion of the Middle East*. New York: Cornell University, 2009.

Marr, Timothy. *The Cultural Roots of American Islamicism*. New York: Cambridge University, 2006.

Marsden, George M. *Jonathan Edwards: A Life*. New Haven: Yale University, 2003.

Marty, Martin. *The Infidel: Free Thought and American Religion*. New York: Meridian, 1961.

Matthews, Jean V. *Toward a New Society: American Thought and Culture, 1800–1830*. Boston: Twayne, 1991.

May, Henry Farnham. *The Enlightenment in America*. New York: Oxford University, 1976.

McCloy, Frank Dixon. "The Founding of Protestant Theological Seminaries in the United States of America, 1784–1840." PhD diss., Harvard University, 1959.

McDermott, Gerald. *Jonathan Edwards Confronts the Gods: Christian Theology, Enlightenment Religion, and Non-Christian Faiths*. Oxford: Oxford University, 2000.

Merrill, E. *What exertions have been made and are now making for introducing the gospel among the heathen* (1813). Unpublished manuscript, Volume7/Dissertations. Franklin Trace Library Special collections, Andover Newton Theological School, Newton Center, MA.

Merrill, Thomas Abbot. *Semi-centennial Sermon, Containing a History of Middlebury, Vt., Delivered Dec. 3, 1840, Being the First Thanksgiving Day, After the Expiration of Half a Century From the Organization of the Congregational Church, Sept. 5, 1790*. Middlebury: E. Maxham, 1841.

Meyer, Donald H. *The Democratic Enlightenment*. New York: Capricorn, 1976.

Miller, Alpha. *Dissertation on the Duty & the best Manner, of extending religious instruction to the black population of the United States* (Jan 28, 1817). Unpublished manuscript, Volume7/Dissertations. Franklin Trace Library Special collections, Andover Newton Theological School, Newton Center, MA.

Miller, Perry. *The Life of the Mind in America: From the Revolution to the Civil War.* New York: Harcourt, Brace & World, 1970.

Miller, Samuel. *Letters on Clerical Manners and Habits: Addressed to a Student in the Theological Seminary, at Princeton, N.J.* Princeton: Moore Baker, 1835.

Mitchell, William. *Asia Minor* (date unknown). ). Unpublished manuscript, Volume7/Dissertations. Franklin Trace Library Special collections, Andover Newton Theological School, Newton Center, MA.

Morse, James King. *Jedidiah Morse: A Champion of New England Orthodoxy.* New York: AMS, 1967.

Morse, Jedidiah. *The Controversy Respecting the Revolution in Harvard College and the Events which have followed it; occasioned by the use which has been made of certain complaints and accusations of Hannah Adams, against the author.* Charlestown: Printed for the Author, 1814.

———. *A Sermon Delivered at the New North Church in Boston in the Morning and In the Afternoon at Charlestown, May 9th, 1798 Being the Day Recommended by John Adams President of the United States of America For Solemn Humiliation, Fasting and Prayer.* Boston: Hall, 1798.

———. *A Sermon Delivered before the Orand Lodge of Free & Accepted Masons of the Commonwealth of Massachusetts.* Leominster, MA: 1798.

———. *A Sermon Exhibiting the Present Dangers, and Consequent Duties of the Citizens of the United States of America.* Charlestown, MA: Etheridge, 1799.

———. *Signs of the Times: A Sermon Preached before the Society for Propagating the Gospel among the Indians and Others in North America at Their Anniversary, Nov. 1, 1810.* Charlestown, MA: Armstrong, 1810.

———. *The True Reasons on Which the election of a Hollis Professor of Divinity in Harvard College was opposed at the board of overseers.* Charlestown, MA: Printed for the Author, 1805.

Morton, Daniel. *Memoir of Rev. Levi Parsons, First Missionary to Palestine from the United States: Containing Sketches of his Early Life and Education, His Missionary Labours in this Country, in Asia Minor and Judea, with an Account of His last Sickness and Death.* Hartford, CT: Cooke and Packard & Butler, 1830.

Murdock, Thomas. *The Present State of the Greek Church in Russia* (March 11, 1817). Unpublished manuscript, Volume7/Dissertations. Franklin Trace Library Special collections, Andover Newton Theological School, Newton Center, MA.

Nash, Gary B. "The American Clergy and the French Revolution." *William and Mary Quarterly* 3, no. 22 (1965) 392–412.

Naylor, Natalie. "The Theological Seminary in the Configuration of American Higher Education: the Ante-Bellum Years." *History of Education Quarterly* 17, no. 1 (1977) 17–30.

Neil Brody Miller, "Proper Subjects for Public Inquiry: The First Unitarian Controversy and the Transformation of Federalist Print Culture." *Early American Literature* 43, no. 1 (2008) 101–35.

Neulip, James W. *Intercultural Communication: A Contextual Approach, Edition 4.* Los Angeles: Sage, 2011.

Noll, Mark. *America's God: From Jonathan Edwards to Abraham Lincoln.* New York: Oxford University, 2002.

———. "Common Sense Tradition and American Evangelical Thought." *American Quarterly* 37, no. 2 (1985) 216–38.

Obenzinger, Hilton. "Holy Land Narrative and American Convenant: Levi Parsons, Pliny Fisk and the Palestine Mission." *Religion & Literature* 35, nos. 2/3 (2003) 241–67.

Ogden, David L. *Present state of popery* (winter, 1817) Unpublished manuscript, Volume7/Dissertations. Franklin Trace Library Special collections, Andover Newton Theological School, Newton Center, MA.

Oren, Michael B. *Faith and Fantasy: American in the Middle East 1776 to the Present.* New York: Norton, 2007.

Packard, Theophilus. *Two Sermons Delivered in Shelburne (Mass.), May 15, 1808, In Which are Plainly Exhibiteed the Scriptural Evidences of the Essential Divinity of our Lord JESUS CHRIST; and the Importance of Viewing and Treating Him Accordin to His Real Character.* Greenfield, MA: Denio, 1808.

Parsons, Levi. *Address to Society* (Sept, 1817). Unpublished manuscript, Dissertations. Volume7/Dissertations. Franklin Trace Library Special collections, Andover Newton Theological School, Newton Center, MA.

———. *Discourse for Professor Jushua Bates, Nov, 1811.* C115. Davis Family Library, Special Collections. Middlebury College, Middlebury, VT.

——— Journal of Levi Parsons *"From the Time of Leaving Smyrna Dec 5, 1820 till arrival at Jerusalem, February 17, 1821."* Slots 6–8.Unit 5 (ABC 16.6). Reel 513

———. Letter to Ira Parsons, September 17, 1814. C115. Davis Family Library, Special Collections. Middlebury College, Middlebury, VT.

———. Letter to Miss Electa May, April 21, 1814. C115. Davis Family Library, Special Collections. Middlebury College, Middlebury, VT.

———. Letter to Miss Electa May, August 12, 1813. C115. Davis Family Library, Special Collections. Middlebury College, Middlebury, VT.

———. Letter to Miss Lucretia Parsons, June 1, 1814 C115.. Davis Family Library, Special Collections. Middlebury College, Middlebury, VT.

———. Letter to Miss Lucretia Parsons, March 17, 1814. C115. Davis Family Library, Special Collections. Middlebury College, Middlebury, VT.

———. Letter to Miss Lucretia Parsons, March 28, 1812. C115. Davis Family Library, Special Collections. Middlebury College, Middlebury, VT.

———. Letter to Miss Lucretia Parsons, May, 1814. C115. Davis Family Library, Special Collections. Middlebury College, Middlebury, VT.

———.Letter to Mrs. Electa Parsons, Oct 2, 1811. C115.Davis Family Library, Special Collections. Middlebury College, Middlebury, VT.

———. Letter to Mrs. Electa Parsons, Oct 30, 1811. C115. Davis Family Library, Special Collections. Middlebury College, Middlebury, VT.

———. Letter to Rev. Daniel O. Morton, June 21, 1815. C115. Davis Family Library, Special Collections. Middlebury College, Middlebury, VT.

———. Letters to Pliny Fisk. Dec. 30, 1814. Oct 23, 1817.Jan 2, 1818. Feb 3, 1818. Aug 19, 1818. C115. Franklin Trask Library. Andover Newton Theological School. Newton Center, MA.

————. *The Peculiar consolations of a Missionary* (July 2, 1816). ). Unpublished manuscript, Dissertations. Volume7/Dissertations Franklin Trace Library Special collections, Andover Newton Theological School, Newton Center, MA.

Perl-Rosenthal, Nathan. "Private Letters and Public Diplomacy: The Adams Network and the Quasi-War, 1797–1798." *Journal of the Early Republic* 31, no. 2 (2011) 283–311.

Pettit, Norman. *The Heart Renewed: Assurance of Salvation in the New England Spiritual Life.* Lewiston, NY: Mellen, 2004.

Philips, Joseph W. *Jedidiah Morse and New England Congregationalism.* New Brunswick, NJ: Rutgers University Press, 1983.

Phillips, Clifton Jackson. *Protestant America and the Pagan World: The First Half Century of the American Board of Commissioners for Foreign Missions, 1810–1860.* Cambridge, MA: President and Fellows of Harvard College, 1969.

Pikkert, Pieter. *Protestant Missionaries to the Middle East: Ambassadors of Christ or Culture?* PhD diss., University of South Africa, 2006.

Pond, Enoch. *Short Missionary Discourses or Monthly Concert Lectures.* Worcester, MA: Dorr and Howland, 1824.

Porter, Ebenezer. *Letters on Revival.* 1832. Reprint, Edinburgh: Banner of Truth Trust, 2004. (Originally published by Andover's professor of Rhetoric.)

*The Panoplist* 1 (1806).

Prideaux, Humphrey. *The True Nature of Imposture Fully Displayed in the Life of Mahomet with a Discourse annex'd, for the Vindicating of Christianity from this Charge; Offered to the Consideration of the Deists of the present Age.* London: Rogers, 1698.

Proudfit, Alexander, *Ministerial Labour and Support: A Sermon Preached at Middlebury, Vermont, Feb. 21, 1810, at the Ordination of Mr. Henry Davis and his Induction as President of the College.* Middlebury, VT: Dodd & Ramsey, 1810.

Rabinowitz, Richard. *The Transformation of Personal Religious Experience in 19th Century New England.* Boston: Northeastern University, 1989.

"Reviews: American Unitarianism; or a Brief History of the Progress and Present State of the Unitarian Churches in America." *Panoplist and Missionary Magazine* 11, no. 6 (1815) 241–71.

"Revival of Religion in Middlebury College." *Panoplist and Missionary Magazine United* 4, NS (1812) 380–81.

Richards, Thomas C. *Samuel J. Mills: Missionary Pathfinder, Pioneer and Promoter.* Boston: Pilgrim, 1906.

Robinson, David. *The Unitarians and the Universalists.* Westport, CT: Greenwood, 1985.

Rogers, Richard Lee. "'A Bright and New Constellation': Millennial Narratives, and the Origins of American Foreign Missions." In *North American Foreign Missions, 1810 –1914: Theology, Theory, and Policy*, edited by Wilbert R. Shenk, 39–60. Grand Rapids: Eerdmans, 2004.

Rowe, Henry. *History of Andover Seminary.* Newton, MA: Todd, 1933.

Rubin, Julius H. *Religious Melancholy and Protestant Experience in America.* New York: Oxford University, 1994.

Said, Edward W. *Orientalism.* New York: Vintage, 1979.

Sale, George. *The Koran, Commonly Called The Alcoran of Mohammed, Translated into English immediately from the original Arabic; with Explanatory notes, taken from the most approved commentators to which is prefixed a Preliminary Discourse in Two Volumes.* London: Tegg, 1825.

Salibi, Kamal, and Yusuf K. Khoury, eds. *The Missionary Herald: Reports from Ottoman Syria, 1819–1870.* Amman, Jordan: Royal Institute for Inter-faith Studies, 1995.

Sargent, John. *Memoir of the Rev. Henry Martyn, B.D., Late Fellow of St. John's College, Cambridge, and Chaplain to the Honourable East India Company.* London: Seeley and Burnside, 1819.

Scales, Jacob. *View of the doctrines of Mohammedism and their influence on the moral character* (July, 1819). Unpublished manuscript, Volume7/Dissertations Franklin Trace Library Special collections, Andover Newton Theological School, Newton Center, MA.

Sha'ban, Fuad. *Islam and Arabs in Early American Thought: The Roots of Orientalism in America.* Dunham, NC: Acorn, 1991.

Shaw, Standford. *Between Old and New: The Ottoman Empire under Sultan Selim III.* Cambridge, MA: Harvard University, 1971.

Sheldon, George. *A History of Deerfield, MA: The Times When and the People by Whom it was Settled, Unsettled and Resettled.* Vol. 2. Greenfield, MA: Hall, 1896.

Shepard, Thomas. *What are the improper motives by which a missionary is in danger of being influenced in devoting himself to the heathen?* (Dec, 1815). Unpublished manuscript, Volume7/Dissertations. Franklin Trace Library Special collections, Andover Newton Theological School, Newton Center, MA.

Shiels, Richard D. "The Second Great Awakening in Connecticut: Critique of the Traditional Interpretation." *Church History* 49, no. 4 (1980) 401–15.

Sloan, Douglas. *The Scottish Enlightenment and the American College Ideal.* New York: Teachers College, 1971.

Smith, Wilson. "William Paley's Theological Utilitarianism in America." *William and Mary Quarterly, Third Series* 2, no. 3 (1954) 402–24.

Snell, Rachel A. *Jedidiah Morse and the Crusade for the New Jerusalem: The Cultural Catalysts of the Bavarian Illuminati Conspiracy.* Paper 8. Orono, ME: University of Maine Honors College, 2006.

Society of Inquiry. *Memoirs of American Missionaries, Formerly Connected with the Society of Inquiry in the Andover Theological Seminary Embracing a History of the Society, etc.* Boston: Pierce and Parker, 1833.

Sprague, William Buell. *Annals of the American Pulpit: Or, Commemorative Notices of Distinguished American Clergymen of Various Denominations.* Vol. 2. New York: Carter & Bros., 1859.

———. *The Life of Jedidiah Morse, D.D.* New York: Randolph, 1813.

Stameshkin, David M. *The Town's College: Middlebury College, 1800–1915.* Middlebury, VT: Middlebury College, 1985.

Stanley, Brian, ed. *Christian Missions and the Enlightenment.* Grand Rapids: Eerdmans, 2001.

Stauffer, Vernon. *New England and the Bavarian Illuminati.* New York: Columbia University, 1918

Steadman, John M. *The Myth of Asia.* New York: Simon and Schuster, 1969.

Swanson, Herb. "Said's Orientalism and the Study of Christian Missions." *International Bulletin of Missionary Research* 28, no. 3 (2004) 107.

Sweet, William Warren. "The Rise of Theological Schools in America." *Church History* 6, no. 3 (1937) 260–73.